FROM THE MAKER OF THE TEST

The Official SAT Subject Test Study Guide

U.S. History

The College Board
New York, N.Y.

About the College Board

The College Board is a mission-driven not-for-profit organization that connects students to college success and opportunity. Founded in 1900, the College Board was created to expand access to higher education. Today, the membership association is made up of over 6,000 of the world's leading educational institutions and is dedicated to promoting excellence and equity in education. Each year, the College Board helps more than seven million students prepare for a successful transition to college through programs and services in college readiness and college success—including the SAT® and the Advanced Placement Program®. The organization also serves the education community through research and advocacy on behalf of students, educators, and schools.

For further information, visit collegeboard.org

Copies of this book are available from your bookseller or may be ordered from College Board Publications at store.collegeboard.org or by calling 800-323-7155.

Editorial inquiries concerning this book should be addressed to the College Board, SAT Program, 250 Vesey Street, New York, New York 10281.

ISBN 13: 978-1-4573-0931-1

Printed in the United States of America

1 2 3 4 5 6 7 8 9   23 22 21 20 19 18 17

Distributed by Macmillan

Contents

The SAT Subject Tests

About SAT Subject Tests

SAT Subject Tests™ are a valuable way to help you show colleges a more complete picture of your academic background and interests. Each year, nearly one million Subject Tests are taken by students throughout the country and around the world to gain admission to the leading colleges and universities in the U.S.

SAT Subject Tests are one-hour exams that give you the opportunity to demonstrate knowledge and showcase achievement in specific subjects. They provide a fair and reliable measure of your achievement in high school—information that can help enhance your college admission portfolio. The U.S. History Subject Test is a great way to highlight your understanding, skills, and strengths in history.

This book provides information and guidance to help you study for and familiarize yourself with the U.S. History Subject Test. It contains actual, previously administered tests and official answer sheets that will help you get comfortable with the tests' format, so you feel better prepared on test day.

The Benefits of SAT Subject Tests

SAT Subject Tests let you put your best foot forward, allowing you to focus on subjects that you know well and enjoy. They can help you differentiate yourself in a competitive admission environment by providing additional information about your skills and knowledge of particular subjects. Many colleges also use Subject Tests for course placement and selection; some schools allow you to place out of introductory courses by taking certain Subject Tests.

Subject Tests are flexible and can be tailored to your strengths and areas of interest. These are the **only** national admission tests where **you** choose the tests that best showcase your achievements and interests. You select the Subject Test(s) and can take up to three tests in one sitting. With the exception of listening tests, you can even decide to change the subject or number of tests you want to take on the day of the test. This flexibility can help you be more relaxed on test day.

Who Should Consider Subject Tests?

Anyone can take an SAT Subject Test to highlight their knowledge of a specific subject. SAT Subject Tests may be especially beneficial for certain students:

- Students applying to colleges that require or recommend Subject Tests—be aware that some schools have additional Subject Test requirements for certain students, majors, or programs of study

- Students who wish to demonstrate strength in specific subject areas

- Students who wish to demonstrate knowledge obtained outside a traditional classroom environment (e.g., summer enrichment, distance learning, weekend study, etc.)

- Students looking to place out of certain classes in college

- Students enrolled in dual-enrollment programs

- Homeschooled students or students taking courses online

- Students who feel that their course grade may not be a true reflection of their knowledge of the subject matter

Who Requires the SAT Subject Tests?

Most college websites and catalogs include information about admission requirements, including which Subject Tests are needed or recommended for admission. Schools have varying policies regarding Subject Tests, but they generally fall into one or more of the following categories:

- Required for admission

- Recommended for admission

- Required or recommended for certain majors or programs of study (e.g., engineering, honors, etc.)

- Required or recommended for certain groups of students (e.g., homeschooled students)

- Required, recommended, or accepted for course placement

- Accepted for course credit

- Accepted as an alternative to fulfill certain college admission requirements

- Accepted as an alternative to fulfill certain high school subject competencies

- Accepted and considered, especially if Subject Tests improve or enhance a student's application

REMEMBER

Subject Tests are a valuable way to help you show colleges a more complete picture of your academic achievements.

In addition, the College Board provides a number of resources where you can search for information about Subject Test requirements at specific colleges.

- Visit the websites of the colleges and universities that interest you.
- Visit College Search at www.collegeboard.org.
- Purchase a copy of *The College Board College Handbook.*

Some colleges require specific tests, such as mathematics or science, so it's important to make sure you understand the policies prior to choosing which Subject Test(s) to take. If you have questions or concerns about admission policies, contact college admission officers at individual schools. They are usually pleased to meet with students interested in their schools.

Subject Tests Offered

SAT Subject Tests measure how well you know a particular subject area and your ability to apply that knowledge. SAT Subject Tests aren't connected to specific textbooks or teaching methods. The content of each test evolves to reflect the latest trends in what is taught in typical high school courses in the corresponding subject.

The tests fall into five general subject areas:

English	History	Mathematics	Science	Languages	
				Reading Only	**with Listening**
Literature	United States History	Mathematics Level 1	Biology E/M	French	Chinese
	World History	Mathematics Level 2	Chemistry	German	French
			Physics	Italian	German
				Latin	Japanese
				Modern Hebrew	Korean
				Spanish	Spanish

Who Develops the Tests

The SAT Subject Tests are part of the SAT® Program of the College Board, a not-for-profit membership association of over 6,000 schools, colleges, universities, and other educational associations. Every year, the College Board serves seven million students and their parents, 24,000 high schools, and 3,800 colleges through major programs and services in college readiness, college admission, guidance, assessment, financial aid, and enrollment.

Each subject has its own test development committee, typically composed of teachers and college professors appointed for the different Subject Tests. The test questions are written and reviewed by each Subject Test Committee, under the guidance of professional test developers. The tests are rigorously developed, highly reliable assessments of knowledge and skills taught in high school classrooms.

Deciding to Take an SAT Subject Test

Which Tests Should You Take?

The SAT Subject Tests that you take should be based on your interests and academic strengths. The tests are a great way to indicate interest in specific majors or programs of study (e.g., engineering, pre-med, cultural studies).

You should also consider whether the colleges that you're interested in require or recommend Subject Tests. Some colleges will grant an exemption from or credit for a freshman course requirement if a student does well on a particular SAT Subject Test. Below are some things for you to consider as you decide which test(s) to take.

Think through your strengths and interests

- List the subjects in which you do well and that truly interest you.

- Think through what you might like to study in college.

- Consider whether your current admission credentials (high school grades, SAT scores, etc.) highlight your strengths.

Consider the colleges that you're interested in

- Make a list of the colleges you're considering.

- Take some time to look into what these colleges require or what may help you stand out in the admission process.

- Use College Search to look up colleges' test requirements.

- If the colleges you're interested in require or recommend SAT Subject Tests, find out how many tests are required or recommended and in which subjects.

Take a look at your current and recent course load

- Have you completed the required coursework? The best time to take SAT Subject Tests is at the end of the course, when the material is still fresh in your mind.

- Check the recommended preparation guidelines for the Subject Tests that interest you to see if you've completed the recommended coursework.

- Try your hand at some SAT Subject Test practice questions on collegeboard.org or in this book.

Don't forget, regardless of admission requirements, you can enhance your college portfolio by taking Subject Tests in subject areas that you know very well.

If you're still unsure about which SAT Subject Tests to take, talk to your teacher or counselor about your specific situation. You can also find more information about SAT Subject Tests on collegeboard.org.

When to Take the Tests

We generally recommend that you take Subject Tests after you complete the relevant course work, prior to your senior year of high school, if possible. This way, you will already have your Subject Test credentials complete, allowing you to focus on your college applications in the fall of your senior year. If you are able to, take the United States History Subject Test right after your course ends, when the content is still fresh in your mind.

Since not all Subject Tests are offered on every test date, be sure to check when the Subject Tests that you're interested in are offered and plan accordingly.

You should also balance this with college application deadlines. If you're interested in applying early decision or early action to any college, many colleges advise that you take the SAT Subject Tests by October or November of your senior year. For regular decision applications, some colleges will accept SAT Subject Test scores through the December administration. Use College Search to look up policies for specific colleges.

This book suggests ways you can prepare for the SAT Subject Tests in U.S. History. Before taking a test in a subject you haven't studied recently, ask your teacher for advice about the best time to take the test. Then review the course material thoroughly over several weeks.

How to Register for the Tests

There are several ways to register for the SAT Subject Tests.

- Visit the College Board's website at collegeboard.org. Most students choose to register for Subject Tests on the College Board website.

- Register by telephone (for a fee) if you have registered previously for the SAT or an SAT Subject Test. Call, toll free from anywhere in the United States, 866-756-7346. From outside the United States, call 212-713-7789.

- If you do not have access to the internet, find registration forms in *The Paper Registration Guide for the SAT and SAT Subject Tests.* You can find the booklet in a guidance office at any high school or by writing to:

> The College Board
> SAT Program
> P.O. Box 025505
> Miami, FL 33102

When you register for the SAT Subject Tests, you will have to indicate the specific Subject Tests you plan to take on the test date you select. You may take one, two, or three tests on any given test date; your testing fee will vary accordingly. Except for the Language Tests with Listening, you may change your mind on the day of the test and instead select from any of the other Subject Tests offered that day.

Student Search Service

The Student Search Service® helps colleges find prospective students. If you take the PSAT/NMSQT®, the SAT, an SAT Subject Test, or any AP® Exam, you can be included in this free service.

Here's how it works: During SAT or SAT Subject Test registration, indicate that you want to be part of the Student Search. Your name is put in a database along with other information such as your address, high school grade point average, date of birth, grade level, high school, email address, intended college major, and extracurricular activities.

Colleges and scholarship programs then use the Student Search to help them locate and recruit students with characteristics that might be a good match with their schools.

Here are some points to keep in mind about the Student Search Service:

- Being part of Student Search is voluntary. You may take the test even if you don't join Student Search.

- Colleges participating in Student Search do not receive your exam scores. Colleges can ask for the names of students within certain score ranges, but your exact score is not reported.

- Being contacted by a college doesn't mean you have been admitted. You can be admitted only after you apply. The Student Search Service is simply a way for colleges to reach prospective students.

- Student Search Service will share your contact information only with approved colleges and scholarship programs that are recruiting students like you. Your name will never be sold to a private company or mailing list.

Keep the Tests in Perspective

Colleges that require Subject Test scores do so because the scores are useful in making admission or placement decisions. Schools that don't have specific Subject Test policies generally review Subject Test scores during the application process because the scores can give a fuller picture of your academic achievement. The Subject Tests are a particularly helpful tool for admission and placement programs because the tests aren't tied to specific textbooks, grading procedures, or instruction methods but are still tied to curricula. The tests provide level ground on which colleges can compare your scores with those of students who come from schools and backgrounds that may be far different from yours.

It's important to remember that test scores are just one of several factors that colleges consider in the admission process. Admission officers also look at your high school grades, letters of recommendation, extracurricular activities, essays, and other criteria. Try to keep this in mind when you're preparing for and taking Subject Tests.

Fee Waivers

Students who face financial barriers to taking the SAT Subject Tests can be granted College Board fee waivers through schools and authorized community-based organizations to cover the cost of testing. Seniors who use a fee waiver to take the SAT will automatically receive four college application fee waivers to use in applying to colleges and universities that accept the waivers. You can learn about eligibility and other benefits offered to help you in the college application process at sat.org/fee-waivers.

Score Choice

In March 2009, the College Board introduced Score Choice™, a feature that gives you the option to choose the scores you send to colleges by test date for the SAT and by individual test for the SAT Subject Tests—at no additional cost. Designed to reduce your test day stress, Score Choice gives you an opportunity to show colleges the scores you feel best represent your abilities. Score Choice is optional, so if you don't actively choose to use it, all of your scores will be sent automatically with your score report. Since most colleges only consider your best scores, you should still feel comfortable reporting scores from all of your tests.

REMEMBER

Score Choice gives you an opportunity to show colleges the scores you feel best represent your abilities.

About collegeboard.org

The College Board website collegeboard.org is a comprehensive tool that can help you be prepared, connected, and informed throughout the college planning and admission process. In addition to registering for the SAT and SAT Subject Tests, you can find information about other tests and services, browse the College Board Store (where you can order *The College Board College Handbook*, *The Official Study Guide for all SAT Subject Tests* and other guides specific to mathematics, science and history), and send emails with your questions and concerns. You can also find free practice questions for each of the 20 SAT Subject Tests. These are an excellent supplement to this Study Guide and can help you be even more prepared on test day.

Once you create a free online account, you can print your SAT admission ticket, see your scores, and send them to schools.

More college planning resources The College Board offers free, comprehensive resources at Big Future™ to help you with your college planing. Visit **bigfuture.org** to put together a step-by-step plan for the entire process, from finding the right college, exploring majors and careers, and calculating costs, to applying for scholarships and financial aid.

How to Do Your Best on the SAT Subject Tests

Get Ready

Give yourself several weeks before the tests to read the course materials and the suggestions in this book. The rules for the SAT Subject Tests may be different than the rules for most of the tests you've taken in high school. You're probably used to answering questions in order, spending more time answering the hard questions and, in the hopes of getting at least partial credit, showing all your work.

When you take the SAT Subject Tests, it's OK to move around within the test section and to answer questions in any order you wish. Keep in mind that the questions go from easier to harder. You receive one point for each question answered correctly. For each question that you try but answer incorrectly, a fraction of a point is subtracted from the total number of correct answers. No points are added or subtracted for unanswered questions. If your final raw score includes a fraction, the score is rounded to the nearest whole number.

Avoid Surprises

Know what to expect. Become familiar with the test and test day procedures. You'll boost your confidence and feel a lot more relaxed.

- **Know how the tests are set up.** All SAT Subject Tests are one-hour multiple-choice tests. The first page of each Subject Test includes a background questionnaire. You will be asked to fill it out before taking the test. The information is for statistical purposes only. It will not influence your test score. Your answers to the questionnaire will assist us in developing future versions of the test. You can see a sample of the background questionnaire at the start of each test in the book.

- **Learn the test directions.** The directions for answering the questions in this book are the same as those on the actual test. If you become familiar with the directions now, you'll leave yourself more time to answer the questions when you take the test.

- **Study the sample questions.** The more familiar you are with the question formats, the more comfortable you'll feel when you see similar questions on the actual test.

- **Get to know the answer sheet.** At the back of this book, you'll find a set of sample answer sheets. The appearance of the answer sheets in this book may differ from the answer sheets you see on test day.

- **Understand how the tests are scored.** You get one point for each right answer and lose a fraction of a point for each wrong answer. You neither gain nor lose points for omitting an answer. Hard questions count the same amount as easier questions.

A Practice Test Can Help

Find out where your strengths lie and which areas you need to work on. Do a run-through of a Subject Test under conditions that are close to what they will be on test day.

- **Set aside an hour so you can take the test without interruption.** You will be given one hour to take each SAT Subject Test.

- **Prepare a desk or table that has no books or papers on it.** No books, including dictionaries, are allowed in the test room.

- **Read the instructions that precede the practice test.** On test day, you will be asked to do this before you answer the questions.

- **Remove and fill in an answer sheet from the back of this book.** You can use one answer sheet for up to three Subject Tests.

- **Use a clock or kitchen timer to time yourself.** This will help you to pace yourself and to get used to taking a test in 60 minutes.

The Day Before the Test

It's natural to be nervous. A bit of a nervous edge can keep you sharp and focused. Below are a few suggestions to help you be more relaxed as the test approaches.

Do a brief review on the day before the test. Look through the sample questions, answer explanations and test directions in this book or on the College Board website. Keep the review brief; cramming the night before the test is unlikely to help your performance and might even make you more anxious.

The night before test day, prepare everything you need to take with you. You will need:

- Your admission ticket.
- An acceptable photo ID. (see page 11)
- Two No. 2 pencils with soft erasers. (Do not bring pens or mechanical pencils.)
- A watch without an audible alarm.
- A snack.

Know the route to the test center and any instructions for finding the entrance.

Check the time your admission ticket specifies for arrival. Arrive a little early to give yourself time to settle in.

Get a good night's sleep.

REMEMBER

You are in control.
Come prepared.
Pace yourself.
Guess wisely.

Acceptable Photo IDs

- Driver's license (with your photo)

- State-issued ID

- Valid passport

- School ID card

- Student ID form that has been prepared by your school on school stationery and includes a recognizable photo and the school seal, which overlaps the photo (go to www.collegeboard.org for more information)

The most up-to-date information about acceptable photo IDs can be found on collegeboard.org.

REMINDER   What I Need on Test Day

Make a copy of this box and post it somewhere noticeable.

I Need   **I Have**

Appropriate photo ID   _____

Admission ticket   _____

Two No. 2 pencils with clean soft erasers   _____

Watch (without an audible alarm)   _____

Snack   _____

Bottled water   _____

Directions to the test center   _____

Instructions for finding the entrance on weekends   _____

I am leaving the house at _____ a.m.

Be on time or you can't take the test.

On Test Day

You have good reason to feel confident. You're thoroughly prepared. You're familiar with what this day will bring. You are in control.

Keep in Mind

You must be on time or you can't take the test. Leave yourself plenty of time for mishaps and emergencies.

Think positively. If you are worrying about not doing well, then your mind isn't on the test. Be as positive as possible.

Stay focused. Think only about the question in front of you. Letting your mind wander will cost you time.

Concentrate on your own test. The first thing some students do when they get stuck on a question is to look around to see how everyone else is doing. What they usually see is that others seem busy filling in their answer sheets. Instead of being concerned that you are not doing as well as everyone else, keep in mind that everyone works at a different pace. Your neighbors may not be working on the question that puzzled you. They may not even be taking the same test. Thinking about what others are doing distracts you from working on your own test.

Making an Educated Guess

Educated guesses are helpful when it comes to taking tests with multiple-choice questions; however, making guesses is not a good idea. To correct for random guessing, a fraction of a point is subtracted for each incorrect answer. That means random guessing—guessing with no idea of an answer that might be correct—could lower your score. The best approach is to eliminate all the choices that you know are wrong. Make an educated guess from the remaining choices. If you can't eliminate any choices, move on.

REMEMBER

All correct answers are worth one point, regardless of the question's difficulty level.

IMPORTANT

Cell phone use is prohibited in the test center or testing room. If your cell phone is on, your scores will be canceled.

10 Tips FOR TAKING THE TEST

1. **Read carefully.** Consider all the choices in each question. Avoid careless mistakes that will cause you to lose points.

2. **Answer the easy questions first.** Work on less time-consuming questions before moving on to the more difficult ones.

3. **Eliminate choices that you know are wrong.** Cross them out in your test book so that you can clearly see which choices are left.

4. **Make educated guesses or skip the question.** If you have eliminated the choices that you know are wrong, guessing is your best strategy. However, if you cannot eliminate any of the answer choices, it is best to skip the question.

5. **Keep your answer sheet neat.** The answer sheet is scored by a machine, which can't tell the difference between an answer and a doodle. If the machine mistakenly reads two answers for one question, it will consider the question unanswered.

6. **Use your test booklet as scrap paper.** Use it to make notes or write down ideas. No one else will look at what you write.

7. **Check off questions as you work on them.** This will save time and help you to know which questions you've skipped.

8. **Check your answer sheet regularly.** Make sure you are in the right place. Check the number of the question and the number on the answer sheet every few questions. This is especially important when you skip a question. Losing your place on the answer sheet will cost you time and even points.

9. **Work at an even, steady pace and keep moving.** Each question on the test takes a certain amount of time to read and answer. Good test-takers develop a sense of timing to help them complete the test. Your goal is to spend time on the questions that you are most likely to answer correctly.

10. **Keep track of time.** During the hour that each Subject Test takes, check your progress occasionally so that you know how much of the test you have completed and how much time is left. Leave a few minutes for review toward the end of the testing period.

IMPORTANT

If you erase all your answers to a Subject Test, that's the same as a request to cancel the test. All Subject Tests taken with the erased test will also be canceled.

REMEMBER

Check your answer sheet. Make sure your answers are dark and completely filled in. Erase completely.

7 Ways TO PACE YOURSELF

1. Set up a schedule. Know when you should be one-quarter of the way through and halfway through. Every now and then, check your progress against your schedule.

2. Begin to work as soon as the testing time begins. Reading the instructions and getting to know the test directions in this book ahead of time will allow you to do that.

3. Work at an even, steady pace. After you answer the questions you are sure of, move on to those for which you'll need more time.

4. Skip questions you can't answer. You might have time to return to them. Remember to mark them in your test booklet, so you'll be able to find them later.

5. As you work on a question, cross out the answers you can eliminate in your test book.

6. Go back to the questions you skipped. If you can, eliminate some of the answer choices, then make an educated guess.

7. Leave time in the last few minutes to check your answers to avoid mistakes.

After the Tests

Most, but not all, scores will be reported online several weeks after the test date. A few days later, a full score report will be available to you online. You can request a paper score report too, which arrives later. Your score report will also be mailed to your high school and to the colleges, universities and scholarship programs that you indicated when you registered or on the correction form attached to your admission ticket. The score report includes your scores, percentiles and interpretive information.

What's Your Score?

Scores are available for free at www.collegeboard.org several weeks after each SAT is given. You can also get your scores—for a fee—by telephone. Call customer service at 866-756-7346 in the United States. From outside the United States, call 212-713-7789.

Some scores may take longer to report. If your score report is not available online when expected, check back the following week. If you have requested a paper score report and you have not received it by eight weeks after the test date (by five weeks for online reports), contact customer service by phone at 866-756-7346 or by e-mail at sat@info.collegeboard.org.

Should You Take the Tests Again?

Before you decide whether or not to retest, you need to evaluate your scores. The best way to evaluate how you really did on a Subject Test is to compare your scores to the admission or placement requirements, or average scores, of the colleges to which you are applying. You may decide that with additional work you could do better taking the test again.

Contacting the College Board

If you have comments or questions about the tests, please write to us at the College Board SAT Program, P.O. Box 025505, Miami, FL 33102, or e-mail us at sat@info.collegeboard.org.

United States History

Purpose

The Subject Test in United States History emphasizes pre-Columbian times to the present as well as basic social science concepts, methods, and generalizations as they are found in the study of history. It is not tied to any textbook or instructional approach, but to your high school curriculum.

Format

This is a one-hour test with 90 to 95 multiple-choice questions. The questions cover political, economic, social, intellectual, and cultural history as well as foreign policy. The chart on the following page shows you what content the test covers and the approximate percentages of questions covering that content.

Content

The questions may require you to:

- recall basic information and require you to know facts, terms, concepts, and generalizations

- analyze and interpret materials such as graphs, charts, paintings, text, cartoons, photographs, and maps

- understand important aspects of U.S. history

- relate ideas to given data

- evaluate data for a given purpose, basing your judgment either on internal evidence, such as proof and logical consistency, or on external criteria, such as comparison with other works, established standards, and theories

Topics Covered

Material Covered*	Approximate Percentage of Test
Political History	32–36
Economic History	18–20
Social History	18–22
Intellectual and Cultural History	10–12
Foreign Policy	13–17
Periods Covered	
Pre-Columbian history to 1789	20
1790 to 1898	40
1899 to the present	40

* Social science concepts, methods, and generalizations are incorporated in this material.

How to Prepare

The only essential preparation is a sound, one-year course in U.S. history at the college-preparatory level. Most of the test questions are based on material commonly taught in U.S. history courses in secondary schools, although some of the material may be covered in other social studies courses. Knowledge gained from social studies courses and from outside reading could be helpful. No one textbook or method of instruction is considered better than another. Familiarize yourself with the directions in advance. The directions in this book are identical to those that appear on the test.

Score

The total score is reported on the 200-to-800 scale.

Sample Questions

All questions on the Subject Test in U.S. History are multiple choice, requiring you to choose the best response from five choices. The following sample questions illustrate the types of questions on the test, their range of difficulty, and the abilities they measure. Questions may be presented as separate items or in sets based on quotations, maps, pictures, graphs, or tables.

Directions: Each of the questions or incomplete statements below is followed by five suggested answers or completions. Select the one that is best in each case and then fill in the corresponding circle on the answer sheet.

1

Which leader of the national women's suffrage movement was responsible for the "winning plan" leading to the enactment of the Nineteenth Amendment?

A) Abigail Adams

B) Carrie Chapman Catt

C) Peggy Eaton

D) Emma Goldman

E) Carrie Nation

Choice (B) is the correct answer to question 1. Carrie Chapman Catt was influential in the 1920 ratification of the Nineteenth Amendment, which gave women the right to vote. In 1916, as president of the National American Woman Suffrage Association, Chapman Catt unveiled her "winning plan" for achieving women's suffrage (voting rights). Her plan was to lobby for suffrage at both the national and state levels. She thought that gaining key states would help persuade legislators at the national level. Her plan and her support of the war effort worked: the Nineteenth Amendment was ratified just four years later. None of the other women were leaders of the U.S. women's suffrage movement. Abigail Adams (A) was the wife of second U.S. President John Adams. Peggy Eaton (C) is known for her involvement in a scandal with John Henry Eaton, a member of President Andrew Jackson's cabinet, whom she eventually married. Emma Goldman (D) was a Lithuanian-born anarchist and radical activist who was deported in 1919. Carrie Nation (E) was a leader of the temperance movement in the United States.

2

The greatest source of federal revenue between 1865 and 1900 was

A) land sales

B) tariffs

C) property and corporate taxes

D) income taxes

E) bond sales

Choice (B) is the correct answer to question 2. The greatest source of federal revenue between 1865 and 1900 was tariffs. Tariffs are duties governments collect on goods that are imported into their country. To raise much-needed funds during the American Civil War, the United States established high tariffs on incoming goods from Europe. After the war, the high tariffs remained to raise federal revenue and to protect American manufacturers from competition with cheaper imported goods. Many opposed high tariffs because they restricted international trade and tended to make consumer goods more expensive, and these tariffs were eventually lowered. The other answers are incorrect. Land sales (A) and bond sales (E) did not generate as much federal revenue as tariffs did during this time period. Federal taxation of property and corporations (C) and of income (D) occurred primarily after the passage of the Sixteenth Amendment was ratified in 1913, ending a long battle about the constitutionality of federal taxation of income.

3

During the Progressive Era, Congress passed legislation to create the

A) Federal Reserve System

B) Interstate Commerce Commission

C) Agricultural Adjustment Act

D) Tennessee Valley Authority

E) Works Progress Administration

Choice (A) is the correct answer to question 3. During the Progressive Era of the early twentieth century, Congress did much to reform the country, including passing legislation to create the Federal Reserve System. President Woodrow Wilson signed this important legislation in 1913, helping to stabilize the nation's economy by setting up a system to control the money supply. The Federal Reserve System is a central U.S. banking system responsible for monetary policy. The Federal Reserve System regulates the creation of currency and sets interest rates. The other answers are incorrect, as none of the other acts or agencies was established during this time period. The Interstate Commerce Commission (B) was created earlier, in 1887. The Agricultural Adjustment Act (C), the Tennessee Valley Authority (D), and the Works Progress Administration (E) were all created later, during the New Deal of the 1930s.

4

Under Chief Justice Earl Warren, the Supreme Court did which of the following?

A) Restricted the rights of dissidents to receive passports

B) Developed a clear definition of obscenity still in use

C) Protected the rights of persons charged with criminal activity

D) Upheld state laws segregating public schools

E) Endorsed prayer in public schools

Choice (C) is the correct answer to question 4. Under Earl Warren, Chief Justice from 1953 to 1969, the Supreme Court ruled in favor of the plaintiff in *Miranda v. Arizona*, thereby protecting the rights of persons charged with criminal activity. With the 1966 Miranda case, the Court ruled that before persons accused of a crime are interrogated by the police, they must be informed of their right to remain silent and to have an attorney present. The decision established what has come to be known as the Miranda warning to arrested persons, famously beginning, "You have the right to remain silent. Anything you say can and will be used against you in a court of law. You have the right to an attorney..." The other answers are incorrect. In the 1958 *Kent v. Dulles* decision, the Supreme Court upheld the rights of dissidents to receive passports (A). Although the Supreme Court did rule on a definition of obscenity in *Roth v. United States* in 1957, Warren argued that the definition was still unclear (B). Clearer criteria for obscenity were established by the Supreme Court in 1973 with *Miller v. California*, after Warren had left the court. Under Warren, the Supreme Court also made the historic *Brown v. Board of Education of Topeka* decision in 1954, overthrowing legal segregation of public schools (D). In *Engel v. Vitale* (1962), the Supreme Court under Warren ruled that prayer in public schools was unconstitutional (E).

5

Louis Sullivan and Frank Lloyd Wright are best known for their work in

A) painting

B) poetry

C) science

D) architecture

E) philosophy

Choice (D) is the correct answer to question 5. Louis Sullivan and Frank Lloyd Wright are best known for their work in architecture. Louis Sullivan (1856–1924) was an American architect known for designing steel-framed buildings. Sullivan is considered to be the originator of the skyscraper. A member of the Chicago School of Architecture, Sullivan's influential buildings include the Wainwright Building in St. Louis and the Carson

Pirie Scott department store in Chicago. Also associated with the Chicago School, Frank Lloyd Wright (1867–1959) was an American architect known for his "prairie houses," clean geometric lines, and style of integrating buildings into their natural surroundings. Among his most famous buildings are the Guggenheim Museum in New York City and the Fallingwater house in Bear Run, Pennsylvania. The other answers are incorrect.

6

"I believe that it must be the policy of the United States to support free peoples who are resisting attempted subjugation by armed minorities or by outside pressures.

I believe that we must assist free peoples to work out their own destinies in their own way. . . .

Should we fail to aid Greece and Turkey in this fateful hour, the effect will be far reaching to the west as well as to the east. We must take immediate and resolute action."

The excerpt above states which of the following foreign policies?

A) The Gentlemen's Agreement

B) The Marshall Plan

C) The Good Neighbor policy

D) The Truman Doctrine

E) The Alliance for Progress

Choice (D) is the correct answer to question 6. The excerpt is taken from President Harry Truman's address to the U.S. Congress on March 12, 1947, in which he expressed what came to be known as the Truman Doctrine. Central to the Truman Doctrine is the idea that it is in the best interests of the United States to help governments resist and repress uprisings and invasions by organizations the United States deems undemocratic, with a focus on stopping the spread of communism. This doctrine was initially used, as the excerpt suggests, to help Greece and Turkey defeat a communist insurgency. Later, the Truman Doctrine was famously cited as an argument for U.S. involvement in Southeast Asia. The other answers are incorrect.

7

The decade following the War of 1812 has been characterized as the Era of Good Feelings for which of the following reasons?

A) All sections of the country supported the aims of the Hartford Convention.

B) Only one political party dominated national elections.

C) International cooperation produced a long period of peace.

D) Women gained political influence with the right to vote.

E) Abolitionists succeeded in restricting slavery in new territories.

Choice (B) is the correct answer to question 7. The decade following the War of 1812 has been characterized as the Era of Good Feelings largely because one political party dominated national elections. President James Monroe of the Democratic–Republican Party, elected with little opposition in 1816, ran unopposed in 1820 and was nearly unanimously reelected. The other main political party, the Federalists, was in the midst of collapse in 1816, and no other party or candidate gained national popularity for years to come. The other answers are incorrect. The Hartford Convention of 1814 (A) was only supported by delegates from New England, who met to discuss their disagreements with the South and the antitrade policies of President James Madison. Although some international peace occurred at the end of the Napoleonic Wars, it was during this decade that many South American nations revolted against Spain (C). Women did not gain the right to vote until 1920 (D). The Missouri Compromise of 1820 prohibited slavery in many territories, but permitted it in the territory of Missouri (E).

8

Puritans who remained within the Church of England founded the colony of

A) Massachusetts Bay

B) New Netherland

C) Plymouth Plantation

D) Rhode Island

E) Virginia

Choice (A) is the correct answer to question 8. Puritans who remained within the Church of England founded the colony of Massachusetts Bay. The term "Puritan" generally refers to a sect of English Christianity that originated in the 16th century. Puritans held beliefs about ethics, biblical interpretation, and church authority that differed from the core beliefs of the Church of England. Of those Puritans who remained within the official church, many, like the founders of the Massachusetts Bay Colony, found it easier to live and worship in the American colonies. The other answers are incorrect. The beliefs of some Puritans, such as the founders of the Plymouth Plantation (C) and Rhode Island (D), led them to separate from the Church of England. The settlers of New Netherland (B) were from the Netherlands and were not members of the Church of England. The founders of Virginia (E) were members of the Church of England who did not hold Puritan beliefs.

9

Michael Harrington's 1962 book, *The Other America*, primarily addresses the

A) growth of Communist Party membership

B) problems of migrant labor

C) failure of secondary education

D) increase in poverty

E) increase in gender inequality

Choice (D) is the correct answer to question 9. Michael Harrington's 1962 book, the full title of which is *The Other America: Poverty in the United States*, addresses the increase in poverty in the United States. A writer and activist, Harrington became an influential voice in U.S. society. *The Other America*, which reveals the impoverished conditions under which many U.S. citizens lived, attracted many readers, including Presidents John F. Kennedy and Lyndon B. Johnson, and is said to have led in part to President Johnson's declaration of a "war on poverty." The other answers are incorrect, as Harrington's book is not primarily focused on the Communist Party (A), migrant labor (B), secondary education (C), or gender inequality (E).

10

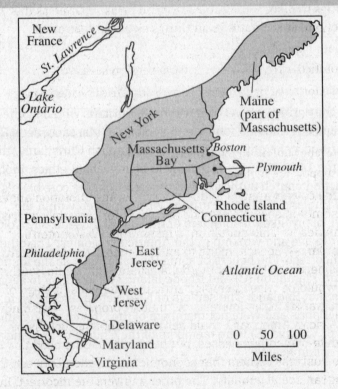

The shaded area in the map above represents the boundaries of

A) King Philip's (Metacom's) domain in 1675

B) the Powhatan Confederacy in 1680

C) the Dominion of New England in 1688

D) the Puritan colonies in 1710

E) the Iroquois Confederacy in 1750

Choice (C) is the correct answer to question 10. The shaded area in the map above represents the boundaries of the Dominion of New England in 1688. The Dominion of New England was an administrative unit of the English colonies established by King James II in 1686. In 1688, New York and New Jersey were acquired by England from the Dutch and added to the Dominion. King James II established the Dominion to centralize military and political rule in order to enforce imperial policies such as the Navigation Acts, which restricted the colonies from trading with non-British companies. Highly unpopular with the colonists, the central administration by the Dominion and its enforcing British soldiers were met with severe resistance, collapsing with the overthrow of James II in the Glorious Revolution of 1688. The other answers are incorrect. In 1675 and 1676, King Philip (Metacom) was at war with colonists throughout the shaded region, but he never took full control of the territories (A). The Powhatan Confederacy was located south of the shaded area (B). Large portions of this area, including New York, were not Puritan colonies in 1710 (D). The Iroquois Confederacy was located west and north of the shaded area (E).

11

"In all things that are purely social we can be as separate as the fingers, yet one as the hand in all things essential to mutual progress."

In the quotation above, Booker T. Washington seeks to

A) provide a formula for economic success for African Americans

B) demand integrated facilities for African Americans

C) promote religious harmony between whites and African Americans

D) promote labor unions in the United States South

E) gather support for abolishing slavery

Choice (A) is the correct answer to question 11. In the quotation above, Booker T. Washington seeks to provide a formula for economic success for African Americans. This quotation is taken from Washington's "Atlanta Compromise" speech, made to an audience of predominately white businessmen in 1895. Washington is arguing that white Southern businessmen would be wise to employ African Americans (instead of European immigrants) in the interests of "mutual progress." Washington believed that African Americans could achieve economic success by laboring for white-owned businesses, but he clearly felt the need to reassure white business owners that economic cooperation between the races did not mean social equality. The other answers are incorrect. In this address, Washington is mainly concerned with the economic cooperation between whites and African Americans, not integrated facilities (B) or religious harmony (C). Washington was seeking greater employment of African Americans, not modification of their working conditions through labor unions (D). Slavery had already been abolished by the time of this address (E).

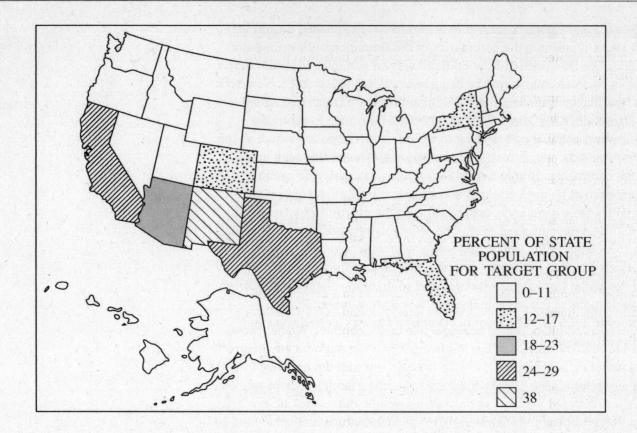

PERCENT OF STATE
POPULATION
FOR TARGET GROUP

0–11
12–17
18–23
24–29
38

12

The late twentieth-century map above shows concentrations of which of the following groups?

A) Conservative Republicans

B) African Americans

C) Liberal Democrats

D) Christian fundamentalists

E) Hispanics

Choice (E) is the correct answer to question 12. This map shows concentrations of Hispanics in the United States in the late twentieth century. The term Hispanic refers to people of Spanish or Latin American heritage. As shown by the map, the states with the highest percentage of Hispanics in the late twentieth century were located along or near the Mexican border, with the exception of Florida and New York, two states with historically large Hispanic populations. The other choices are incorrect. None of the other groups were represented demographically in the late twentieth century as shown on the map: there were higher proportions of Conservative Republicans (A), African Americans (B), and Christian fundamentalists (D) in Southern states such as South Carolina and Georgia, and higher proportions of Liberal Democrats (C) in such states as New Jersey, Massachusetts, and Illinois.

13

In the seventeenth century, women serving as indentured laborers had to

A) remain unmarried until their indenture was over

B) give their inheritance to their employers

C) renounce all legal ties to their families

D) pledge to produce specified amounts of spun wool and cotton thread

E) live in separate buildings or dormitories supervised by matrons

Choice (A) is the correct answer to question 13. In the seventeenth century, women serving as indentured laborers had to remain unmarried until their terms of indenture were over. Indentured laborers were laborers who undertook contract work for an employer for a period of time without pay, in exchange for housing, food, training, and, in the case of many American indentured laborers, the cost of coming to a new country. Because the indentured servants were legally bound to their masters, they were prohibited from marrying while under contract. Women were also prohibited from becoming pregnant. The other answers are incorrect. Indentured servants were otherwise free persons and did not have to give up their inheritances (B), or renounce ties to their families (C). Most female indentured servants performed household duties and did not have to produce wool or cotton thread (D). Female indentured servants often lived in the main houses of their masters rather than in separate buildings or dormitories (E).

United States History – Practice Test 1

Practice Helps

The test that follows is an actual, previously administered SAT Subject Test in United States History. To get an idea of what it's like to take this test, practice under conditions that are much like those of an actual test administration.

- Set aside an hour when you can take the test uninterrupted.

- Sit at a desk or table with no other books or papers. Dictionaries, other books, or notes are not allowed in the test room.

- Tear out an answer sheet from the back of this book and fill it in just as you would on the day of the test. One answer sheet can be used for up to three Subject Tests.

- Read the instructions that precede the practice test. During the actual administration, you will be asked to read them before answering test questions.

- Use a clock or kitchen timer to time yourself.

- After you finish the practice test, read the sections "How to Score the SAT Subject Test in United States History" and "How Did You Do on the Subject Test in United States History?"

- The appearance of the answer sheet in this book may differ from the answer sheet you see on test day.

UNITED STATES HISTORY TEST

The top portion of the page of the answer sheet that you will use to take the United States History Test must be filled in exactly as illustrated below. When your supervisor tells you to fill in the circle next to the name of the test you are about to take, mark your answer sheet as shown.

○ Literature	○ Mathematics Level 1	○ German	○ Chinese Listening	○ Japanese Listening
○ Biology E	○ Mathematics Level 2	○ Italian	○ French Listening	○ Korean Listening
○ Biology M	● U.S. History	○ Latin	○ German Listening	○ Spanish Listening
○ Chemistry	○ World History	○ Modern Hebrew		
○ Physics	○ French	○ Spanish	**Background Questions:** ① ② ③ ④ ⑤ ⑥ ⑦ ⑧ ⑨	

After filling in the circle next to the name of the test you are taking, locate the Background Questions section, which also appears at the top of your answer sheet (as shown above). This is where you will answer the following Background Questions on your answer sheet.

BACKGROUND QUESTIONS

Please answer the two questions below by filling in the appropriate circle in the Background Questions box on your answer sheet. <u>The information you provide is for statistical purposes only and will not affect your test score.</u>

Question _____ I

How many semesters of United States History have you taken from grade 9 to the present? (If you are taking United States History this semester, count it as a full semester.) Fill in only <u>one</u> circle of circles 1-4.

- One semester or less   —Fill in circle 1.
- Two semesters   —Fill in circle 2.
- Three semesters   —Fill in circle 3.
- Four or more semesters   —Fill in circle 4.

Question _____ II

Which, if any, of the following social studies courses have you taken from grade 9 to the present? (Fill in ALL circles that apply.)

- One or more semesters of government   —Fill in circle 5.
- One or more semesters of economics   —Fill in circle 6.
- One or more semesters of geography   —Fill in circle 7.
- One or more semesters of psychology   —Fill in circle 8.
- One or more semesters of sociology or anthropology   —Fill in circle 9.

If you have taken none of these social studies courses, leave the circles 5 through 9 blank.

When the supervisor gives the signal, turn the page and begin the United States History Test. There are 100 numbered circles on the answer sheet and 90 questions in the United States History Test. Therefore, use only circles 1 to 90 for recording your answers.

UNITED STATES HISTORY TEST

Directions: Each of the questions or incomplete statements below is followed by five suggested answers or completions. Select the one that is best in each case and then fill in the corresponding circle on the answer sheet.

1. The first example of a representative legislative assembly among the British colonies in North America was the

    (A) New England Confederation
    (B) Virginia House of Burgesses
    (C) Albany Congress
    (D) Virginia Company
    (E) Society of Friends

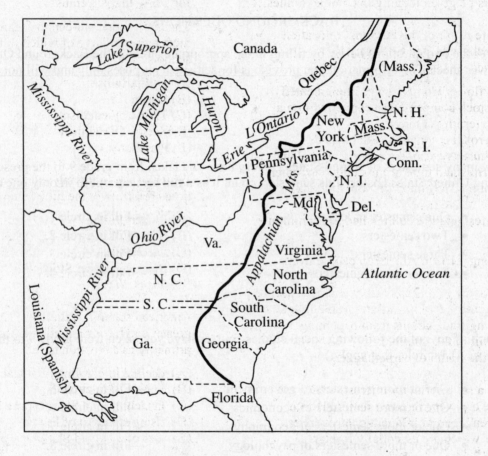

2. The heavy line on the map above represents the western boundary established by the

    (A) Proclamation of 1763
    (B) Quebec Act of 1774
    (C) Treaty of Paris of 1783
    (D) Jay Treaty of 1794
    (E) Treaty of Ghent of 1814

GO ON TO THE NEXT PAGE

3. Which of the following is true of the Stamp Act of 1765 ?

    (A) It established the first comprehensive postal service for the colonies.
    (B) It provided new financial resources for the colonies.
    (C) It was repealed in 1766, although Britain still claimed the right to tax the colonies.
    (D) It was accepted by the colonists with only mild resistance.
    (E) It established the requirement that British soldiers be given lodging in colonial homes.

4. An immediate result of the Puritans' relocation of the Massachusetts Bay Company to North America was that

    (A) the Mayflower Compact was implemented
    (B) a joint-stock company was converted into a self-governing colony
    (C) the first royal colony was established
    (D) Massachusetts became a proprietary colony
    (E) the Pilgrims and the Puritans joined together to form the Dominion of New England

5. The literacy test and the poll tax had the common purpose of

    (A) preventing African American people from voting
    (B) turning away immigrants from southern ports
    (C) assisting the Republican Party in the South
    (D) preventing trade unions from becoming powerful in the South
    (E) ridding the South of carpetbaggers

6. "Europe has a set of primary interests which to us have none or a very remote relation. Hence she must be engaged in frequent controversies, the causes of which are essentially foreign to our concerns."

    George Washington's Farewell Address

    A similar position to that taken in the statement above was expressed in

    (A) the Monroe Doctrine
    (B) the congressional declaration of war against Spain in 1898
    (C) the congressional declaration of war in 1917
    (D) Franklin Roosevelt's Lend-Lease policy
    (E) the Marshall Plan

7. In the colonial period, which of the following was the most valuable export from the Chesapeake colonies?

    (A) Cotton
    (B) Rice
    (C) Sugar
    (D) Timber
    (E) Tobacco

8. "To believe your own thought, to believe that what is true for you in your private heart is true for all, —that is genius."

    The mid-nineteenth-century statement above is most representative of which of the following schools of thought?

    (A) Utilitarianism
    (B) Deism
    (C) Transcendentalism
    (D) Social Darwinism
    (E) Pragmatism

9. Which of the following was a prominent educational reformer in the nineteenth century?

    (A) Robert Fulton
    (B) Horace Mann
    (C) Jacob Riis
    (D) Harriet Beecher Stowe
    (E) Ida B. Wells

10. American schools in the late 1950s began to put greater emphasis on mathematics and science primarily as a reaction to the

    (A) decline in enrollment at teachers' colleges
    (B) impact of television
    (C) launching of a Soviet space satellite
    (D) rising standard of living
    (E) loss of a United States spy plane

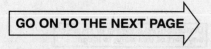
GO ON TO THE NEXT PAGE

11. "[G]overnments are instituted among men, deriving their just powers from the consent of the governed; that, whenever any form of government becomes destructive of these ends, it is the right of the people to alter or to abolish it, and to institute a new government."

The quotation above is from the

(A) Constitution
(B) Bill of Rights
(C) Declaration of Independence
(D) Monroe Doctrine
(E) Articles of Confederation

12. During the Revolutionary War, George Washington did which of the following?

(A) He relied on the American navy.
(B) He believed that colonial militias were more dependable than the Continental army.
(C) He commanded an army better equipped and better trained than Britain's army.
(D) He understood that the army was a symbol of the republican cause.
(E) He encouraged planters to form slave militias for colonial defense.

13. Which of the following is a major reason that the Anti-Federalists opposed ratification of the Constitution?

(A) They believed it did not create a sufficiently strong central government.
(B) They believed it disproportionately benefited rural and agricultural interests.
(C) They suspected it represented an excessive concentration of political power.
(D) They desired a founding document that would guarantee the abolition of slavery.
(E) They favored a return to monarchy.

14. Jeffersonian republicanism included the belief that

(A) the United States needed a strong standing army
(B) United States territory should be enlarged to create more family farms
(C) women should have the right to vote
(D) the urban monied class was the source of republican virtue
(E) property should be owned by the state and loaned to individuals as needed

15. In the period from 1500 to 1750, a direct result of the European interaction with the New World was

(A) the roughly equal increases in the wealth of societies in the Americas and in Europe
(B) the stagnation of the world economic system due to war and conflict
(C) the expansion of world trade due to resources extracted from the Americas
(D) the stabilization of world trade for the first time in more than a century
(E) a decrease in the international slave trade

16. In 1775, British author Samuel Johnson asked, "How is it that we hear the loudest yelps for liberty among the drivers of Negroes?" His comment was

(A) a reflection of British support for the slave trade
(B) an expression of a desire to extend slavery to Great Britain
(C) a demonstration of support for the 1689 Bill of Rights
(D) a criticism of colonial slaveholders who protested against British policies
(E) a statement of support for the emergent antislavery movement in Great Britain

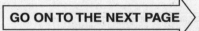
GO ON TO THE NEXT PAGE

17. "RUN away from the subscriber in Albemarle, a Mulatto slave called Sandy, about 35 years of age, his stature is rather low, inclining to corpulence, and his complexion light; he is a shoemaker by trade . . . can do coarse carpenters work . . . in his behavior [he] is artful and knavish. He took with him . . . his shoemakers tools. . . . Whoever conveys the said slave to me . . . shall have 40 shillings reward . . . from THOMAS JEFFERSON."

Virginia Gazette, advertisement, September 14, 1769

The advertisement above reveals

(A) a slaveholder's public description of a slave's individual personality traits and work skills
(B) Jefferson's early commitment to abolishing slavery
(C) the slave's loyalty to the slaveholder, Jefferson
(D) the slave's inability to escape successfully from a slaveholder
(E) the slave's knowledge of advanced agricultural techniques

18. Which of the following effects did both Bacon's Rebellion (1676) and King Philip's War (Metacom's War, 1675–1676) have in common?

(A) The subsequent decline of Native American power
(B) The revival of Puritan influence in the colonies
(C) A reduction in the power of colonial governors
(D) An increase in indentured servitude
(E) The end of building fortified towns for protection

19. "They do much extol and wonder at the English for their strange inventions. . . . The Indians, seeing the plow tear up more ground in a day than their clam-shells could scrape up in a month, desired to see the workmanship of it."

William Wood, *New England's Prospect*, 1634

The statement above best makes which of the following arguments?

(A) American Indians provided information that helped English colonists increase the yields on their crops.
(B) English agricultural practices were far more intensive than those of American Indians.
(C) American Indians' agricultural practices were more sustainable and consistent with the ecology of North America.
(D) American Indians rapidly adopted English behavioral norms and cultural practices.
(E) English settlers engaged in extensive trade with American Indians.

20. Some politicians in the 1820s criticized the Missouri Compromise because it

(A) merely postponed decisions regarding the issue of slavery
(B) increased the area south of latitude 36°30' that was free of slavery
(C) resulted in representatives of slave states outnumbering those of free states in Congress
(D) only affected slaves in the immediate Missouri Territory
(E) would lead immediately to renewed hostility with Spain

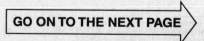 **GO ON TO THE NEXT PAGE**

21. "We, therefore, . . . do declare and ordain, . . . That the several acts . . . are unauthorized by the Constitution of the United States . . . and are null, void, and no law, nor binding upon this State, its officers or citizens."

The quotation above reflects the political doctrine developed by

(A) George Washington
(B) John C. Calhoun
(C) Daniel Webster
(D) Andrew Jackson
(E) Abraham Lincoln

22. In the 1500s, contact between Native Americans and European explorers on the North American mainland led to which of the following developments?

(A) Growing resistance to Native American diseases by Europeans
(B) Discovery of a system of navigable waterways to Asia through North America
(C) Widespread adoption of Native American cultures and religions by Europeans
(D) Forced migration of large numbers of Native Americans to Europe as slaves
(E) Spread of European epidemic diseases among Native Americans

23. George Whitefield was a major figure in which of the following movements?

(A) First Great Awakening
(B) Second Great Awakening
(C) The temperance movement
(D) The abolitionist movement
(E) The Social Gospel movement

24. By the late 1600s, the greatest cultural difference between the New England colonies and the southern colonies was the

(A) influence of the English language on culture
(B) level of government support for the arts
(C) influence of Native American customs on colonists
(D) extent of literacy among White colonists
(E) impact of Catholicism on religious practices

25. Which of the following was the most important immediate result of the Jay Treaty (1794) ?

(A) End of the Federalist Party's control of the national government
(B) Maintenance of a fragile peace with Great Britain
(C) Recall of the United States minister to France
(D) Redefinition of neutral rights by the United States government
(E) Passage of the Alien and Sedition Acts

26. In contrast to the Democratic-Republicans, the Federalists in the 1790s were more likely to support

(A) states' rights
(B) a strong national government
(C) an alliance with France
(D) the financial interests of farmers
(E) rapid expansion of slavery

GO ON TO THE NEXT PAGE

27. The United States intervened in the First World War immediately following

   (A) Germany's refusal to apologize for sinking the Lusitania
   (B) Germany's resumption of unrestricted submarine warfare
   (C) France's decision to surrender
   (D) President Wilson's enunciation of his Fourteen Points
   (E) Germany's invasion of neutral Belgium

28. Which of the following did NOT involve a controversy between advocates of strict and loose construction of the Constitution? ·

   (A) Hamilton's report on the public credit
   (B) Jefferson's purchase of the Louisiana Territory
   (C) Marshall's decision in *McCulloch* v. *Maryland*
   (D) Pierce's acquisition of land in the Gadsden Purchase
   (E) Lincoln's suspension of habeas corpus

29. Which of the following best describes the primary objective of the Roosevelt administration when it took office in 1933 ?

   (A) To curtail runaway inflation and restore the buying power of American wages
   (B) To provide short-term relief as well as long-range solutions to the nation's economic problems
   (C) To force European countries to repay their First World War loans in order to infuse the United States economy with cash
   (D) To restore a sound currency by putting the United States onto the gold standard
   (E) To eliminate the agencies and measures that President Herbert Hoover had created to counteract the Depression

30. Which of the following political parties included supporters of Henry Clay's American System, opponents of Andrew Jackson, and Northern industrialists?

   (A) Anti-Federali sts
   (B) Democr ats
   (C) Free Soilers
   (D) Know-Nothin gs
   (E) Whigs

31. Which of the following was a direct effect of the Second Great Awakening in the United States?

   (A) A greater faith in scientific reason and expert knowledge
   (B) A rejection of European religious ideas
   (C) The increased participation of women in reform movements
   (D) The establishment of many state-supported churches
   (E) A widespread disillusionment with organized churches

32. Which of the following was a response to religious intolerance in the early decades of the nineteenth century?

   (A) The Mormon journey westward
   (B) The transcendentalist movement
   (C) The division between the northern and southern Baptists
   (D) The growth of evangelical revivalism
   (E) The passage of the Chinese Exclusion Act

GO ON TO THE NEXT PAGE

POPULATION IN AND IMMIGRATION TO THE UNITED STATES, 1820–1860

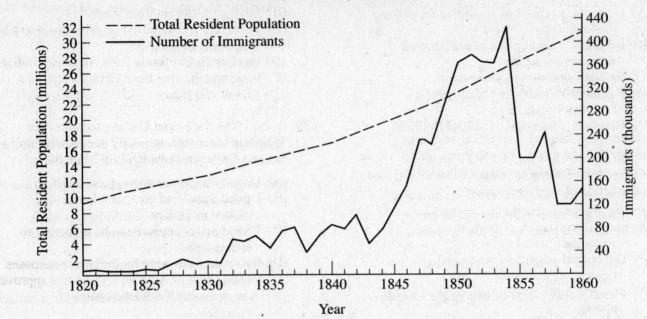

33. Which of the following statements is supported by the graph above?

   (A) Between 1845 and 1855, the number of immigrants to the United States was greater than the total resident population.

   (B) Immigration to the United States grew at a steady rate throughout the antebellum period.

   (C) The total resident population of the United States quadrupled between 1820 and 1860.

   (D) From the early 1840s to the mid-1850s, the number of immigrants to the United States increased sharply.

   (E) In the 1850s the total resident population of the United States dropped dramatically.

GO ON TO THE NEXT PAGE

34. Which of the following popular mid-nineteenth-century pastimes best reveal the pervasive influence of slavery in the culture of cities in the northern United States?

    (A) Circuses
    (B) Operas
    (C) Baseball games
    (D) Minstrel shows
    (E) Horse races

35. Which of the following accurately describes a major form of government support for economic development from the 1820s to the 1850s?

    (A) State governments invested in canal and railroad construction.
    (B) Federal legislation authorized a transcontinental railroad.
    (C) The federal government nationalized the Massachusetts textile industry.
    (D) Congress authorized a minimum wage for workers.
    (E) State governments created a coordinated national banking system.

36. All of the following statements about slavery in the antebellum South are correct EXCEPT:

    (A) Many plantation slaves and slaveholders attended the same religious services.
    (B) The number of slaves increased dramatically during the first half of the nineteenth century.
    (C) The majority of White Southerners held slaves.
    (D) Slave families were often broken up by the sale of family members.
    (E) Slaves worked in a variety of occupations other than agriculture.

37. Which of the following best describes the role played by the Border States in the Civil War?

    (A) The cotton they produced provided important financial resources for the Union.
    (B) Their high concentration of slaves attracted the interest of Northern abolitionists.
    (C) Their strategic location generally benefited the Union.
    (D) They were located next to the Mississippi River and controlled its navigation.
    (E) They surrounded the capital of the Confederacy.

38. The United States acquired California by

    (A) fighting a war with Mexico
    (B) buying California from Spain
    (C) claiming the area based on prior discovery by United States settlers
    (D) purchasing California from American Indians
    (E) acquiring the area from Great Britain as a result of a treaty

39. In the 1960s the Soviet Union used all of the following arguments to justify the presence of Soviet missiles in Cuba EXCEPT that the

    (A) United States was an aggressive nation
    (B) United States had comparable missiles located in Turkey
    (C) United States appeared to be preparing to invade Cuba
    (D) Soviet missiles were for defensive purposes
    (E) Organization of American States had approved the presence of Soviet missiles

40. The Emancipation Proclamation was significant because it

    (A) abolished slavery throughout the United States
    (B) instituted equal protection before the law
    (C) formally ended the Civil War
    (D) guaranteed equal pay for African American soldiers
    (E) proclaimed the end of slavery in areas in rebellion against the United States government

41. All of the following motivated the Puritan settlement of New England EXCEPT

    (A) a search for expanded economic opportunities
    (B) dissatisfaction with the Church of England
    (C) the intention to create a church organization around the principles of congregationalism
    (D) a commitment to the religious doctrines of John Calvin
    (E) a belief in the principle of religious toleration

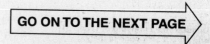

PARDON.
Columbia—"Shall I Trust These Men,

Courtesy of Library of Congress #LC-DIG-ds-07129

FRANCHISE.
and Not This Man?"

Courtesy of Library of Congress #LC-DIG-ds-07129

42. The 1865 cartoon above by Thomas Nast criticizes

(A) the Dred Scott decision
(B) the Reconstruction plan of President Andrew Johnson
(C) the Reconstruction plan of the Radical Republicans
(D) the end of Reconstruction
(E) Jim Crow laws

GO ON TO THE NEXT PAGE

43. Which of the following statements about the antislavery movement of the 1840s and 1850s is most accurate? ·

   (A) The movement's primary goal was to help former slaves resettle in Africa.

   (B) The movement was closely allied with the Jacksonian wing of the Democratic Party.

   (C) Black abolitionists consistently rejected armed self-defense or violent action as a means of ending slavery.

   (D) Many opponents of slavery became involved in political action to limit the spread of slavery.

   (E) Abolitionist organizations were fully integrated racially.

44. "We mean to make things over, we are tired of toil for naught,
With but bare enough to live upon, and never an hour for thought;
We want to feel the sunshine, and we want to smell the flowers,
We are sure that God has will'd it, and we mean to have eight hours.
We're summoning our forces from the shipyard, shop and mill,
Eight hours for work, eight hours for rest, eight hours for what we will!"

   The song lyrics above, written in the late 1860s, expressed the goals of

   (A) business owners

   (B) labor union members

   (C) temperan ce advocates

   (D) farmers

   (E) women's rights activists

45. Between 1800 and 1860, the Northern states had all of the following advantages that enabled them to surpass the Southern states in industrialization EXCEPT

   (A) raw materials for the textile industry

   (B) more readily available capital

   (C) better transportation systems

   (D) larger urban markets for industrial products

   (E) a larger immigrant labor force

46. In the late nineteenth century, the concentration of the meatpacking industry in Chicago led to all of the following effects EXCEPT

   (A) heavy pollution of a tributary of the Chicago River

   (B) bankruptcies of independent small-town butchers

   (C) development of a militant labor movement among the stockyard workers

   (D) improvement in the quality of meat available to consumers

   (E) criticism of practices in the food industry by muckrakers

47. All of the following statements about education in the United States before 1900 are true EXCEPT:

   (A) Soon after the American Revolution, many academies were founded for elite young men and women.

   (B) Very few Black people received public education before the Civil War.

   (C) In the North, education through high school became compulsory at the time of the Civil War.

   (D) Land grants under the Morrill Act strengthened higher education.

   (E) Law and medical schools admitted few women.

GO ON TO THE NEXT PAGE

48. Which of the following was NOT a major source of conflict between capital and labor in the late nineteenth century?

   (A) Cuts in wages in response to poor market conditions
   (B) Replacement of striking workers with strike-breakers from different ethnic groups
   (C) Technological innovations that displaced skilled workers
   (D) Strike intervention by the government on the side of capital
   (E) Equal pay for men and women doing the same work

49. Which of the following territories, whose inhabitants later became citizens, did the United States annex as a direct result of the Spanish-American War?

   (A) Cuba
   (B) Puerto Rico
   (C) Samoa
   (D) The Virgin Islands
   (E) Panama

50. Members of which of the following groups were most eager to have immigrants enter the United States during the 1890s?

   (A) Factory workers
   (B) Free silverites
   (C) Former slaves
   (D) Populists
   (E) Industrialists

GO ON TO THE NEXT PAGE

THE CONSUMER CONSUMED.

Courtesy of Library of Congress # LC-USZ62-99122

51. The 1888 cartoon above was most likely intended to suggest that

(A) United States military expansion was imposing a significant cost on the economy

(B) domestic producers saved consumers from tariff-inflated prices

(C) the federal government protected consumers by eliminating tariffs

(D) United States trusts produced goods at low prices beneficial to consumers

(E) United States consumers could not escape paying the federal government or the trusts

GO ON TO THE NEXT PAGE ⟩

52. "[A]bout 23,000,000 acres have been separated from Indian reservations and added to the public domain for the use of those who desired to secure free homes under our beneficent laws. It is difficult to estimate the increase of wealth which will result from the conversion of these waste lands into farms. . . . [T]his work has proceeded upon lines of justice toward the Indian, and . . . he may now, if he will, secure to himself the good influences of a settled habitation, the fruits of industry, and the security of citizenship."

In the quote above, President Benjamin Harrison describes the desired effects of which of the following?

(A) Dawes Severalty Act
(B) Homest ead Act
(C) Newlands Reclamation Act
(D) Indian Reorganization Act
(E) Soil Conservation and Domestic Allotment Act

53. Which of the following contributed to the North's victory in the Civil War?

(A) The South failed to manage its economic resources effectively.
(B) The South lacked a strong military tradition.
(C) Great Britain provided military aid to the North.
(D) Northern public opinion was united in support of the war.
(E) European powers boycotted Southern cotton.

54. The 1964 Gulf of Tonkin incident was used as justification for

(A) CIA covert operations in Guatemala
(B) NATO involvement in the Suez crisis
(C) United States military escalation in Vietnam
(D) United States peacekeeping operations in Lebanon
(E) United Nations intervention in the Congo

55. The primary motive for establishing the first permanent English colony was to

(A) make an economic profit
(B) achieve political freedom
(C) ensure religious freedom
(D) challenge France's power in the New World
(E) convert American Indians to Christianity

56. During his administration, Theodore Roosevelt did all of the following EXCEPT

(A) launch antitrust action against the Northern Securities Company
(B) ask Congress to consider a constitutional amendment granting women the vote
(C) add millions of acres to the system of national parks
(D) secure passage of the Hepburn Act to regulate the railroads
(E) intervene in the 1902 United Mine Workers' strike

57. In the early twentieth century, federal or state governments enacted all of the following People's (Populist) Party platform reforms EXCEPT the

(A) secr et ballot
(B) income tax
(C) government ownership of railroads
(D) direct election of senators
(E) initiative and referendum

58. Unlike Populist reformers of the late nineteenth century, Progressive reformers of the early twentieth century were most typically

(A) middle-clas s city dwellers
(B) African Americans
(C) struggling farmers
(D) new immigrants
(E) factory workers

GO ON TO THE NEXT PAGE

PERCENT OF POPULAR VOTE
IN THE 1912 PRESIDENTIAL ELECTION

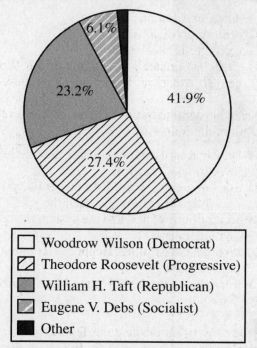

☐	Woodrow Wilson (Democrat)
▨	Theodore Roosevelt (Progressive)
▧	William H. Taft (Republican)
▨	Eugene V. Debs (Socialist)
■	Other

59. Based on the graph above and an understanding of United States history, which of the following conclusions can be drawn regarding the presidential election of 1912 ?

(A) The split in the Republican Party allowed the Democrat to win with less than a majority of the popular vote.

(B) Voters elected the candidate who sought the most sweeping federal involvement in the nation's economy.

(C) The candidate who received the greatest number of popular votes did not win the election.

(D) The contest was decided along regional lines.

(E) The majority of voters desired a decrease in the size and power of the federal government.

60. Which of the following occurred during the Progressive Era in the early twentieth century?

(A) Congress enacted a law making lynching a federal crime.

(B) Segregation of the races in federal civil service was abolished.

(C) The National Association for the Advancement of Colored People was formed.

(D) Black workers returned in large numbers from the North to the South.

(E) The Fourteenth Amendment was repealed.

GO ON TO THE NEXT PAGE ⟩

MUST LIBERTY'S LIGHT GO OUT?

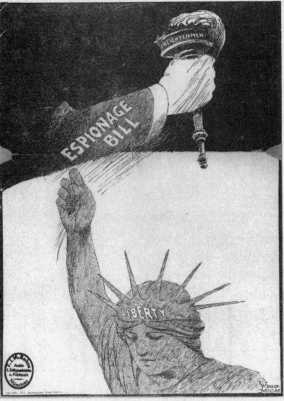

Courtesy of Library of Congress # LC-USZ62-90457

61. The 1917 cartoon above was most likely intended
to suggest which of the following?

(A) Immigrant quotas were needed to protect the
ideals of the Constitution.

(B) Civil liberties were being unnecessarily
compromised during the First World War.

(C) Imprisonment of dissenters was necessary
to maintain national security in wartime.

(D) German spying was a serious threat to the
United States war effort.

(E) Wartime rationing undermined United States
freedoms.

GO ON TO THE NEXT PAGE

THE AWAKENING

62. The 1915 cartoon above suggests that

   (A) western states were seen as leaders in granting woman suffrage

   (B) female employment in eastern factories inhibited the spread of woman suffrage

   (C) states east of the Mississippi had so many immigrants that their governments refused to allow woman suffrage

   (D) Civil War constitutional amendments balanced granting former slaves voting rights by expanding woman suffrage

   (E) success in achieving woman suffrage followed the same pattern as success in state temperance movements

GO ON TO THE NEXT PAGE

Remember Your First Thrill of
AMERICAN LIBERTY

YOUR DUTY-*Buy*
United States Government *Bonds*
2ⁿᵈ Liberty Loan of 1917

National Archives

63. The poster above represents an appeal based on

(A) colonialism
(B) imperialism
(C) racism
(D) capitalism
(E) patriotism

64. All of the following occurred in the Union during the Civil War EXCEPT

(A) an increase in prices for goods and services
(B) the establishment of a national banking system
(C) the suppression of habeas corpus
(D) an increase in the war powers of the presidency
(E) the abolition of racial segregation

GO ON TO THE NEXT PAGE

The Granger Collection, New York

65. The cartoon above from 1922 is a reference to which of the following situations?

(A) The Teapot Dome incident
(B) The breakup of the Standard Oil Company
(C) Publication of Ida Tarbell's exposé about the business practices of John D. Rockefeller
(D) The oil embargo following the Yom Kippur War
(E) Publicity resulting from the Exxon oil spill in Alaska

GO ON TO THE NEXT PAGE

66. Which of the following is true of the United States immigration laws of 1921 and 1924 ?

    (A) They imposed literacy tests on immigrants in order to bar those who did not speak English.
    (B) They created quotas that curtailed the immigration of people from southern and eastern Europe.
    (C) They allowed only as many Asians to enter the United States each year as had lived in the country in 1890.
    (D) They permitted unrestricted immigration from Great Britain and Ireland.
    (E) They encouraged immigration by people with highly sought-after job skills.

67. The Dust Bowl of the 1930s was centered in

    (A) Arizona and Southern California
    (B) Utah and Nevada
    (C) Missouri and Iowa
    (D) Texas and Louisiana
    (E) Oklahoma and Kansas

68. The increasing tensions between the United States and Japan prior to the Second World War primarily concerned Japan's

    (A) demands for unrestricted immigration to the United States for Japanese citizens
    (B) refusal to sign a nonaggression pact with the Soviet Union
    (C) fears of an air attack on the Japanese fleet
    (D) efforts to promote communism in Indochina
    (E) invasion of China and its efforts to alter the balance of power in the Pacific

69. A basic change occurred in United States economic relations with the rest of the world during the First World War when the United States

    (A) became the world's leading steel producer
    (B) acquired preferential trading rights from the Soviet Union
    (C) changed from a debtor nation to a creditor nation
    (D) refused to go off the gold standard
    (E) adopted a policy of gradual tariff reduction

70. During the 1960s and 1970s, which of the following resulted directly from the feminist movement?

    (A) Ratification of the Equal Rights Amendment
    (B) Elimination of male-female pay differentials
    (C) Establishment of federally funded day-care centers
    (D) Use of women as combat soldiers in the Vietnam War
    (E) Significant growth in the number of women admitted to professional schools

GO ON TO THE NEXT PAGE

WASTE HELPS THE ENEMY

CONSERVE MATERIAL

© Boeing

71. The Second World War poster above best exemplifies which of the following?

(A) Use of propaganda to portray the enemy as inhuman
(B) Mobilization of the home front in support of the war effort
(C) The technological superiority enjoyed by the United States
(D) Tensions within the United States concerning priorities in the war effort
(E) The wartime prosperity brought about by government spending

72. According to the writings of James Madison, a federal republic with a large population and an extensive territory would provide an effective check on the problem of

(A) factionalism
(B) populatio n growth
(C) chronic shortages of hard currency
(D) rapid industrial development
(E) foreign entanglement

73. "I believe that it must be the policy of the United States to support free peoples who are resisting attempted subjugation by armed minorities or by outside pressures. I believe that we must assist free peoples to work out their own destinies in their own way."

The statement above is an expression of which of the following?

(A) The Truman Doctrine
(B) The Gulf of Tonkin Resolution
(C) The Fourteen Points
(D) The Monroe Doctrine
(E) The Open Door policy

74. Between 1945 and 1980, the United States labor force changed significantly in that the percentage of

(A) white-collar workers increased
(B) industrial workers increased
(C) agricultural workers increased
(D) women workers decreased
(E) service workers decreased

GO ON TO THE NEXT PAGE

75. "The security, the success of our country . . . rests squarely upon the media, which disseminates the truth on which the decisions of democracy are made. You are the keepers of a trust and you must be just. You must guard and you must defend your media . . . against the works of divisiveness, against bigotry, against the corrupting evils of partisanship in any guise."

In this excerpt from his "Power of the Media" speech delivered in 1968, President Lyndon Johnson argued which of the following?

(A) The power of the media had decreased rapidly in the post-Second World War period.
(B) True democracy can be protected only if the government is allowed to prevent the media from causing divisiveness.
(C) Most newspapers are guilty of placing too much emphasis on international events.
(D) National security requires that the media support the government in all of its policies.
(E) The media plays a major role in shaping public opinion and must cover events responsibly.

76. All of the following social activists from the 1960s and 1970s are matched correctly with the groups they led EXCEPT

(A) Betty Friedan . . National Organization for Women
(B) Russell Means . . American Indian Movement
(C) César Chávez . . United Farm Workers Organizing Committee
(D) Stokely Carmichael . . National Association for the Advancement of Colored People
(E) Martin Luther King, Jr., . . Southern Christian Leadership Conference

77. All of the following were provided for in the peace treaty that resulted from the Versailles peace conference in 1919 EXCEPT a

(A) League of Nations
(B) reconstructed Poland
(C) state of Czechoslovakia
(D) system of mandates over former German colonies
(E) rearmament limitation on all major powers

78. Which of the following was evidence of the influence of business on federal policy in the late 1940s?

(A) The passage of the Taft-Hartley Act in 1947
(B) The liberalization of the Social Security system
(C) The reelection of President Truman in 1948
(D) The acceptance of Keynesian economic analysis
(E) The establishment of a Fair Employment Practices Committee

GO ON TO THE NEXT PAGE

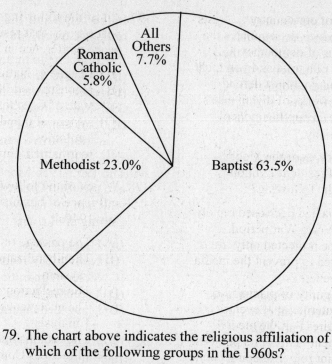

79. The chart above indicates the religious affiliation of which of the following groups in the 1960s?

(A) Polish Americans
(B) Scandinavian Americans
(C) Irish Americans
(D) African Americans
(E) Mexican Americans

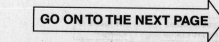

80. James Hagerty, press secretary to President Eisenhower, made the following entry in his diary concerning an April 1954 meeting of the National Security Council: "situation getting critical—Fr[ench] want 50 more bombers—and they are running short of pilots—could use 'American volunteers'—also considering use of [American] troops eventually."

Hagerty's diary entry above referred to a developing crisis in

(A) Korea
(B) Indochina
(C) the Middle East
(D) Africa
(E) South America

81. Which of the following was most responsible for President Carter's declining approval rating in public opinion polls in the last year of his administration?

(A) The Iran hostage crisis
(B) The boycott of the 1980 Olympic Games
(C) A major scandal in the attorney general's office
(D) His Supreme Court nominations
(E) The Camp David Accords

82. The doctrine of states' rights is illustrated by all of the following EXCEPT the

(A) *Marbury* v. *Madison* decision
(B) Hartford Convention
(C) Virginia and Kentucky Resolutions
(D) Nullification Ordinance
(E) "personal liberty" laws

83. In the 1820s and 1830s, owners of the textile mills in Lowell, Massachusetts, were generally

(A) reluctant to hire women workers
(B) quick to develop new product lines
(C) eager to recruit immigrant workers
(D) slow to invest in new technology
(E) concerned about the moral environment of their workers

84. The 1955-1956 Montgomery bus boycott and the 1960 Greensboro sit-in represent which of the following approaches to gaining civil rights for African Americans?

(A) Black Power
(B) Nonviolent resistance
(C) Voter registration
(D) Freedom Rides
(E) Mass demonstrations

85. In *Miranda* v. *Arizona* (1966), the Supreme Court ruled that

(A) police must inform accused individuals of the right to remain silent
(B) defendants in minor criminal cases are not entitled to legal counsel
(C) items seized illegally by the police cannot be used as evidence
(D) teenagers enjoy the rights to attorneys and to juries in juvenile courts
(E) the death penalty cannot be applied to individuals who were juveniles when they committed their crimes

GO ON TO THE NEXT PAGE

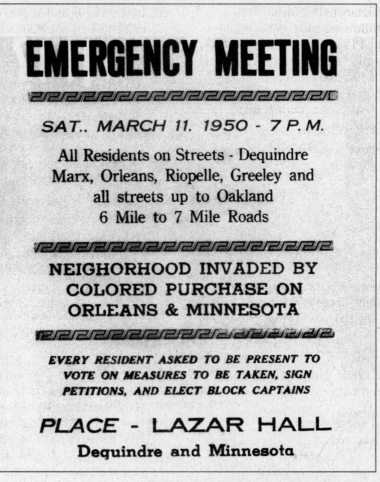

EMERGENCY MEETING

SAT., MARCH 11, 1950 - 7 P.M.

All Residents on Streets - Dequindre
Marx, Orleans, Riopelle, Greeley and
all streets up to Oakland
6 Mile to 7 Mile Roads

NEIGHORHOOD INVADED BY
COLORED PURCHASE ON
ORLEANS & MINNESOTA

*EVERY RESIDENT ASKED TO BE PRESENT TO
VOTE ON MEASURES TO BE TAKEN, SIGN
PETITIONS, AND ELECT BLOCK CAPTAINS*

PLACE - LAZAR HALL

Dequindre and Minnesota

Courtesy of the Archives of Labor and Urban Affairs,
Wayne State University, Detroit, Michigan

86. The poster above represented a movement intended to

(A) organize resistance to United States participation in the
    Korean War
(B) preserve segregation of neighborhoods
(C) deport undocumented immigrants
(D) establish a local anticommunist committee
(E) support urban redevelopment projects

87. Students at Kent State University and Jackson State College protested which of the following in the spring of 1970 ?

(A) President Johnson's escalation of the Vietnam War
(B) President Nixon's call for a military draft
(C) President Nixon's invasion of Cambodia
(D) The leaking of the Pentagon Papers to *The New York Times*
(E) The Watergate scandal

88. Which of the following was the most immediate catalyst for Congressional passage of the Civil Rights Act in 1964 ?

(A) The assassination of President John F. Kennedy months after he gave a nationally televised speech on civil rights
(B) The sit-ins organized by college students protesting segregated lunch counters in Greensboro, North Carolina
(C) The Supreme Court's decision in *Brown* v. *Board of Education of Topeka*, which held that school segregation is unconstitutional
(D) The Montgomery bus boycott, which led to desegregated seating on public buses in Montgomery, Alabama
(E) The founding of civil rights groups such as the National Association for the Advancement of Colored People

89. The United States government used the alleged presence of weapons of mass destruction (WMDs) to justify the

(A) Korean War (1950–1953)
(B) invasion of Grenada (1983)
(C) Persian Gulf War (1991)
(D) invasion of Afghanistan (2001)
(E) invasion of Iraq (2003)

90. Which of the following musical genres is most closely associated with the gay rights movement?

(A) Jazz in the 1920s
(B) Rock and roll in the 1950s
(C) Disco in the 1970s
(D) Heavy metal in the 1980s
(E) Hip-hop in the 1990s

S T O P

IF YOU FINISH BEFORE TIME IS CALLED, YOU MAY CHECK YOUR WORK ON THIS TEST ONLY. DO NOT TURN TO ANY OTHER TEST IN THIS BOOK.

How to Score the SAT Subject Test in United States History

When you take an actual SAT Subject Test in United States History, your answer sheet will be "read" by a scanning machine that will record your response to each question. Then a computer will compare your answers with the correct answers and produce your raw score. You get one point for each correct answer. For each wrong answer, you lose one-fourth of a point. Questions you omit (and any for which you mark more than one answer) are not counted. This raw score is converted to a scaled score that is reported to you and to the colleges you specify.

Worksheet 1. Finding Your Raw Test Score

STEP 1: Table A on the following page lists the correct answers for all the questions on the Subject Test in United States History that is reproduced in this book. It also serves as a worksheet for you to calculate your raw score.

- Compare your answers with those given in the table.
- Put a check in the column marked "Right" if your answer is correct.
- Put a check in the column marked "Wrong" if your answer is incorrect.
- Leave both columns blank if you omitted the question.

STEP 2: Count the number of right answers.

Enter the total here: _____

STEP 3: Count the number of wrong answers.

Enter the total here: _____

STEP 4: Multiply the number of wrong answers by .250.

Enter the product here: _____

STEP 5: Subtract the result obtained in Step 4 from the total you obtained in Step 2.

Enter the result here: _____

STEP 6: Round the number obtained in Step 5 to the nearest whole number.

Enter the result here: _____

The number you obtained in Step 6 is your raw score.

Answers to Practice Test 1 for United States History

Table A

Answers to the Subject Test in United States History - Practice Test 1 and Percentage of Students Answering Each Question Correctly

Question Number	Correct Answer	Right	Wrong	Percent Answering Correctly*	Question Number	Correct Answer	Right	Wrong	Percent Answering Correctly*
1	B			84	31	C			45
2	A			85	32	A			66
3	C			93	33	D			79
4	B			28	34	D			54
5	A			96	35	A			40
6	A			74	36	C			61
7	E			85	37	C			70
8	C			68	38	A			78
9	B			70	39	E			85
10	C			94	40	E			82
11	C			60	41	E			47
12	D			52	42	B			25
13	C			85	43	D			70
14	B			57	44	B			96
15	C			91	45	A			83
16	D			82	46	D			61
17	A			69	47	C			44
18	A			52	48	E			71
19	B			71	49	B			78
20	A			78	50	E			84
21	B			61	51	E			91
22	E			96	52	A			41
23	A			53	53	A			60
24	D			53	54	C			80
25	B			61	55	A			71
26	B			86	56	B			77
27	B			78	57	C			51
28	D			28	58	A			76
29	B			90	59	A			78
30	E			68	60	C			66

Table A continued on next page

Table A continued from previous page

Question Number	Correct Answer	Right	Wrong	Percent Answering Correctly*	Question Number	Correct Answer	Right	Wrong	Percent Answering Correctly*
61	B			76	76	D			38
62	A			90	77	E			43
63	E			87	78	A			51
64	E			70	79	D			62
65	A			78	80	B			49
66	B			72	81	A			68
67	E			84	82	A			52
68	E			79	83	E			24
69	C			60	84	B			91
70	E			48	85	A			77
71	B			66	86	B			92
72	A			32	87	C			37
73	A			62	88	A			41
74	A			71	89	E			55
75	E			83	90	C			78

* These percentages are based on an analysis of the answer sheets for a random sample of 17,729 students who took the original administration of this test and whose mean score was 643. They may be used as an indication of the relative difficulty of a particular question. Each percentage may also be used to predict the likelihood that a typical Subject Test in United States History candidate will answer correctly that question on this edition of this test.

Finding Your Scaled Score

When you take SAT Subject Tests, the scores sent to the colleges you specify are reported on the College Board scale, which ranges from 200–800. You can convert your practice test score to a scaled score by using Table B. To find your scaled score, locate your raw score in the left-hand column of Table B; the corresponding score in the right-hand column is your scaled score. For example, a raw score of 50 on this particular edition of the Subject Test in United States History corresponds to a scaled score of 620.

Raw scores are converted to scaled scores to ensure that a score earned on any one edition of a particular Subject Test is comparable to the same scaled score earned on any other edition of the same Subject Test. Because some editions of the tests may be slightly easier or more difficult than others, College Board scaled scores are adjusted so that they indicate the same level of performance regardless of the edition of the test taken and the ability of the group that takes it. Thus, for example, a score of 500 on one edition of a test taken at a particular administration indicates the same level of achievement as a score of 500 on a different edition of the test taken at a different administration.

When you take the SAT Subject Tests during a national administration, your scores are likely to differ somewhat from the scores you obtain on the tests in this book. People perform at different levels at different times for reasons unrelated to the tests themselves. The precision of any test is also limited because it represents only a sample of all the possible questions that could be asked.

Table B
Scaled Score Conversion Table
Subject Test in United States History - Practice Test 1

Raw Score	Reported Score	Raw Score	Reported Score	Raw Score	Reported Score
90	800	50	620	10	380
89	800	49	610	9	370
88	800	48	610	8	360
87	800	47	600	7	360
86	800	46	600	6	350
85	800	45	590	5	350
84	800	44	580	4	340
83	800	43	580	3	340
82	800	42	570	2	330
81	800	41	570	1	330
80	790	40	560	0	320
79	790	39	550	−1	320
78	780	38	550	−2	310
77	780	37	540	−3	310
76	770	36	530	−4	300
75	760	35	530	−5	300
74	760	34	520	−6	290
73	750	33	510	−7	290
72	750	32	510	−8	280
71	740	31	500	−9	280
70	730	30	500	−10	270
69	730	29	490	−11	270
68	720	28	480	−12	260
67	720	27	480	−13	250
66	710	26	470	−14	240
65	710	25	460	−15	240
64	700	24	460	−16	230
63	690	23	450	−17	220
62	690	22	450	−18	220
61	680	21	440	−19	210
60	680	20	430	−20	200
59	670	19	430	−21	200
58	670	18	420	−22	200
57	660	17	420		
56	650	16	410		
55	650	15	400		
54	640	14	400		
53	640	13	390		
52	630	12	390		
51	630	11	380		

How Did You Do on the Subject Test in United States History?

After you score your test and analyze your performance, think about the following questions:

Did you run out of time before reaching the end of the test?

If so, you may need to pace yourself better. For example, maybe you spent too much time on one or two hard questions. A better approach might be to skip the ones you can't answer right away and try answering all the questions that remain on the test. Then if there's time, go back to the questions you skipped.

Did you take a long time reading the directions?

You will save time when you take the test by learning the directions to the Subject Test in United States History ahead of time. Each minute you spend reading directions during the test is a minute that you could use to answer questions.

How did you handle questions you were unsure of?

If you were able to eliminate one or more of the answer choices as wrong and guess from the remaining ones, your approach probably worked to your advantage. On the other hand, making haphazard guesses or omitting questions without trying to eliminate choices could cost you valuable points.

How difficult were the questions for you compared with other students who took the test?

Table A shows you how difficult the multiple-choice questions were for the group of students who took this test during its national administration. The right-hand column gives the percentage of students that answered each question correctly.

A question answered correctly by almost everyone in the group is obviously an easier question. For example, 82 percent of the students answered question 16 correctly. But only 43 percent answered question 77 correctly.

Keep in mind that these percentages are based on just one group of students. They would probably be different with another group of students taking the test.

If you missed several easier questions, go back and try to find out why: Did the questions cover material you haven't yet reviewed? Did you misunderstand the directions?

Answer Explanations

For Practice Test 1

Question 1

Choice (B) is the correct answer. Beginning in 1619, county and town representatives (burgesses) in the Virginia colony met as the first democratically elected assembly in British North America. The House of Burgesses would continue until 1776.

Question 2

Choice (A) is the correct answer. In an effort to minimize future conflicts with American Indian groups over westward expansion, the British government enacted the Proclamation of 1763 to restrict colonial settlement to east of the Appalachian Mountains, increasing resentment among many colonists.

Question 3

Choice (C) is the correct answer. The Stamp Act was the first attempt of the British government to directly tax the American colonies to help pay for the expenses incurred during the French and Indian War (Seven Years' War). Although the British Parliament repealed the act the following year due to an influx of petitions, widespread American refusal to obey the act, and British merchant complaints of lost income, Parliament issued the Declaratory Act in 1766 to reassert its authority to tax its colonies.

Question 4

Choice (B) is the correct answer. Like the Virginia Company's establishment of the Jamestown Colony, the Massachusetts Bay Company was funded and governed by stockholders and settlers, although in Massachusetts they were primarily Puritan refugees. Over time, the increasing importance of commercial activity and the efforts by the English Crown to assert more authority in the region resulted in the merging of the colony with Plymouth and other territories in New England, turning Massachusetts Bay into the self-governing colony known as the Province of Massachusetts Bay.

Question 5

Choice (A) is the correct answer. As part of Jim Crow legislation across the South following Reconstruction and into the 1960s, many states employed a variety of legal avenues such as rigged literacy tests and prohibitively expensive poll taxes to prevent African Americans from voting, thereby ensuring White dominance of Southern politics.

Question 6

Choice (A) is the correct answer. George Washington's Farewell Address warned United States citizens to avoid political entanglements with European nations. The Monroe Doctrine is the most similar option because it was the policy established to prevent any expansion of European influence in the Western Hemisphere in order to limit conflict with European empires.

Question 7

Choice (E) is the correct answer. Tobacco was the most valuable commodity produced in the Chesapeake region until after the Revolutionary War when the invention of the cotton gin increased the profitability of cotton production.

Question 8

Choice (C) is the correct answer. Transcendentalists believed that to fully understand the real world one should not rely on the senses because knowledge came from the innate divinity of each person's soul. The idea that all men and women were, by nature, equally capable resulted in many Transcendentalists becoming involved in mid-nineteenth-century reform movements.

Question 9

Choice (B) is the correct answer. Horace Mann pioneered the idea of the common school, whereby taxes would be used to fund and operate public schools. He also initiated reforms that professionalized teaching and allowed women to become teachers.

Question 10

Choice (C) is the correct answer. The successful launch of Sputnik in 1957 set in motion huge federal investments in math and science education as a means of competing against the Soviet Union in all manner of technological innovations.

Question 11

Choice (C) is the correct answer. Relying on Enlightenment ideas of government, this excerpt from the Declaration of Independence outlines some of the justifications for separation from Great Britain.

Question 12

Choice (D) is the correct answer. George Washington knew when the Continental army won victories against the well-trained and well-funded British military it could provide symbolic proof of the viability of the republican cause. In addition, Continental army victories resulted in practical support in terms of raising funds, encouraging volunteers, and garnering international backing.

Question 13

Choice (C) is the correct answer. Many Anti-Federalists feared that the new Constitution would grant too much authority to the national government at the expense of states or individuals. In addition, in an effort to guarantee individual rights against the expansion of the central government that the Constitution represented, Anti-Federalists pushed for a series of ten amendments to the Constitution known as the Bill of Rights.

Question 14

Choice (B) is the correct answer. Thomas Jefferson believed in an agriculture-centered vision of the United States, where most citizens would live on small farms. In this view, productive work on the land was a source of civic virtue. This vision conflicted with the urban and commerce-centric policies proposed by others such as Alexander Hamilton.

Question 15

Choice (C) is the correct answer. The establishment of European colonies in the Western Hemisphere and the increased usage of enslaved and indentured labor resulted in massive resource extraction (e.g., agricultural crops, timber, minerals) and the creation of the triangular trade exchange of goods, resources, and human labor across the Atlantic region.

Question 16

Choice (D) is the correct answer. The quotation references the perceived moral hypocrisy that many of the most vocal supporters of American independence (including leaders such as Patrick Henry and George Washington) were themselves slaveholders who deprived others of their freedom.

Question 17

Choice (A) is the correct answer. The excerpt describes the skills and personality of a runaway enslaved man and the price that would be paid if the man were captured and returned to the slaveholder, Thomas Jefferson.

Question 18

Choice (A) is the correct answer. In King Philip's War tensions over territory and religion erupted into direct conflict between Native American settlements and English settlers and their Native American allies in Massachusetts, Connecticut, and Rhode Island. In Bacon's Rebellion, frontier settlers clashed with the colonial government and Native Americans over their desire to settle additional territory claimed by the Virginia colony. Both conflicts concluded with an expansion of White settlement at the expense of Native American territorial claims.

Question 19

Choice (B) is the correct answer. The excerpt asserts that English agricultural practices—namely the introduction of plows—impressed American Indians because the practice allowed English settlers to farm larger areas more intensively than American Indians had previously.

Question 20

Choice (A) is the correct answer. The Missouri Compromise allowed the simultaneous incorporation of Missouri and Maine as states in order to maintain the balance of slave and free states. The compromise also established the latitude of 36 degrees 30 minutes as the dividing line between any future free and slave states. The compromise later would be overturned by the Kansas-Nebraska Act, which determined that the inhabitants of a territory, not its location, would determine whether slavery would be permitted, resulting in increased sectional tension and outright conflict over the issue.

Question 21

Choice (B) is the correct answer. John C. Calhoun advocated for the concept of nullification, the contention that states had the constitutional right to nullify any federal law that they deemed unconstitutional. This particular excerpt, from the South Carolina Ordinance of Nullification of 1832, rejects the federal tariff. Many debates as to the validity of nullification arose over the issue of whether or not states could ignore federal laws prohibiting or limiting slavery before the Civil War.

Question 22

Choice (E) is the correct answer. Because the distance between North America and Europe created a buffer for diseases prevalent in Europe, the initial contact between Europeans and American Indians following 1492 resulted in the widespread transmission of diseases such as smallpox to the Americas. The lack of immunity resulted in extreme population declines and the destabilization of many American Indian societies.

Question 23

Choice (A) is the correct answer. George Whitefield was an English preacher who helped popularize outdoor religious revivals and Methodism in the American colonies in the 1740s during the First Great Awakening.

Question 24

Choice (D) is the correct answer. Owing to the Puritans' focus on being able to read the Bible to improve religious understanding, they were generally supportive of the establishment of public school systems. This resulted in basic literacy rates that were much higher in New England than in any other region of the early American colonies.

Question 25

Choice (B) is the correct answer. The Jay Treaty settled several outstanding disputes between the United States and Great Britain that had not been resolved by the Treaty of Paris (1783). Although unpopular with many, the treaty maintained peace between the two states.

Question 26

Choice (B) is the correct answer. Members of the Federalist Party generally supported having a stronger federal government, rejected the idea of states' rights, wanted to avoid entanglement with revolutionary France, supported the development of urban economic centers, and were opposed to the expansion of slavery.

Question 27

Choice (B) is the correct answer. The decision of Germany to resume unrestricted submarine warfare in January 1917 resulted in the sinking of several unarmed American merchant and passenger ships even though the United States was a neutral nation in the war. Woodrow Wilson asked for Congressional approval to declare war against Germany in April 1917.

Question 28

Choice (D) is the correct answer. Although the treaty contributed to debates over the potential expansion of slavery into new territories, the Gadsden Purchase (Gadsden Treaty) was generally supported by those who wanted to resolve boundary issues remaining from the Mexican-American War and those who wanted to establish a southern route for the transcontinental railroad through the region. By contrast, the options in choices (A), (B), (C), and (E) did all involve controversies between strict and loose constructions of the Constitution.

Question 29

Choice (B) is the correct answer. Following his inauguration, Franklin D. Roosevelt immediately set out to establish poverty relief programs (e.g., Federal Emergency Relief Administration), employment programs (e.g., Civilian Conservation Corps), and economic controls (e.g., Agricultural Adjustment Administration, National Industry Recovery Act) to stem the worst impacts of the Great Depression. Shortly after, his administration began implementing legislation to address long-term issues, including increasing regulation of the economic system (e.g., Securities Exchange Act) and establishing a national pension system to reduce endemic poverty among senior citizens (e.g., Social Security Act).

Question 30

Choice (E) is the correct answer. Composed of a loose collection of political groups opposed to the growing executive power of Andrew Jackson, the Whig Party supported the use of federal power to establish a national infrastructure project (the American System), to create a protective tariff, and to reestablish a national bank system.

Question 31

Choice (C) is the correct answer. The Second Great Awakening established a sentiment of reform in the United States based on arguments of moral improvement. What resulted was a burgeoning of reform movements with a wide range of agendas (e.g., abolition, temperance, female suffrage). As many of these issues dealt directly with the day-to-day lives of women, their participation and leadership naturally grew over time.

Question 32

Choice (A) is the correct answer. Although its origins came at a time of other revivalist religious movements in the early nineteenth century, conflict between adherents of Mormonism and non-Mormons resulted in the resettlement of Mormon communities, first from Missouri to Illinois, then to the Utah Territory.

Question 33

Choice (D) is the correct answer. Sharp increases in immigration beginning in the 1840s depicted on the graph resulted from the significant influx of German and Irish immigrants to the United States. This substantially contributed to overall population growth in the United States in the antebellum period.

Question 34

Choice (D) is the correct answer. Minstrel shows were performed by White actors who portrayed African American characters by wearing blackface makeup. Through their emphasis on song and dance, these shows relied upon heavily racialized stereotypes of African and African American cultures and often utilized themes that justified slavery.

Question 35

Choice (A) is the correct answer. Like Henry Clay and his American System, many politicians in the first half of the nineteenth century argued for subsidies and other support for infrastructure improvements to better connect port, industrial, and agricultural regions. As a result, state governments invested in expanded canal and rail construction, particularly in the Northeast and Midwest.

Question 36

Choice (C) is the correct answer. Most White Southerners did not hold any enslaved people directly, though many were related to slaveholders or their livelihoods relied upon slavery in one form or another. Historians have calculated that approximately 25 percent of White households in the South were slaveholders, though this rate varied in different parts of the South.

Question 37

Choice (C) is the correct answer. The Border States that maintained slavery during the Civil War but did not secede from the United States (Missouri, Kentucky, West Virginia, Maryland, and Delaware) were the most politically divided areas over the issues of secession and slavery before and during the war. Their position adjacent to the Confederate States, their significance in maintaining Union access to Washington, D.C., and their importance in holding the Ohio and Mississippi Rivers for troop and supply transport made continuing to control these states a priority for the United States war effort.

Question 38

Choice (A) is the correct answer. After the Mexican-American War (1846–1848), Mexico ceded the area that is now California to the United States in the Treaty of Guadalupe Hidalgo.

Question 39

Choice (E) is the correct answer. When the presence of Soviet missiles became public, the Organization of American States approved the United States quarantine of Cuba to prevent the installation of any additional missiles.

Question 40

Choice (E) is the correct answer. The Emancipation Proclamation declared an end to slavery in the states that had seceded from the United States to become the Confederate States, but it did not apply in the Border States that maintained slavery but did not secede (Missouri, Kentucky, West Virginia, Maryland, and Delaware).

Question 41

Choice (E) is the correct answer. Puritan religious communities required strict adherence to their religious doctrine in order to participate in local political and church governance. As with Roger Williams and the establishment of Rhode Island, oftentimes those banished from Puritan colonies instituted religious toleration laws in their new colonies as a reaction to their treatment by the Puritans.

Question 42

Choice (B) is the correct answer. The cartoon depicts Columbia (a symbol of the United States) unenthusiastically receiving pardon requests from Southern White men while wondering why an injured African American soldier does not earn the right to vote. In so doing, the cartoon echoes criticism of Andrew Johnson's Reconstruction plan (also known as Presidential Reconstruction), which pardoned most White Southern men and restored their right to vote but did not extend citizenship or voting rights to emancipated Black men.

Question 43

Choice (D) is the correct answer. Although many leaders tried to maintain the equal addition of free and slave states outlined in the Missouri Compromise (1820), antislavery advocates began to attempt to limit the expansion of slave states into new territories. For example, the Wilmot Proviso proposed unsuccessfully to bar slavery from any territory acquired from Mexico as a result of the Mexican-American War.

Question 44

Choice (B) is the correct answer. The song lyrics express one of the main goals of nineteenth-century labor unions—the call for a standard eight-hour workday and the desire for leisure time.

Question 45

Choice (A) is the correct answer. The vast majority of raw materials for the Northern textile industry—i.e. cotton—was produced by enslaved labor in the South rather than in the North.

Question 46

Choice (D) is the correct answer. The industrialized nature of the Chicago meatpacking industry and a lack of governmental or corporate oversight contributed to the low, sometimes dangerous quality of the meat produced. These conditions were revealed to the public in works such as *The Jungle* by Upton Sinclair.

Question 47

Choice (C) is the correct answer. Compulsory high school education did not come into effect in most states until after 1900 as part of Progressive Era reforms meant to limit child labor and expand educational opportunities.

Question 48

Choice (E) is the correct answer. Equal pay for men and women was not an issue in the late nineteenth century. Federal equal pay protections for women would not be implemented in the United States until the Equal Pay Act of 1963.

Question 49

Choice (B) is the correct answer. As a result of the Insular Cases (1901) and the enactment of the Jones Act (1917), the United States affirmed the citizenship of the residents of Puerto Rico, which the United States annexed from Spain following the Spanish-American War.

Question 50

Choice (E) is the correct answer. Industrialists encouraged immigration because they could pay less money to low-skilled immigrants with few legal protections than they could pay other groups.

Question 51

Choice (E) is the correct answer. By showing a consumer caught between paying trusts or tariffs, the cartoon suggests the difficulty in which consumers found themselves. The image represents the dominance that trusts had over the prices of domestic goods while at the same time suggesting that foreign goods were equally expensive because of government tariffs on products. Consumers were forced to pay inflated costs for goods in either scenario.

Question 52

Choice (A) is the correct answer. The Dawes Severalty Act attempted to undermine tribal cohesion by dividing reservations and assigning land—usually the poorest in the area—to individual American Indians with the assumption that permanent agricultural work would help promote assimilation. Remaining land not distributed to American Indians was then sold to White settlers.

Question 53

Choice (A) is the correct answer. The South's continued reliance on the production of raw materials for export—which was limited by the war—and the relative lack of industrial production and transportation infrastructure compared with the North left the South at a considerable economic disadvantage during the Civil War.

Question 54

Choice (C) is the correct answer. Allegations of two unprovoked attacks against United States naval ships in the Gulf of Tonkin off of the coast of North Vietnam resulted in the passage of the Gulf of Tonkin Resolution. The resolution permitted President Lyndon Johnson to escalate United States involvement against North Vietnam by authorizing aerial bombardment and deploying ground troops in an attempt to contain the spread of communism into South Vietnam.

Question 55

Choice (A) is the correct answer. The Virginia Company was a joint-stock venture meant to provide profit for investors through resource extraction and the production of cash crops. The Virginia Company established the first English settlement in North America in 1607. Tobacco was introduced as a cash crop as a means of obtaining a profit, but because of death, disease, and frequent conflict with the Powhatan Confederacy, the Virginia Company was rarely profitable and the Crown dissolved its charter in 1624.

Question 56

Choice (B) is the correct answer. Although Theodore Roosevelt did come to support woman suffrage earlier than many other political leaders of his time, he did not ask Congress to consider a constitutional amendment granting women the right to vote. Congress did not approve the Nineteenth Amendment for woman suffrage until 1919. Roosevelt did all of the other actions mentioned in the question, advocating for greater regulation of large corporations and for the conservation of natural resources.

Question 57

Choice (C) is the correct answer. Although many Populist political reforms were adopted, neither state nor the federal governments took control of the railroads.

Question 58

Choice (A) is the correct answer. With their focus on pressing urban issues such as immigration, sanitation, and antitrust activity, middle-class city dwellers were typically the greatest advocates of Progressive Era reforms, unlike the more rural-focused reforms of the Populist movement.

Question 59

Choice (A) is the correct answer. The decision of former President Theodore Roosevelt to leave the Republican Party and run for president as a member of the Progressive (Bull Moose) Party resulted in a split in the electorate that allowed Democrat Woodrow Wilson to win the election with a plurality of the popular vote rather than a majority.

Question 60

Choice (C) is the correct answer. The National Association for the Advancement of Colored People (NAACP) formed during the Progressive Era in 1909 as a response to the continued issues of lynching, segregation, and discrimination across the United States.

Question 61

Choice (B) is the correct answer. The image depicts the 1917 Espionage Act, passed at the onset of the United States involvement in the First World War, as unnecessarily restricting civil liberties such as free speech. The act made it a crime to interfere with or encourage insubordination against military or naval forces, including advocating men to refuse service if drafted into the military.

Question 62

Choice (A) is the correct answer. The image represents the figure of woman suffrage moving from the West, where women could vote in most state and local elections, toward the East where women were seeking representation.

Question 63

Choice (E) is the correct answer. The image attempts to elicit a patriotic sentiment among many immigrants to get them to donate in support of United States participation in the First World War. The image attempts to evoke their memories of arriving in the United States and sailing past the Statue of Liberty on their way to Ellis Island.

Question 64

Choice (E) is the correct answer. The Civil War did not result in the end of racial segregation in the United States. Although the Thirteenth, Fourteenth, and Fifteenth Amendments ended slavery, granted citizenship to former enslaved people, and granted universal male suffrage, the end of Reconstruction in 1877 saw the establishment of segregationist laws and practices across the United States that would persist well into the twentieth century.

Question 65

Choice (A) is the correct answer. The image represents the political fallout from the discovery that the secretary of the interior had been bribed by oil companies to allow leases to drill for oil on federal land in areas such as the Teapot Dome region in Wyoming. The scandal undermined Warren Harding's administration and the public's confidence in the government.

Question 66

Choice (B) is the correct answer. The Emergency Quota Act of 1921 and the Immigration Act of 1924 established quotas based on the percentage of United States citizens who could trace their ancestry to different European nations based on earlier census data. The quota favored immigrants from Great Britain and western Europe, and limited immigration from southern and eastern Europe because their populations in the United States increased most only after the 1890 census.

Question 67

Choice (E) is the correct answer. The exposure of topsoil across vast areas of the American prairie due to extensive agricultural use and over plowing resulted in winds picking up and scattering much of the topsoil in Oklahoma and Kansas as massive dust storms, causing significant ecological and economic damage.

Question 68

Choice (E) is the correct answer. Japan's invasion of northeastern China in 1931 culminated in condemnation of the action by the United States as a violation of the Open Door Policy. As a result, the United States gradually increased economic and resource sanctions against Japan, contributing as some historians have argued to the impetus for the Japanese decision to attack Pearl Harbor in December 1941.

Question 69

Choice (C) is the correct answer. Even before entering the First World War as a belligerent, the United States used its position as a neutral party to offer loans to the warring nations, primarily Britain and France, to buy American-made goods. As a result, by the end of the war the United States became the largest creditor nation.

Question 70

Choice (E) is the correct answer. In addition to entering the overall workforce in numbers not seen since the Second World War, women made significant inroads in terms of access to professional schools (law schools, medical schools, etc.) in the 1960s and 1970s.

Question 71

Choice (B) is the correct answer. The figurative image of Adolph Hitler represents how the waste of materials on the home front that could be used for the war effort helped the enemies of the United States during the Second World War.

Question 72

Choice (A) is the correct answer. In *The Federalist* number 10, James Madison wrote that while the causes of factionalism could not be stopped, its negative effects could be controlled by fostering a large and ideologically diverse population in a republican system of government.

Question 73

Choice (A) is the correct answer. The Truman Doctrine argued that it was the responsibility of the United States to protect and supply anticommunist forces—or the "free peoples"—in nations around the world in the years following the Second World War. The policy would be carried out initially in Turkey and Greece, but the doctrine represented the bedrock principle of containment that guided United States foreign policy throughout the Cold War.

Question 74

Choice (A) is the correct answer. After the Second World War, the number of middle-management, professional, and office workers (or, "white-collar workers") grew as a college education became more accessible and as mechanization further decreased the economic need for less-skilled industrial and agricultural workers.

Question 75

Choice (E) is the correct answer. The excerpt indicates that it is the responsibility of the media to honestly report the truth in order to prevent "divisiveness," "bigotry," and "partisanship" in the United States.

Question 76

Choice (D) is the correct answer. Stokely Carmichael was a social activist most notably associated with his leadership of the Student Nonviolent Coordinating Committee (SNCC).

Question 77

Choice (E) is the correct answer. The Treaty of Versailles limited the military capability of only Germany (but not the other major powers) after the conclusion of the First World War. This represented an attempt by the Allies to hinder potential German aggression in the future.

Question 78

Choice (A) is the correct answer. The Taft-Harley Act (1947) stated that workers had a right to refrain from union activity and placed other restrictions on the actions and structure of unions, oftentimes to the benefit of businesses.

Question 79

Choice (D) is the correct answer. The vast majority of African Americans in the 1960s were affiliated with historically Black Baptist and Methodist Protestant denominations.

Question 80

Choice (B) is the correct answer. Despite efforts to combat communism in North Vietnam, in 1954 France lost control of its colonial holdings throughout Indochina as North and South Vietnam, Laos, and Cambodia gained their independence through the Geneva Accords. The United States and South Vietnam rejected the accords because of the proposal for reunification of Vietnam through nationwide elections and the concern that communism would then spread to the South. This resulted in an increased United States political and military presence in the region.

Question 81

Choice (A) is the correct answer. The taking of American hostages from the United States Embassy in Tehran, Iran for 444 days undermined the public perception of President Jimmy Carter. The inability of the administration to negotiate the release of the hostages and a failed rescue attempt further eroded his credibility at a time of growing global instability.

Question 82

Choice (A) is the correct answer. *Marbury* v. *Madison* clarified the Supreme Court's right to exercise judicial review, or the process by which the Court can determine whether or not laws are constitutional as part of the system of checks and balances in the federal government. It does not illustrate the concept of states' rights.

Question 83

Choice (E) is the correct answer. As the majority of workers in the Lowell mills were young girls and unmarried women, the owners went to great lengths to ensure that these mill girls behaved appropriately. The majority of these workers lived in company-owned boarding houses and the mills exerted a great deal of control over the women. Any deviation from the rules (e.g., intemperance, not attending services on the Sabbath) could result in termination.

Question 84

Choice (B) is the correct answer. Inspired by the tactics of Mohandas Gandhi in India, the Montgomery boycott and the Greensboro sit-in represent economic and physical resistance to Jim Crow era segregation laws, using moral arguments and active nonviolent challenges to try to gain support for the Civil Rights movement and to encourage the laws to be changed.

Question 85

Choice (A) is the correct answer. In *Miranda* v. *Arizona*, the Supreme Court ruled that those under arrest are required to be informed of their Fifth Amendment right against self-incrimination before being questioned by authorities, and therefore they have "the right to remain silent" and the right to have an attorney present to protect them from self-incrimination.

Question 86

Choice (B) is the correct answer. The image represents an attempt by members of a White community to maintain their segregated neighborhood after an African American purchased a home in the area.

Question 87

Choice (C) is the correct answer. The United States public learned that President Richard Nixon approved aerial bombardment to target North Vietnamese military forces in Cambodia in 1969 and had authorized the use of ground forces in 1970. This escalation of the Vietnam War intensified antiwar sentiment and resulted in protests across the country, including protests that turned violent at Kent State and Jackson State.

Question 88

Choice (A) is the correct answer. President Kennedy's speech on civil rights in June 1963 set the stage for the passage of the Civil Rights Act of 1964 by his successor, Lyndon Johnson.

Question 89

Choice (E) is the correct answer. President George W. Bush's administration alleged that Iraq illegally maintained chemical and biological weapons of mass destruction and that it was attempting to develop nuclear weapons. The potential threat of Iraq using those weapons was used to justify the United States invasion of Iraq in 2003.

Question 90

Choice (C) is the correct answer. With its origins following the Stonewall Riot (1969), the modern gay rights movement is closely associated with disco music, since it gained popularity at the same time.

United States History – Practice Test 2

Practice Helps

The test that follows is an actual, previously administered SAT Subject Test in United States History. To get an idea of what it's like to take this test, practice under conditions that are much like those of an actual test administration.

- Set aside an hour when you can take the test uninterrupted.

- Sit at a desk or table with no other books or papers. Dictionaries, other books, or notes are not allowed in the test room.

- Tear out an answer sheet from the back of this book and fill it in just as you would on the day of the test. One answer sheet can be used for up to three Subject Tests.

- Read the instructions that precede the practice test. During the actual administration, you will be asked to read them before answering test questions.

- Use a clock or kitchen timer to time yourself.

- After you finish the practice test, read the sections "How to Score the SAT Subject Test in United States History" and "How Did You Do on the Subject Test in United States History?"

- The appearance of the answer sheet in this book may differ from the answer sheet you see on test day.

UNITED STATES HISTORY TEST

The top portion of the page of the answer sheet that you will use to take the United States History Test must be filled in exactly as illustrated below. When your supervisor tells you to fill in the circle next to the name of the test you are about to take, mark your answer sheet as shown.

○ Literature	○ Mathematics Level 1	○ German	○ Chinese Listening	○ Japanese Listening
○ Biology E	○ Mathematics Level 2	○ Italian	○ French Listening	○ Korean Listening
○ Biology M	● U.S. History	○ Latin	○ German Listening	○ Spanish Listening
○ Chemistry	○ World History	○ Modern Hebrew		
○ Physics	○ French	○ Spanish	**Background Questions:** ① ② ③ ④ ⑤ ⑥ ⑦ ⑧ ⑨	

After filling in the circle next to the name of the test you are taking, locate the Background Questions section, which also appears at the top of your answer sheet (as shown above). This is where you will answer the following Background Questions on your answer sheet.

BACKGROUND QUESTIONS

Please answer the two questions below by filling in the appropriate circle in the Background Questions box on your answer sheet. <u>The information you provide is for statistical purposes only and will not affect your test score.</u>

Question   I

How many semesters of United States History have you taken from grade 9 to the present? (If you are taking United States History this semester, count it as a full semester.) Fill in only <u>one</u> circle of circles 1-4.

- One semester or less   —Fill in circle 1.
- Two semesters   —Fill in circle 2.
- Three semesters   —Fill in circle 3.
- Four or more semesters   —Fill in circle 4.

Question   II

Which, if any, of the following social studies courses have you taken from grade 9 to the present? (Fill in ALL circles that apply.)

- One or more semesters of government   —Fill in circle 5.
- One or more semesters of economics   —Fill in circle 6.
- One or more semesters of geography   —Fill in circle 7.
- One or more semesters of psychology   —Fill in circle 8.
- One or more semesters of sociology
  or anthropology   —Fill in circle 9.

If you have taken none of these social studies courses, leave the circles 5 through 9 blank.

When the supervisor gives the signal, turn the page and begin the United States History Test. There are 100 numbered circles on the answer sheet and 90 questions in the United States History Test. Therefore, use only circles 1 to 90 for recording your answers.

Directions: Each of the questions or incomplete statements below is followed by five suggested answers or completions. Select the one that is best in each case and then fill in the corresponding circle on the answer sheet.

1. One way in which colonial Pennsylvania differed from colonial Massachusetts was that Pennsylvania

   (A) had an established principle of religious toleration
   (B) was founded by people seeking relief from religious persecution
   (C) had more densely populated settlements
   (D) had less fertile and profitable farmland
   (E) had a much more homogenous population

2. At the Constitutional Convention of 1787, the establishment of a bicameral Congress resolved the dispute between

   (A) the North and the South
   (B) the East and the West
   (C) rich states and poor states
   (D) states with large populations and states with small populations
   (E) states with large territory and states with little territory

3. The Imperial Wars (1688-1763) affected the British colonies in which of the following ways?

   (A) Defense of the colonies required the British to hire Hessian mercenaries.
   (B) The colonies drew closer to the French as the conflict dragged on for decades.
   (C) British preoccupation in Europe enabled the colonies to practice greater self-government.
   (D) The New England colonies were overrun repeatedly by the forces of both the French and the Spanish.
   (E) The New England colonies gave up hopes of obtaining land in the area around the Saint Lawrence River.

4. "Manifest Destiny" was first used as a slogan by people who

   (A) defended slavery in the territories
   (B) advocated the annexation of Hawaii
   (C) urged United States expansion to the Pacific Coast in the 1840s
   (D) worked for independence from England in the 1750s
   (E) advocated war with Spain in 1898

5. Which of the following was proposed by the Albany Conference of 1754 ?

   (A) A union among British colonies for defense against American Indians
   (B) Independence from Britain
   (C) The removal of American Indians to reservations west of the Mississippi River
   (D) Repeal of the Stamp Act
   (E) A boycott against British goods

6. In the colonial era, the most common form of employment for free women was as

   (A) schoolteacher s
   (B) domestic servants
   (C) tavern keepers
   (D) hatmakers
   (E) field hands

GO ON TO THE NEXT PAGE

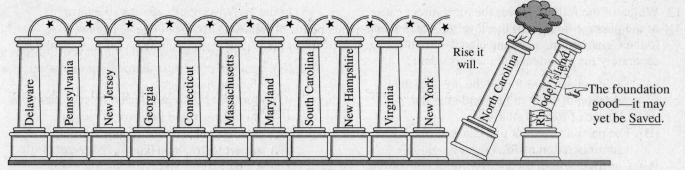

Rise it will.

The foundation good—it may yet be <u>Saved</u>.

The Federal Edifice

7. The image above was originally created to promote which of the following?

    (A) The signing of the Declaration of Independence
    (B) The passage of the Articles of Confederation
    (C) The ratification of the United States Constitution
    (D) The declaration of the War of 1812
    (E) The Southern movement for secession

8. Of the following North American Indian groups, Spanish colonists in the New World interacted most with

    (A) Pequot
    (B) Iroquois
    (C) Wampanoag
    (D) Huron
    (E) Pueblo

9. Which of the following authors was NOT known for writings that responded to contemporary United States social problems?

    (A) Harriet Beecher Stowe
    (B) Upton Sinclair
    (C) Ida B. Wells
    (D) Emily Dickinson
    (E) Frederick Douglass

10. Which of the following was true of the Battle of New Orleans?

    (A) It resulted in a draw between the British and the American forces.
    (B) The Americans won, but with very heavy losses of life and property.
    (C) The British burned the city as they retreated.
    (D) General Jackson received little national appreciation for his victory.
    (E) The victory boosted Americans' confidence in their nation.

11. Which of the following religious denominations was founded out of the desire to create separate Black institutions?

    (A) Society of Friends (Quaker)
    (B) African Methodist Episcopal
    (C) Southern Baptist
    (D) Methodist
    (E) Church of Jesus Christ of Latter-day Saints (Mormon)

GO ON TO THE NEXT PAGE

12. Which of the following was the most direct cause of the passage in 1804 of the Twelfth Amendment to the Constitution, requiring electors to vote separately for president and vice president?

    (A) The deadlock that forced the presidential election of 1800 to be decided in the House of Representatives
    (B) The partisan conflict that characterized the administration of John Adams
    (C) Conflicts within the United States concerning whether to support Britain or France during the Napoleonic Wars
    (D) George Washington's warning about the dangers of political parties
    (E) Criticism of Thomas Jefferson's purchase in 1803 of the Louisiana Territory

13. Which of the following most directly led to the formation of the Republican Party before the Civil War?

    (A) The Wilmot Proviso (1846)
    (B) The Compromise of 1850
    (C) The presidential election of 1852
    (D) The Kansas-Nebraska Act (1854)
    (E) The presidential election of 1856

14. Which of the following has NOT been an important historical source for understanding the lives of slaves in the United States?

    (A) Narratives written by runaway slaves such as Frederick Douglass
    (B) Archaeologic al evidence
    (C) African American songs and folktales
    (D) Daily diaries written by enslaved people
    (E) Plantation records and documents kept by slaveholders

15. Which of the following labor organizations represented both skilled and unskilled workers during the nineteenth century?

    (A) American Federation of Labor
    (B) Brotherhood of Sleeping Car Porters
    (C) Knights of Labor
    (D) United Mine Workers of America
    (E) Congress of Industrial Organizations

16. In the early twentieth century, the term "muckrakers" referred to

    (A) women who organized against prostitution
    (B) agrarian protesters demanding increased federal assistance
    (C) journalists who publicized corrupt practices in business and politics
    (D) government sanitation inspectors
    (E) painters who depicted everyday urban life

17. Which of the following was NOT typical of the experience of industrial laborers in the late nineteenth century?

    (A) Membership in strong unions that protected the rights of most workers
    (B) Physically dangerous workplace conditions
    (C) Increasing presence of women, children, and immigrants in the workplace
    (D) Workers' loss of control of how and when they worked
    (E) Slowly rising median wages

18. Between 1865 and 1900, the largest women's organization in the United States advocated which of the following causes?

    (A) Woman suffrage
    (B) Pacifism
    (C) The rights of former slaves
    (D) Consumer protection
    (E) Temper ance

19. Which of the following is closest to a Marxist interpretation of the Civil War?

    (A) The war was prompted by Northern moral outrage over the South's persistent support of slavery.
    (B) The war was inevitable in view of long-standing cultural differences between the North and South.
    (C) The war could have been avoided if Northern politicians had compromised with Southern politicians.
    (D) The war resulted from tension between the North's wage-labor economy and the South's slave-labor economy.
    (E) The war was the fault of unapologetic Southern leaders who promoted slavery in the face of worldwide opposition.

 GO ON TO THE NEXT PAGE

20. The Populist Party of the 1890s advocated which of the following?

 (A) Adoption of the gold standard for currency
 (B) Government ownership of railroads
 (C) Federal subsidies for industry
 (D) Expansion of male suffrage
 (E) Abolition of the income tax

21. Which of the following actions was NOT considered by expansionists such as Theodore Roosevelt, Henry Cabot Lodge, and Alfred Mahan to be necessary for the national greatness of the United States?

 (A) Developing a strong navy
 (B) Building a canal through Central America
 (C) Acquiring possessions and fueling stations in the Pacific Ocean
 (D) Acquiring possessions in the Caribbean
 (E) Acquiring Alaska

22. The progressive administrations of Theodore Roosevelt and Woodrow Wilson were similar in that they both

 (A) took an active role in curtailing immigration from Asia
 (B) sought to limit corporations that had become very large and powerful
 (C) sought to implement a full program of social welfare
 (D) sought to focus foreign policy on Latin America
 (E) took steps to desegregate federal agencies

23. All of the following were causes of the Great Depression of the 1930s EXCEPT

 (A) overextension of credit
 (B) technological unemployment due to new laborsaving equipment in factories
 (C) problems in the European economy that adversely affected international trade
 (D) underproduction on farms leading to a shortage of agricultural products
 (E) unequal distribution of wealth and income

24. Franklin D. Roosevelt's New Deal coalition secured significant support from all of the following groups EXCEPT

 (A) union members
 (B) ethnic urban voters
 (C) corporate executives
 (D) African Americans
 (E) southern White voters

25. Franklin D. Roosevelt's first "Hundred Days" legislation dealt with all of the following EXCEPT

 (A) the National Recovery Administration
 (B) lend-lease
 (C) the Civilian Conservation Corps
 (D) agricultural adjustment
 (E) the Tennessee Valley Authority

GO ON TO THE NEXT PAGE

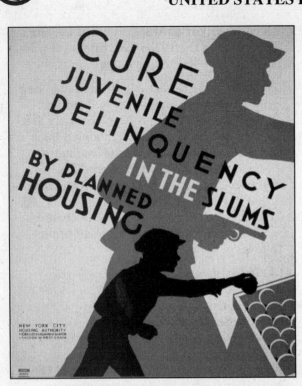

Courtesy of the Library of Congress #LC-USZ62-59985

26. The 1930s Works Progress Administration poster above is best understood in the context of which of the following efforts of the New Deal?

   (A) Creating new economic regulations to restore financial stability
   (B) Using government intervention to resolve social problems
   (C) Establishing federal jobs to support young people
   (D) Providing new social services for rural youth
   (E) Improving law enforcement to reduce crime

27. Which of the following curtailed some of the rights given to unions in the Wagner Act?

   (A) The Fair Deal
   (B) The Taft-Hartley Act
   (C) The GI Bill
   (D) The New Deal
   (E) The Great Society program

28. During the Second World War, African Americans experienced

   (A) an official end to racial segregation in the United States military
   (B) access to most military ranks and occupations
   (C) exclusion from the military draft
   (D) equal access to education
   (E) expanded opportunities to work in manufacturing industries

29. Which of the following was an immediate effect of the Korean War?

   (A) Anticommunism lost influence in United States politics.
   (B) The United States experienced extensive antiwar protests.
   (C) The United States Army was resegregated.
   (D) The idea of global containment gained credibility among policy makers.
   (E) The United States established diplomatic relations with China.

30. President John F. Kennedy called his national defense strategy

   (A) massive retaliation
   (B) détente
   (C) brinkmanship
   (D) flexible response
   (E) appease ment

31. A basic principle of President Lyndon Johnson's War on Poverty was that

   (A) the federal government should enhance economic opportunities for people below the poverty line
   (B) state governments should take on primary responsibility for the care of people below the poverty line
   (C) the private sector should guarantee employment for all people who wish to work
   (D) poverty should be addressed primarily by increasing military spending and creating jobs in defense industries
   (E) the unrestrained functioning of the free market would eliminate poverty

GO ON TO THE NEXT PAGE

32. In pre-Columbian North American cultures, all of the following could be found EXCEPT

(A) irrigation systems
(B) cultivated maize
(C) multifamily dwellings
(D) herbal medical treatment
(E) water wheels

- *Mapp* v. *Ohio* (1961)
- *Gideon* v. *Wainwright* (1963)
- *Escobedo* v. *Illinois* (1964)
- *Miranda* v. *Arizona* (1966)

33. The Supreme Court rulings listed above all address which of the following issues?

(A) Rights of criminal suspects
(B) Protection of voting rights
(C) Freedom of speech and assembly
(D) Separation of church and state
(E) Challenges to racial segregation

34. Between 1979 and 1989, the United States was involved in all of the following in its relationship with Iran under the Ayatollah Khomeini EXCEPT the

(A) downing of an Iranian passenger airliner by a surface-to-air missile
(B) attempted helicopter rescue of hostages held in the United States embassy
(C) freezing of Iranian assets
(D) sale of new armaments and replacement parts to Iran
(E) resumption of diplomatic relations

35. "A few days later, Doris was back. She had tried to help get Negroes in Natchez organized and failed. From what she said, the Klan ruled the entire area. CORE didn't get enough cooperation from the Negroes to be able to stay. . . . Back at the Freedom House that evening, I found another letter from Mama. As usual, it was full of pleas, begging me to leave Mississippi."

The quotation above is from a memoir of events in

(A) 1884
(B) 1926
(C) 1945
(D) 1963
(E) 1974

36. Which of the following describes an important action of the United Farm Workers organization in the 1960s and 1970s?

(A) It supported the passage of the Agricultural Adjustment Act.
(B) It fought against environmental legislation in order to protect farmers' profits.
(C) It demanded equal rights for African American sharecroppers.
(D) It organized grape and lettuce boycotts to help migrant workers.
(E) It campaigned for the Populist Party and for currency based on free silver.

37. Which of the following people is correctly matched with the organization that she or he led?

(A) Frances Willard . . National American Woman Suffrage Association
(B) Carrie Chapman Catt . . Woman's Christian Temperance Union
(C) Samuel Gompers . . American Federation of Labor
(D) W. E. B. Du Bois . . Black Panther Party
(E) Black Elk . . American Indian Movement

GO ON TO THE NEXT PAGE

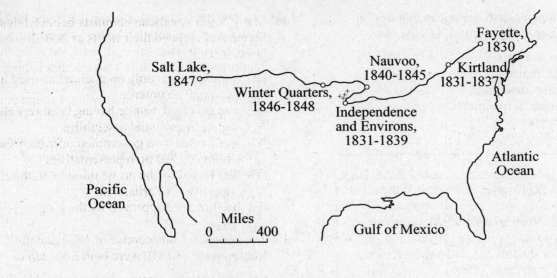

Fayette, 1830

Salt Lake, 1847

Nauvoo, 1840-1845

Kirtland 1831-1837

Winter Quarters, 1846-1848

Independence and Environs, 1831-1839

Atlantic Ocean

Pacific Ocean

Miles
0   400

Gulf of Mexico

38. The map above traces the nineteenth-century movements or migrations of

(A) the Cherokee
(B) the Iroquois
(C) gold prospectors
(D) Franciscan missionaries
(E) the Mormons

39. Which of the following developments played the most important role in the creation of the American (Know-Nothing) Party?

(A) Massive migration of Southern ex-slaves to Northern cities
(B) An influx of German and Irish immigrants, many of whom were Roman Catholic
(C) The loss of jobs due to an economic depression
(D) A controversial proposal to establish free public education
(E) The increasing demands of women for political power after Seneca Falls

40. The term "de facto segregation" refers to

(A) late-nineteenth-century segregation laws of southern and border states
(B) segregation that exists without being written into law
(C) the Supreme Court's decision invalidating the "separate but equal" principle
(D) a system that establishes racial and ethnic quotas for employment
(E) the tendency of immigrant populations to settle in southern states

GO ON TO THE NEXT PAGE

41. The first European colony on the site of present-day New York City was founded by the

    (A) Dutch
    (B) English
    (C) French
    (D) Spanish
    (E) Swedish

42. "These pious [people], who . . . would rather have died than lift a hand for defense against the most dangerous enemies, were now all of a sudden willing to . . . [enter into conflict with] a small group of their poor, oppressed, driven, and suffering fellow inhabitants and citizens from the frontier."

    The eyewitness account above lends support to which of the following conclusions about the Pennsylvania colony in the 1760s?

    (A) Increasing factionalism in the colony undermined religious ideals.
    (B) Some religious groups renounced land ownership in order to abide by their principles.
    (C) Colonists and frontier settlers were able to resolve their differences without taking up arms.
    (D) Colonists encouraged Native Americans to attack frontier settlements.
    (E) Tolerance of religious diversity had led to a community in which different groups respected the rights of others.

43. The Ghost Dance is best described as

    (A) a ritual created by the Shakers
    (B) a Native American religious movement in the 1890s
    (C) part of the Salem witch trials
    (D) a movement during the 1960s
    (E) a practice among utopian communities in the 1840s

44. Many North American colonists believed that the Stamp Act violated their rights as British subjects because it

    (A) imposed taxes only on documents used in colonial commerce
    (B) was enforced despite having been repealed by all of the colonial assemblies
    (C) was passed by a government in which the colonists had no representatives
    (D) was levied by the prime minister without the approval of Parliament
    (E) had not been approved by the king

45. The Missouri Compromise of 1820 and the Compromise of 1850 were both intended to

    (A) settle border disputes between the United States and its neighbors
    (B) establish a political party system that could withstand the pressures of a presidential election
    (C) resolve the conflicts that surrounded the admission of new states to the Union
    (D) settle disputes between the executive and legislative branches
    (E) ease the growing conflict between urban and rural areas

46. "The growth of a large business corporation is merely survival of the fittest. . . . The American Beauty rose can be produced in the splendor and fragrance which bring cheer to its beholder only by sacrificing the early buds which grow up around it. This is not an evil tendency in business. It is merely the working-out of a law of nature and a law of God."

    These sentiments are most characteristic of

    (A) socialism
    (B) anarchism
    (C) pragmatism
    (D) Social Darwinism
    (E) utopianism

47. A stated purpose of the Proclamation of 1763 was to

   (A) encourage settlement of the trans-Appalachian region
   (B) diminish the powers of the colonial governors
   (C) limit conflict between Native Americans and colonists
   (D) acknowledge French primacy in the fur trade
   (E) stimulate friendly contact between Native Americans and the Dutch

48. The Roosevelt Corollary to the Monroe Doctrine called for the United States to

   (A) remain aloof from the affairs of European countries
   (B) stay out of the affairs of Central American countries
   (C) intervene in the internal affairs of Asian countries
   (D) act as an international police power in Central and South America
   (E) arbitrate differences between European countries and China

49. What role did women play in the American colonists' resistance to Parliament's passage of the Stamp Act and Townshend Acts?

   (A) They took up arms in protest.
   (B) They participated in boycotts against British goods.
   (C) They voted for independence against Britain.
   (D) They had no role in the resistance movement.
   (E) They refused to associate with non-British settlers.

50. Which of the following was established at the end of the First World War?

   (A) North Atlantic Treaty Organization (NATO)
   (B) Pan-American Union
   (C) United Nations
   (D) League of Nations
   (E) World Bank

51. During the American Revolution, enslaved and free African Americans fought for

   (A) both Great Britain and the United States
   (B) the United States only
   (C) Great Britain only
   (D) American Indian autonomy
   (E) the independence of Haiti

52. "One ever feels his twoness,—an American, a Negro; two souls, two thoughts, two unreconciled strivings; two warring ideals in one dark body, whose dogged strength alone keeps it from being torn asunder. . . . He simply wishes to make it possible for a man to be both a Negro and an American, without being cursed and spit upon by his fellows, without having the doors of opportunity closed roughly in his face."

   The excerpt above is from which of the following works?

   (A) The Gettysburg Address by Abraham Lincoln
   (B) The Atlanta Compromise speech by Booker T. Washington
   (C) *The Souls of Black Folk* by W. E. B. Du Bois
   (D) The "Letter from Birmingham Jail" by Martin Luther King, Jr.
   (E) *The Autobiography of Malcolm X* by Malcolm X and Alex Haley

53. In *Marbury* v. *Madison*, the United States Supreme Court established the precedent of

   (A) stare decisis
   (B) judicial review
   (C) separate but equal
   (D) implied powers
   (E) sanctity of contracts

GO ON TO THE NEXT PAGE

54. President George Washington sent troops to put down the Whiskey Rebellion of 1794 because he

(A) believed in the need for standing armies to manage the civilian population
(B) wished to stop the use of alcohol on the Pennsylvania frontier
(C) wanted to assert the power of the national government in the face of armed resistance
(D) yielded to pressure from the Senate to use force against the uprising
(E) feared that British troops were inciting the rebels

55. As a member of George Washington's cabinet, Alexander Hamilton did which of the following?

(A) He promoted a literal interpretation of the Constitution.
(B) He encouraged compromise among political factions.
(C) He shaped the United States economic system.
(D) He protected the interests of individual states.
(E) He forged an enduring United States alliance with France.

56. The Articles of Confederation differed from the Constitution in which of the following ways?

(A) The articles took effect upon ratification by a majority of the states.
(B) Under the articles, members of the Senate were appointed rather than elected.
(C) The articles barred the federal government from printing paper currency.
(D) The articles did not provide for a strong executive branch of government.
(E) The articles did not give the federal government authority to conduct foreign policy.

57. The Monroe Doctrine was a pronouncement associated with all of the following EXCEPT the United States

(A) desire to become formally allied with Great Britain
(B) fear of French intervention in the New World through the Holy Alliance
(C) opposition to further European colonization in the New World
(D) belief in republican governments for the New World
(E) intent to refrain from involvement in European rivalries

GO ON TO THE NEXT PAGE

© Hulton Fine Art Collection/ Getty Images

58. Asher Durand's 1849 painting *Kindred Spirits*, above, is typical of the Hudson River School in its

   (A) endorsement of the religious revivalism of the Second Great Awakening
   (B) portrayal of the wilderness as a defining characteristic of the United States
   (C) endorsement of the industrial development of unused land
   (D) visual warning about the dangers in nature
   (E) patriotic celebration of the recent United States victory in the Mexican-American War

GO ON TO THE NEXT PAGE

59. President Lyndon B. Johnson's policy regarding Vietnam differed most from those of Presidents Truman, Eisenhower, and Kennedy in that Johnson's policy

   (A) was intended to contain communism
   (B) assumed that if Vietnam fell to communism, the other countries in Southeast Asia would follow
   (C) assumed that the Soviet Union controlled the government of North Vietnam
   (D) sent military advisors to train South Vietnamese forces
   (E) put large numbers of American ground troops into combat

60. Massive demonstrations and student strikes followed the 1970 American invasion of

   (A) Vietnam
   (B) the Dominican Republic
   (C) Cambodia
   (D) Nicar agua
   (E) El Salvador

61. Which of the following contributed most to the commercial development of the English colony of Virginia in the seventeenth century?

   (A) Slaves imported directly from Africa
   (B) The glassblowing industry established at Jamestown
   (C) The improved tobacco developed by John Rolfe
   (D) Jamestown's diversified agriculture
   (E) The introduction of cotton as a staple product

62. The English Navigation Acts did which of the following?

   (A) Listed colonial products that could be shipped only to England
   (B) Placed tariffs on all goods that colonists imported
   (C) Encouraged manufacturing in the North American colonies
   (D) Limited all foreign trade to a few designated harbors
   (E) Prohibited shipbuilding in the North American colonies

63. When William Lloyd Garrison called the United States Constitution "a covenant with death, an agreement with hell," he was referring to the Constitution's treatment of

   (A) soldiers
   (B) slaves
   (C) women
   (D) workers
   (E) prisoners

64. A visitor to the United States wishing to understand the development of industry during the 1820s would most likely have visited

   (A) Savannah, Georgia
   (B) St. Louis, Missouri
   (C) Columbus, Ohio
   (D) Frankfort, Kentucky
   (E) Lowell, Massachusetts

GO ON TO THE NEXT PAGE

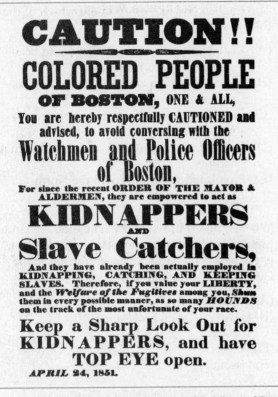

CAUTION!!

COLORED PEOPLE

OF BOSTON, ONE & ALL,

You are hereby respectfully CAUTIONED and advised, to avoid conversing with the

Watchmen and Police Officers of Boston,

For since the recent ORDER OF THE MAYOR & ALDERMEN, they are empowered to act as

KIDNAPPERS

AND

Slave Catchers,

And they have already been actually employed in KIDNAPPING, CATCHING, AND KEEPING SLAVES. Therefore, if you value your LIBERTY, and the *Welfare of the Fugitives* among you, *Shun* them in every possible manner, as so many *HOUNDS* on the track of the most unfortunate of your race.

Keep a Sharp Look Out for KIDNAPPERS, and have TOP EYE open.

APRIL 24, 1851.

Courtesy of the Library of Congress

65. The poster above expressed northern outrage over

(A) the reestablishment of the slave trade
(B) the migration of Black people to the North
(C) the strengthened Fugitive Slave Act
(D) an outbreak of kidnappings and ransom demands
(E) Boston's political machine

66. The United States annexed territory in southern Arizona via the Gadsden Purchase in order to acquire

(A) a waterway to the Pacific Ocean
(B) gold and iron deposits
(C) land upon which to build a railroad
(D) additional grasslands for ranching
(E) fertile farmland for agriculture

67. All of the following statements about urban political machines in the late nineteenth and early twentieth centuries are correct EXCEPT:

(A) Machines rewarded party workers with patronage jobs and favors.
(B) Most machines campaigned to restrict suffrage.
(C) Machines flourished with the rapid growth of cities.
(D) Most machines were rooted in immigrant constituencies.
(E) Machines provided a rudimentary form of social security.

68. Why did some leaders of the women's rights movement oppose the Fifteenth Amendment, which gave African American men the right to vote?

(A) They believed that the Fifteenth Amendment was not passed in a constitutional manner.
(B) They believed that only property owners should be allowed to vote.
(C) They believed that all women as well as African American men should be allowed to vote.
(D) They opposed equal political rights for African American people and White people.
(E) They feared that the amendment might produce racial conflict.

69. The Black Codes following the Civil War were intended to

(A) eliminate racial segregation
(B) limit the rights of former slaves
(C) impose limits on coal mining
(D) restrict immigration
(E) expand electoral suffrage

GO ON TO THE NEXT PAGE

Courtesy of the Library of Congress #LC-USZ62-100543

70. The 1884 image above of a female pupil of Carlisle Indian Industrial School in Pennsylvania visiting her home at the Pine Ridge Indian Reservation in South Dakota promotes the policy of

(A) seculari zation
(B) assi milation
(C) cultural preservation
(D) segregation
(E) land restoration

71. Immigration to the United States in the late nineteenth century differed from immigration in the early nineteenth century because the largest numbers of the immigrants in the later period were from

(A) northern and western Europe
(B) the Middle East
(C) South America
(D) sub-Saharan Africa
(E) southern and eastern Europe

HARPER'S WEEKLY.

E PLURIBUS UNUM (EXCEPT THE CHINESE).

Courtesy of HarpWeek

72. The 1882 cartoon above was most likely intended to suggest that

(A) the United States sought to expand trade with nations abroad
(B) few Chinese people sought to immigrate to the United States
(C) the United States restricted immigration from all parts of the world
(D) restrictions on Chinese immigration contradicted United States principles
(E) the United States imposed military control over parts of China

GO ON TO THE NEXT PAGE

73. The Virginia and Kentucky Resolutions, the demands made at the Hartford Convention, and the South Carolina Exposition and Protest were all similar in their

   (A) support of the Union to the detriment of the states
   (B) demands for a strong federal foreign policy
   (C) challenge to the laws of the federal government
   (D) call for federal economic policies in support of opening up the West
   (E) disagreement with the immigration policies of the federal government

74. Henry Clay was involved in all of the following EXCEPT the

   (A) Three-Fifths Compromise
   (B) War Hawks
   (C) Missouri Compromise
   (D) Ameri can System
   (E) Compromise of 1850

75. "If the Democratic Party has had one cardinal principle beyond all others, it has been that of pushing forward the boundaries of the United States. Under this administration, this great principle has been utterly abandoned. . . . Mr. Cleveland has labored to overthrow American interests and American control in Hawaii. Andrew Jackson fought for Florida but Mr. Cleveland is eager to abandon Samoa."

   The purpose of the quotation above by Henry Cabot Lodge was to

   (A) express his support for the Democratic Party
   (B) urge the United States to adopt an expansionist foreign policy
   (C) attack Republican foreign policy
   (D) call for the impeachment of President Cleveland
   (E) call for a veto of Hawaiian annexation

76. The federal government has directly taxed personal income continuously since the

   (A) ratification of the Constitution
   (B) adoption of Alexander Hamilton's fiscal program in the 1790s
   (C) introduction of measures to raise revenue during the Civil War
   (D) ratification of an amendment to the federal Constitution during the Progressive era
   (E) inauguration of New Deal measures to finance federal spending

GO ON TO THE NEXT PAGE

Scientific American, March 1, 1879

77. The illustration above depicts which of the following aspects of early American industrialization?

(A) Gender equality in the workplace
(B) The use of the factory system
(C) The central role of new technology
(D) The beginnings of the labor movement
(E) The use of convict labor

78. In the antebellum North, the cultural ideal of middle-class womanhood was best represented by a woman who was

(A) increasingly educated and articulate about public affairs
(B) primarily concerned with domestic, religious, and family affairs
(C) actively involved in abolitionism and women's rights
(D) the economic partner of her husband inside and outside the home
(E) a participant in the art of painting, sculpture, and music

79. The United States annexed the Philippines and Puerto Rico by which of the following means?

(A) Defeating Japan in the Second World War
(B) Defeating Spain in the late nineteenth century
(C) Concluding treaties with Russia in the late nineteenth century
(D) Concluding treaties with Britain in the late nineteenth century
(E) Purchasing them from Spain in the late nineteenth century in return for military equipment

GO ON TO THE NEXT PAGE

80. "We consider the underlying fallacy of the plaintiff's argument to consist in the assumption that the enforced separation of the two races stamps the colored race with a badge of inferiority. If this be so, it is not by reason of anything found in the act, but solely because the colored race chooses to put that construction upon it."

The excerpt above is from which of the following Supreme Court decisions?

(A) *Dred Scott* v. *Sandford*
(B) *Plessy* v. *Ferguson*
(C) *Brown* v. *Board of Education of Topeka*
(D) *Korematsu* v. *United States*
(E) *Regents of the University of California* v. *Bakke*

81. John Steinbeck's novel *The Grapes of Wrath* depicted which of the following events?

(A) The migration of African Americans from the South
(B) The deportation of Chinese immigrants
(C) The movement of displaced farmers to California
(D) The internment of Japanese residents
(E) The relocation of Cherokee Indians

GO ON TO THE NEXT PAGE

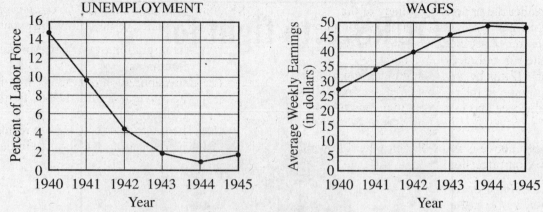

UNEMPLOYMENT

WAGES

82. The graphs above best support which of the following conclusions?

(A) The Second World War ended the Great Depression in the United States, as unemployment declined and wages increased.
(B) Industrial production in the United States stabilized during the years 1940–1945.
(C) As average weekly earnings in the United States declined from 1940 to 1945, unemployment in the United States increased.
(D) United States entry into the Second World War had a negative impact on the economy.
(E) Inflation eroded all of the gains made by workers in the United States during the years 1940–1945.

---

83. President Harry S. Truman announced that it was necessary to drop the atomic bomb on Hiroshima and Nagasaki because

(A) Japan was preparing to launch attacks on the United States mainland
(B) foreign allies pressured the United States to do so
(C) doing so would save American lives
(D) doing so would justify expenses associated with the weapon's development
(E) doing so would take revenge for Japan's attack on Pearl Harbor

GO ON TO THE NEXT PAGE ⟩

OURS...to fight for

FREEDOM FROM WANT

84. The poster above reflects a war aim articulated by

    (A) Abraham Lincoln during the Civil War
    (B) William McKinley during the Spanish-American War
    (C) Woodrow Wilson during the First World War
    (D) Franklin Roosevelt during the Second World War
    (E) Lyndon Johnson during the Vietnam War

GO ON TO THE NEXT PAGE

85. Congress passed the War Powers Act (1973) in order to limit presidential actions such as the

    (A) sale of arms to Iran and diversion of money to the contra resistance in Nicaragua
    (B) expansion of United States military operations in Vietnam
    (C) provision of Marshall Plan aid to countries in Eastern Europe
    (D) formation of the League of Nations
    (E) establishment of internment camps for Japanese Americans

86. The communist defeat of the Chinese Nationalists in 1949 led the United States to do all of the following EXCEPT

    (A) refuse to recognize the new government in Beijing
    (B) interpret the Chinese Revolution as part of a menacing monolith
    (C) come to value Japanese naval power as a check to the spread of communism in Asia
    (D) recognize the government of Taiwan as representing all of China
    (E) experience heightened anticommunist hysteria

87. The Beat Generation can be described as a group of

    (A) labor negotiators concerned with improving workers' material conditions
    (B) critics of the Free Speech movement
    (C) religious fundamentalists from rural areas of the United States
    (D) supporters of increased presidential power
    (E) young writers and artists opposed to the conformity of their era

88. "No person shall be elected to the office of the President more than twice."

    The excerpt above is from a constitutional amendment that was passed as the result of the presidential tenure of

    (A) Woodrow Wilson
    (B) Franklin Roosevelt
    (C) Dwight Eisenhower
    (D) Richard Nixon
    (E) Ronald Reagan

89. Which of the following statements regarding the 1950s is correct?

    (A) Increased economic productivity led to a higher standard of living.
    (B) The Midwest experienced the greatest population increase compared with other regions.
    (C) Women found employment mainly in manufacturing and industrial establishments.
    (D) Inner cities attracted a new influx of middle-class residents.
    (E) Military budgets decreased steadily in the decade following the Second World War.

90. The Second Great Awakening differed from the First Great Awakening in that the Second Great Awakening

    (A) focused on ideas about predestination
    (B) grew out of conflict within the Catholic Church
    (C) influenced only New England
    (D) excluded African Americans
    (E) inspired a variety of reform movements

S T O P

IF YOU FINISH BEFORE TIME IS CALLED, YOU MAY CHECK YOUR WORK ON THIS TEST ONLY. DO NOT TURN TO ANY OTHER TEST IN THIS BOOK.

How to Score the SAT Subject Test in United States History

When you take an actual SAT Subject Test in United States History, your answer sheet will be "read" by a scanning machine that will record your response to each question. Then a computer will compare your answers with the correct answers and produce your raw score. You get one point for each correct answer. For each wrong answer, you lose one-fourth of a point. Questions you omit (and any for which you mark more than one answer) are not counted. This raw score is converted to a scaled score that is reported to you and to the colleges you specify.

Worksheet 1. Finding Your Raw Test Score

STEP 1: Table A on the following page lists the correct answers for all the questions on the Subject Test in United States History that is reproduced in this book. It also serves as a worksheet for you to calculate your raw score.

- Compare your answers with those given in the table.

- Put a check in the column marked "Right" if your answer is correct.

- Put a check in the column marked "Wrong" if your answer is incorrect.

- Leave both columns blank if you omitted the question.

STEP 2: Count the number of right answers.

Enter the total here: _____

STEP 3: Count the number of wrong answers.

Enter the total here: _____

STEP 4: Multiply the number of wrong answers by .250.

Enter the product here: _____

STEP 5: Subtract the result obtained in Step 4 from the total you obtained in Step 2.

Enter the result here: _____

STEP 6: Round the number obtained in Step 5 to the nearest whole number.

Enter the result here: _____

The number you obtained in Step 6 is your raw score.

Answers to Practice Test 2 for United States History

Table A
Answers to the Subject Test in United States History - Practice Test 2 and Percentage of Students Answering
Each Question Correctly

Question Number	Correct Answer	Right	Wrong	Percent Answering Correctly*	Question Number	Correct Answer	Right	Wrong	Percent Answering Correctly*
1	A			70	26	B			63
2	D			90	27	B			54
3	C			76	28	E			51
4	C			93	29	D			58
5	A			47	30	D			28
6	B			52	31	A			71
7	C			64	32	E			77
8	E			58	33	A			72
9	D			70	34	E			25
10	E			67	35	D			41
11	B			62	36	D			27
12	A			50	37	C			57
13	D			26	38	E			69
14	D			15	39	B			64
15	C			39	40	B			74
16	C			94	41	A			84
17	A			53	42	A			57
18	E			42	43	B			63
19	D			58	44	C			91
20	B			43	45	C			87
21	E			60	46	D			90
22	B			59	47	C			68
23	D			54	48	D			77
24	C			68	49	B			81
25	B			59	50	D			81

Table A continued on next page

Table A continued from previous page

Question Number	Correct Answer	Right	Wrong	Percent Answering Correctly*	Question Number	Correct Answer	Right	Wrong	Percent Answering Correctly*
51	A			70	71	E			75
52	C			60	72	D			93
53	B			85	73	C			69
54	C			84	74	A			42
55	C			83	75	B			61
56	D			72	76	D			47
57	A			66	77	B			73
58	B			85	78	B			65
59	E			56	79	B			72
60	C			29	80	B			61
61	C			74	81	C			73
62	A			40	82	A			92
63	B			76	83	C			79
64	E			78	84	D			70
65	C			88	85	B			67
66	C			62	86	C			44
67	B			53	87	E			78
68	C			87	88	B			89
69	B			91	89	A			75
70	B			85	90	E			81

* These percentages are based on an analysis of the answer sheets for a random sample of 6,174 students who took the original administration of this test and whose mean score was 622. They may be used as an indication of the relative difficulty of a particular question. Each percentage may also be used to predict the likelihood that a typical Subject Test in United States History candidate will answer correctly that question on this edition of this test.

Finding Your Scaled Score

When you take SAT Subject Tests, the scores sent to the colleges you specify are reported on the College Board scale, which ranges from 200–800. You can convert your practice test score to a scaled score by using Table B. To find your scaled score, locate your raw score in the left-hand column of Table B; the corresponding score in the right-hand column is your scaled score. For example, a raw score of 50 on this particular edition of the Subject Test in United States History corresponds to a scaled score of 600.

Raw scores are converted to scaled scores to ensure that a score earned on any one edition of a particular Subject Test is comparable to the same scaled score earned on any other edition of the same Subject Test. Because some editions of the tests may be slightly easier or more difficult than others, College Board scaled scores are adjusted so that they indicate the same level of performance regardless of the edition of the test taken and the ability of the group that takes it. Thus, for example, a score of 500 on one edition of a test taken at a particular administration indicates the same level of achievement as a score of 500 on a different edition of the test taken at a different administration.

When you take the SAT Subject Tests during a national administration, your scores are likely to differ somewhat from the scores you obtain on the tests in this book. People perform at different levels at different times for reasons unrelated to the tests themselves. The precision of any test is also limited because it represents only a sample of all the possible questions that could be asked.

Table B
Scaled Score Conversion Table
Subject Test in United States History - Practice Test 2

Raw Score	Reported Score	Raw Score	Reported Score	Raw Score	Reported Score
90	800	50	600	10	390
89	800	49	600	9	390
88	800	48	590	8	380
87	800	47	580	7	380
86	800	46	580	6	380
85	800	45	570	5	370
84	800	44	570	4	370
83	800	43	560	3	360
82	800	42	560	2	360
81	800	41	550	1	350
80	790	40	550	0	350
79	790	39	540	−1	340
78	780	38	540	−2	330
77	770	37	530	−3	330
76	770	36	530	−4	320
75	760	35	520	−5	320
74	750	34	520	−6	310
73	750	33	510	−7	310
72	740	32	510	−8	300
71	730	31	500	−9	300
70	720	30	500	−10	290
69	720	29	490	−11	290
68	710	28	480	−12	280
67	700	27	480	−13	280
66	700	26	470	−14	270
65	690	25	470	−15	260
64	680	24	460	−16	250
63	680	23	460	−17	250
62	670	22	450	−18	240
61	670	21	450	−19	230
60	660	20	440	−20	220
59	650	19	440	−21	210
58	650	18	430	−22	200
57	640	17	430		
56	640	16	420		
55	630	15	420		
54	620	14	410		
53	620	13	410		
52	610	12	400		
51	610	11	400		

How Did You Do on the Subject Test in United States History?

After you score your test and analyze your performance, think about the following questions:

Did you run out of time before reaching the end of the test?

If so, you may need to pace yourself better. For example, maybe you spent too much time on one or two hard questions. A better approach might be to skip the ones you can't answer right away and try answering all the questions that remain on the test. Then if there's time, go back to the questions you skipped.

Did you take a long time reading the directions?

You will save time when you take the test by learning the directions to the Subject Test in United States History ahead of time. Each minute you spend reading directions during the test is a minute that you could use to answer questions.

How did you handle questions you were unsure of?

If you were able to eliminate one or more of the answer choices as wrong and guess from the remaining ones, your approach probably worked to your advantage. On the other hand, making haphazard guesses or omitting questions without trying to eliminate choices could cost you valuable points.

How difficult were the questions for you compared with other students who took the test?

Table A shows you how difficult the multiple-choice questions were for the group of students who took this test during its national administration. The right-hand column gives the percentage of students that answered each question correctly.

A question answered correctly by almost everyone in the group is obviously an easier question. For example, 94 percent of the students answered question 16 correctly. But only 40 percent answered question 62 correctly.

Keep in mind that these percentages are based on just one group of students. They would probably be different with another group of students taking the test.

If you missed several easier questions, go back and try to find out why: Did the questions cover material you haven't yet reviewed? Did you misunderstand the directions?

Answer Explanations

For Practice Test 2

Question 1

Choice (A) is the correct answer. Unlike the Puritan colonists of colonial Massachusetts who required strict religious adherence, the Pennsylvania colony established a principle of religious toleration as a result of the influence of its Quaker founders and the diverse community that settled there.

Question 2

Choice (D) is the correct answer. The Connecticut Compromise established a legislative balance between the New Jersey Plan, which proposed the same number of representatives for each state, favoring small states, and the Virginia Plan, which proposed proportional representation favoring the most populous states. The compromise resulted in the creation of the Senate and the House of Representatives as a bicameral legislative assembly utilizing each approach.

Question 3

Choice (C) is the correct answer. From King William's War to the French and Indian War, persistent conflict among European states over control of Europe and overseas colonies led to greater autonomy from British oversight for American colonists.

Question 4

Choice (C) is the correct answer. Attributed to journalist John O'Sullivan, the term "Manifest Destiny" refers to the belief that the United States had a divine responsibility and right to extend its political, cultural, and moral influence across the North American continent.

Question 5

Choice (A) is the correct answer. The proposed Albany Plan of Union would have established a loose confederation of colonies with the power to levy taxes to ensure common defense against American Indians and in times of war.

Question 6

Choice (B) is the correct answer. Due to the prevailing belief that only men belonged in the public sphere, women's employment was limited to areas that kept them within the domestic sphere, such as servant work.

Question 7

Choice (C) is the correct answer. The image represents the order in which states ratified the Constitution to replace the Articles of Confederation. It implies that the "foundation" of the nation was solid, but that a federal structure was needed to ensure its success.

Question 8

Choice (E) is the correct answer. Spanish colonists most frequently interacted with the Pueblo peoples in what is currently the southwestern United States. This occurred as Spanish colonists moved northward in the sixteenth and seventeenth centuries in the colony of Mexico when trying to settle in the region, initiate trade, and convert indigenous inhabitants.

Question 9

Choice (D) is the correct answer. Unlike the work of Stowe and Douglass addressing issues of slavery, Wells' work on lynching, and Sinclair's work on the need for regulation in the meatpacking industry, Emily Dickinson is best known for her poetry, not for contributing writing that addressed United States social problems.

Question 10

Choice (E) is the correct answer. Although significantly outnumbered, United States forces in the Battle of New Orleans were able to defeat the British military with limited casualties, boosting national morale as the War of 1812 was coming to its end.

Question 11

Choice (B) is the correct answer. Founded by free Black men and women, the African Methodist Episcopal (AME) denomination separated from Methodist Episcopal Church in the early nineteenth century in response to racial discrimination.

Question 12

Choice (A) is the correct answer. In an unexpected flaw of the electoral system where each elector cast two votes for the presidency, both Thomas Jefferson and Aaron Burr received the same number of votes in the Electoral College in 1800. Although the deadlock was finally broken in the House of Representatives after six ballots, the Twelfth Amendment was ratified in 1804 to create separate votes in the Electoral College for president and vice president.

Question 13

Choice (D) is the correct answer. The passage of the Kansas-Nebraska Act eliminated limitations against slavery expanding into new territories established by the Missouri Compromise. As a result, a number of antislavery parties—including former Whigs—coalesced into the Republican Party shortly thereafter.

Question 14

Choice (D) is the correct answer. Given laws against teaching enslaved people to read or write, and the punishments for doing so, writings of people from the period when they were enslaved are extremely rare.

Question 15

Choice (C) is the correct answer. Unlike organizations that only represented skilled (American Federation of Labor, Brotherhood of Sleeping Car Porters) or unskilled (United Mine Workers of America) labor, the Knights of Labor represented craftspeople and unskilled workers in the nineteenth century. In addition, the Congress of Industrial Organizations (which predominantly represented unskilled workers) was not founded until the twentieth century.

Question 16

Choice (C) is the correct answer. "Muckraker" was a term applied to writers and investigative journalists primarily during the Progressive Era who attempted to expose corruption and dangerous business practices to instigate reforms.

Question 17

Choice (A) is the correct answer. Despite growing membership in the late nineteenth century, union membership remained atypical and unions were usually unable to protect workers' rights from companies that had the support of state and federal governments.

Question 18

Choice (E) is the correct answer. The Woman's Christian Temperance Union (WCTU) emerged in the late nineteenth century as one of the most influential political movements in the United States because of its efforts to convince individuals to reduce their consumption of alcohol as well as the organization's eventual encouragement of alcohol prohibition. Although the organization embraced other causes as well, it did not actively pursue woman suffrage until after 1900.

Question 19

Choice (D) is the correct answer. Marxist historical interpretations traditionally focus on the economic drivers of events, therefore many Marxist historians trace the origins of the Civil War to the friction between wage-labor and slave-labor economics.

Question 20

Choice (B) is the correct answer. The Populist Party generally advocated for policies that would improve the economic conditions of farmers. Many farmers believed that private rail companies unfairly controlled shipping costs and access to markets for their goods, therefore the Populist Party called for government control of the railroads to make transporting agricultural products cheaper.

Question 21

Choice (E) is the correct answer. The Alaska purchase occurred shortly after the Civil War in 1867, well before the expansionist policies of Roosevelt, Lodge, and Mahan were undertaken in order to create a network of territorial control and naval stations that would allow for greater United States access and influence around the world.

Question 22

Choice (B) is the correct answer. The rise of corporate monopolies and trusts resulted in allegations of unfair business practices and the manipulation of prices. Both Theodore Roosevelt and Woodrow Wilson attempted to limit the power and reach of these corporations by dividing them up (called trust-busting) and by advocating for reforms that prevented their establishment.

Question 23

Choice (D) is the correct answer. Farmers in the United States consistently overproduced crops (rather than underproducing them), resulting in oversupply and a decline in crop prices. The persistent loss of income drove many farms out of business.

Question 24

Choice (C) is the correct answer. Many business executives rejected the policies of the New Deal as having created undue governmental influence and control over the economy.

Question 25

Choice (B) is the correct answer. The Lend-Lease Act passed in 1941 as a response to the developing conflicts in Europe during the Second World War. Roosevelt's first "Hundred Days" legislation addressed issues concerning economic recovery during the Great Depression.

Question 26

Choice (B) is the correct answer. The image asserts that without intervention a young thief could turn into an armed robber. Planned housing—supported by the federal government under the New Deal— would help address the social factors that contributed to delinquency and crime.

Question 27

Choice (B) is the correct answer. The 1947 Taft-Hartley Act limited union power by allowing workers to refrain from union activity, and it placed other restrictions on the actions and structure of unions, curtailing some of the freedoms allowed unions under the 1935 Wagner Act.

Question 28

Choice (E) is the correct answer. The leader of the Brotherhood of Sleeping Car Porters, A. Philip Randolph, proposed a civil rights march in Washington, D.C., in 1941 to protest employment discrimination. President Franklin Roosevelt issued Executive order 8802, which banned hiring discrimination in defense industries. In this context, African American workers gained increased employment in manufacturing.

Question 29

Choice (D) is the correct answer. During and after the Korean War, the United States adopted the official policy of containing the spread of communism by any means necessary so as to prevent other nations from falling under the ideology in the future.

Question 30

Choice (D) is the correct answer. President John F. Kennedy's policy of flexible response was in contrast to President Eisenhower's policy of massive retaliation, which focused on establishing an insurmountable advantage over the Soviet Union in nuclear weapon stockpiles. Because Kennedy wanted more options than simply an enhanced nuclear arsenal to deal with the emergence of communism in the developing world, the flexible response included diplomacy, economic pressure, and a range of military options.

Question 31

Choice (A) is the correct answer. President Lyndon Johnson's policies for the War on Poverty focused on expanding the role of the federal government in order to create a "Great Society." These programs included job training and early-childhood education programs to provide solutions to short and long-term causes of poverty.

Question 32

Choice (E) is the correct answer. Europeans introduced the technology for the waterwheel to North America after the beginning of the Columbian Exchange.

Question 33

Choice (A) is the correct answer. The Supreme Court rulings listed address the rights of criminal suspects in regards to the validity of police searches, having access to counsel during trial and interrogation, and the right to remain silent to prevent self-incrimination.

Question 34

Choice (E) is the correct answer. The United States and Iran did not resume normal diplomatic relations after breaking off relations in April 1980 in the aftermath of the taking of hostages from the United States embassy in Tehran in 1979.

Question 35

Choice (D) is the correct answer. Civil rights activists began the process of organizing ways to overcome segregationist laws and to promote voting rights. Although the Freedom Summer would happen the following year, much of the groundwork was laid in 1963 despite fierce resistance and physical threats.

Question 36

Choice (D) is the correct answer. The United Farm Workers and its leader Cesar Chavez addressed the poor treatment of agricultural and migratory laborers by orchestrating boycotts of agricultural products they produced.

Question 37

Choice (C) is the correct answer. Samuel Gompers was the first leader of the American Federation of Labor (AFL) union.

Question 38

Choice (E) is the correct answer. The map traces the movement of adherents of Mormonism from its founding in Fayette, New York, to their settlement of Missouri and Illinois, to their eventual relocation to Salt Lake City in the Utah Territory following conflicts with non-Mormons.

Question 39

Choice (B) is the correct answer. The American, or Know-Nothing, Party was a nativist political organization that opposed the immigration of people other than Protestants to the United States.

Question 40

Choice (B) is the correct answer. Segregation often occurred because of a combination of *de jure* (by law) and *de facto* (by practice) actions. Segregation by practice, such as housing restrictions in the North, did not originate from the passage of laws but still resulted in social, cultural, and economic divisions.

Question 41

Choice (A) is the correct answer. In 1624 the Dutch West India Company established a settlement on the southern end of the island of Manhattan in what is now New York City.

Question 42

Choice (A) is the correct answer. The excerpt indicates how issues of westward expansion and the tensions that this created between colonists and American Indians resulted in even pacifist Quakers taking up arms to stop the settlers.

Question 43

Choice (B) is the correct answer. The Ghost Dance was a religious movement fostered by American Indian groups in the northern Great Plains in the late nineteenth century.

Question 44

Choice (C) is the correct answer. The colonial phrase "no taxation without representation" emerged out of the belief that the colonies deserved to have representation in Parliament, particularly in regards to taxation legislation such as the Stamp Act.

Question 45

Choice (C) is the correct answer. Both compromises focused on resolving the debates over the admission of new states into the United States, particularly in regards to maintaining a balance between states that did permit slavery and those that did not.

Question 46

Choice (D) is the correct answer. Social Darwinism applied the concept of natural selection to human society and posited that only the strongest people and institutions deserved to survive. This concept was particularly popular among wealthy individuals in their attempt to explain why social programs to address poverty were generally unnecessary.

Question 47

Choice (C) is the correct answer. The British government issued the Proclamation of 1763 as a means to restrict colonial settlement to east of the Appalachian mountains in an effort to reduce tensions and prevent conflict with Native American groups in the region.

Question 48

Choice (D) is the correct answer. The Roosevelt Corollary extended the Monroe Doctrine by asserting that not only were European nations prohibited from expanding their colonial holdings in the Western Hemisphere, but that the United States had a right and responsibility to act as an international police power to intervene in the region to ensure its interests there.

Question 49

Choice (B) is the correct answer. Women—such as those who founded the Daughters of Liberty—were often the largest and most vocal leaders and supporters of boycotts against British goods in responses to the taxes imposed on items imported into the colonies.

Question 50

Choice (D) is the correct answer. Envisioned by Woodrow Wilson, but not joined by the United States, the League of Nations was meant to be an institution where international problems could be addressed diplomatically to avoid the outbreak of conflicts like those that instigated the First World War.

Question 51

Choice (A) is the correct answer. African Americans participated in the American Revolution on both sides of the conflict. In particular, enslaved people fought for the British after the royal governor of Virginia, Lord Dunmore, offered freedom to any slave who ran away from Patriot slaveholders and agreed to fight for the Loyalists.

Question 52

Choice (C) is the correct answer. Du Bois' text highlights the difficulties that African Americans faced at the turn of the twentieth century in the United States with the continuation of segregationist laws that undermined their citizenship and prevailing racist sentiments that challenged their humanity.

Question 53

Choice (B) is the correct answer. In the ruling of *Marbury* v. *Madison*, the Supreme Court asserted its authority to determine the constitutionality of laws through the process known as judicial review.

Question 54

Choice (C) is the correct answer. In response to one of the first major challenges to federal power—in this instance the power to levy taxes—George Washington's actions during the Whiskey Rebellion strongly asserted the power of the federal government at the state and local level.

Question 55

Choice (C) is the correct answer. As the first Secretary of the Treasury, Alexander Hamilton had a very strong influence in the construction of the economic system of the newly formed United States, promoting the financial credit of the federal government and encouraging manufacturing.

Question 56

Choice (D) is the correct answer. The Articles of Confederation established the office of the president, which was a member of Congress who presided over the body for a one-year term. There was no separate executive branch of the federal government until the ratification of the Constitution.

Question 57

Choice (A) is the correct answer. The Monroe Doctrine grew out of fears that continued colonial expansion in the Americas would undermine the power of the United States. It was part of a larger trend toward shunning foreign alliances and asserting the power of the United States in the region.

Question 58

Choice (B) is the correct answer. The Hudson River School was a nineteenth-century art movement that focused on images of landscapes that emphasized the beauty of nature in the United States.

Question 59

Choice (E) is the correct answer. After the Gulf of Tonkin Incident (1964), Congress permitted President Johnson to increase the presence of United States forces in Vietnam. As a result, Johnson ordered an extensive aerial bombardment of North Vietnam and a proliferation of United States ground forces in South Vietnam.

Question 60

Choice (C) is the correct answer. After it was discovered that President Nixon had expanded combat from the Vietnam War into neighboring Cambodia, demonstrations and strikes proliferated in protest of the war.

Question 61

Choice (C) is the correct answer. The Virginia Colony, originally a joint-stock company, struggled to find a source of income until John Rolfe introduced tobacco production as a cash crop and the colony began to make a profit selling it in Britain. By contrast, slaves in Virginia were relatively limited in numbers and most often brought from other parts of the Americas rather than directly from Africa; the glassblowing industry at Jamestown never became successful; Jamestown did not diversify its agriculture in a significant way in the seventeenth century (focusing instead on tobacco); and cotton was not widely grown in Virginia in the seventeenth century.

Question 62

Choice (A) is the correct answer. The Navigation Acts were mercantilist laws meant to increase the dependency of the North American colonies on Britain by limiting where they could sell their products. These restrictions as to whom colonists could sell products is cited as one of the factors that contributed to increasing anti-British sentiment in the colonies before the American Revolution.

Question 63

Choice (B) is the correct answer. William Lloyd Garrison was a prominent abolitionist who believed that the Constitution's language of freedom and rights were at odds with its acceptance of slavery and the counting of enslaved peoples as three-fifths of a person for the census.

Question 64

Choice (E) is the correct answer. With their ability to harness moving water to power industrial machinery, the textile mills of Lowell, Massachusetts, were at the heart of the burgeoning industrial revolution in the United States in the early nineteenth century.

Question 65

Choice (C) is the correct answer. The image represents the response that Northern abolitionists had to the expansion of the Fugitive Slave Act. As part of the Compromise of 1850, the Fugitive Slave Act required northern law enforcement to help aid in the capture of runaway slaves from the South.

Question 66

Choice (C) is the correct answer. The United States approved the Gadsden Purchase in order to clarify the border with Mexico and to provide a route for the construction of a southern transcontinental railroad.

Question 67

Choice (B) is the correct answer. Political machines encouraged voting as a means of expanding and consolidating their base of support and enhancing their own political power, so they favored wide voting rights. In particular, many states did not use the secret ballot system, so machines could ensure voters' support through persuasion or intimidation.

Question 68

Choice (C) is the correct answer. Many advocates for woman suffrage were angry that African American men were given the right to vote before White women were, resulting in their resistance to the passage of an amendment that only guaranteed universal male suffrage.

Question 69

Choice (B) is the correct answer. Black Codes were laws established in the South after the Civil War to prevent former enslaved people from exercising the rights they had gained and to ensure continued White supremacy. Although many Black Codes would be overturned during Reconstruction, the end of Reconstruction saw the emergence of similar laws and restrictions known as Jim Crow laws.

Question 70

Choice (B) is the correct answer. The image represents the policy of assimilation carried out at the Carlisle Indian Industrial School. American Indian children were removed from their homes, prohibited from wearing traditional clothes and speaking in their own languages, and were instructed in unskilled or domestic labor. By breaking these cultural ties, the United States government believed that American Indians would be Americanized and assimilated into society.

Question 71

Choice (E) is the correct answer. Immigrants in the early to mid-nineteenth century primarily came from western and northern Europe (mostly Ireland and Germany). At the turn of the twentieth century, the majority of immigrants to the United States arrived from southern and eastern Europe.

Question 72

Choice (D) is the correct answer. The image criticizes the passage of the Chinese Exclusion Act of 1882, which barred the immigration of the majority of Chinese people to the United States, as a violation of the "Liberty" that the United States was supposed to represent.

Question 73

Choice (C) is the correct answer. The rejection of the Alien and Sedition Acts in the Virginia and Kentucky Resolutions, the rejection of the War of 1812 and the threat of secession at the Hartford Convention, and the assertion of South Carolina's rights to nullify national tariff rules all represent moments where states asserted the right to challenge the authority of the federal government.

Question 74

Choice (A) is the correct answer. Henry Clay was first elected to the Senate from Kentucky in 1806. This was well after the 1787 Constitutional Convention was held where the Three-Fifths Compromise was approved, counting enslaved peoples as 3/5 of a person in the census.

Question 75

Choice (B) is the correct answer. Henry Cabot Lodge was a Republican senator who, while known for his isolationist foreign politics after the First World War, supported the territorial expansion of the United States, particularly in the late nineteenth century.

Question 76

Choice (D) is the correct answer. The ratification of the Sixteenth Amendment in 1913 allowed for the creation of a federal income tax that was assessed based on an individual's wages, profits, and other money earned, which was a major Progressive Era goal.

Question 77

Choice (B) is the correct answer. Rather than goods being produced by craftspeople or by simple tasks being done in the home (also known as the putting-out system), many semiskilled and unskilled laborers performed small steps of the production process in factories, allowing for increased production and decreased labor costs.

Question 78

Choice (B) is the correct answer. In the decades immediately prior to the Civil War, the concept of domesticity focused on an ideal woman who stayed in the home, was pious, and instructed sons how to be good citizens and daughters how to be good wives and mothers.

Question 79

Choice (B) is the correct answer. The defeat of Spain in the Spanish-American War (1898) resulted in the United States gaining control of a number of Spain's island colonies in the Caribbean and the Pacific, including Puerto Rico and the Philippines.

Question 80

Choice (B) is the correct answer. The excerpt is from the Supreme Court ruling in *Plessy* v. *Ferguson*, where the Court asserted that separate public spaces and public institutions for White and Black people were constitutional so long as the separate amenities were equal. The ruling of "separate but equal" reinforced segregationist Jim Crow laws across the United States until the 1950s.

Question 81

Choice (C) is the correct answer. *The Grapes of Wrath* depicts the movement of farmers (known as Okies) displaced from Oklahoma to California in search of employment during the Great Depression and Dust Bowl.

Question 82

Choice (A) is the correct answer. As the United States entered the Second World War, the demand for war supplies led to increased industrial production and the drafting of young men into the military created near-zero unemployment, which caused employers to increase wages to entice workers. These factors resulted in new opportunities for groups like women and minorities who had previously been kept out of many sectors of the labor market.

Question 83

Choice (C) is the correct answer. Harry Truman's official statement regarding the justification for dropping atomic bombs was that it was calculated that the number of American soldiers who would die if the United States attempted to invade the home islands of Japan would have been too great.

Question 84

Choice (D) is the correct answer. In a speech to Congress as Nazi Germany expanded its power in Europe, Franklin Roosevelt articulated the "Four Freedoms" to which he believed all people of the world had the inherent right (freedom of speech, of religion, from want, from fear).

Question 85

Choice (B) is the correct answer. During the Vietnam War, the expansion of military combat into neighboring Cambodia and Laos by Richard Nixon's administration led many representatives in Congress to challenge the extent of the president's power to wage war, resulting in limitations enacted in the War Powers Act.

Question 86

Choice (C) is the correct answer. As the post-Second World War constitution of Japan explicitly renounced maintaining a military, the United States stationed its own military forces in Japan to prevent the resurgence of Japanese imperialism and to establish bases of operation from which to contain the expansion of communism in East Asia.

Question 87

Choice (E) is the correct answer. The Beat Generation was a countercultural movement that criticized United States culture and society, particularly the conformity of the ideal suburban lifestyle, in the postwar era of the 1950s and 1960s.

Question 88

Choice (B) is the correct answer. Franklin Roosevelt's unprecedented fourth election as president of the United States led many leaders to call for a constitutional amendment to limit the presidency to two terms. Although there was no official law until the ratification of the Twenty-second Amendment in 1951, many presidents had previously adhered to George Washington's precedent of voluntarily stepping down after two terms.

Question 89

Choice (A) is the correct answer. The economic boom the United States experienced after the Second World War resulted in higher productivity, a higher standard of living for many people, and the creation of a consumer culture that encouraged the creation and purchase of new products that would further enhance leisure time.

Question 90

Choice (E) is the correct answer. The religious revivalism of the Second Great Awakening encouraged people to work more actively toward social change and moral improvement. This increased activism led to the creation and intensification of nineteenth-century reform movements such as abolitionism, temperance, and woman suffrage.

United States History – Practice Test 3

Practice Helps

The test that follows is an actual, previously administered SAT Subject Test in United States History. To get an idea of what it's like to take this test, practice under conditions that are much like those of an actual test administration.

- Set aside an hour when you can take the test uninterrupted.

- Sit at a desk or table with no other books or papers. Dictionaries, other books, or notes are not allowed in the test room.

- Tear out an answer sheet from the back of this book and fill it in just as you would on the day of the test. One answer sheet can be used for up to three Subject Tests.

- Read the instructions that precede the practice test. During the actual administration, you will be asked to read them before answering test questions.

- Use a clock or kitchen timer to time yourself.

- After you finish the practice test, read the sections "How to Score the SAT Subject Test in United States History" and "How Did You Do on the Subject Test in United States History?"

- The appearance of the answer sheet in this book may differ from the answer sheet you see on test day.

UNITED STATES HISTORY TEST

The top portion of the page of the answer sheet that you will use to take the United States History Test must be filled in exactly as illustrated below. When your supervisor tells you to fill in the circle next to the name of the test you are about to take, mark your answer sheet as shown.

○ Literature	○ Mathematics Level 1	○ German	○ Chinese Listening	○ Japanese Listening
○ Biology E	○ Mathematics Level 2	○ Italian	○ French Listening	○ Korean Listening
○ Biology M	● U.S. History	○ Latin	○ German Listening	○ Spanish Listening
○ Chemistry	○ World History	○ Modern Hebrew		
○ Physics	○ French	○ Spanish		

Background Questions: ① ② ③ ④ ⑤ ⑥ ⑦ ⑧ ⑨

After filling in the circle next to the name of the test you are taking, locate the Background Questions section, which also appears at the top of your answer sheet (as shown above). This is where you will answer the following Background Questions on your answer sheet.

BACKGROUND QUESTIONS

Please answer the two questions below by filling in the appropriate circle in the Background Questions box on your answer sheet. <u>The information you provide is for statistical purposes only and will not affect your test score.</u>

Question I

How many semesters of United States History have you taken from grade 9 to the present? (If you are taking United States History this semester, count it as a full semester.) Fill in only <u>one</u> circle of circles 1-4.

- One semester or less   —Fill in circle 1.
- Two semesters   —Fill in circle 2.
- Three semesters   —Fill in circle 3.
- Four or more semesters   —Fill in circle 4.

Question II

Which, if any, of the following social studies courses have you taken from grade 9 to the present? (Fill in ALL circles that apply.)

- One or more semesters of government   —Fill in circle 5.
- One or more semesters of economics   —Fill in circle 6.
- One or more semesters of geography   —Fill in circle 7.
- One or more semesters of psychology   —Fill in circle 8.
- One or more semesters of sociology
  or anthropology   —Fill in circle 9.

If you have taken none of these social studies courses, leave the circles 5 through 9 blank.

When the supervisor gives the signal, turn the page and begin the United States History Test. There are 100 numbered circles on the answer sheet and 90 questions in the United States History Test. Therefore, use only circles 1 to 90 for recording your answers.

UNITED STATES HISTORY TEST

<u>Directions:</u> Each of the questions or incomplete statements below is followed by five suggested answers or completions. Select the one that is best in each case and then fill in the corresponding circle on the answer sheet.

1. During the seventeenth and eighteenth centuries, the English colonial system was based most explicitly on the economic and political principles of

    (A) mercantilism
    (B) free trade
    (C) salutary neglect
    (D) enlightened despotism
    (E) physiocracy

2. The concept of the separation of powers, as articulated by the framers of the Constitution, refers to the

    (A) right of free speech
    (B) right of freedom of assembly
    (C) organization of the national government in three branches
    (D) separation of church and state
    (E) political rights of confederated states

3. The Trail of Tears refers to the

    (A) movement of slaves from eastern states into the West after the 1820's
    (B) relocation of Cherokee Indians from the Southeast to settlements in what is now Oklahoma
    (C) difficult movement of settlers over the Oregon Trail
    (D) Lewis and Clark's expedition during the Jefferson presidency
    (E) movement of thousands of people across the Great Plains during the California gold rush

4. All of the following reformers are correctly paired with the reform issue with which they were most involved EXCEPT

    (A) Elizabeth Cady Stanton . . suffrage
    (B) Sojourner Truth . . antislavery
    (C) Harriet Beecher Stowe . . prohibition
    (D) Emma Willard . . women's education
    (E) Dorothea Dix . . treatment of people with mental and emotional disabilities

GO ON TO THE NEXT PAGE

BLACK POPULATION IN THE UNITED STATES, 1820 – 1850
FREE AND SLAVE (in thousands)

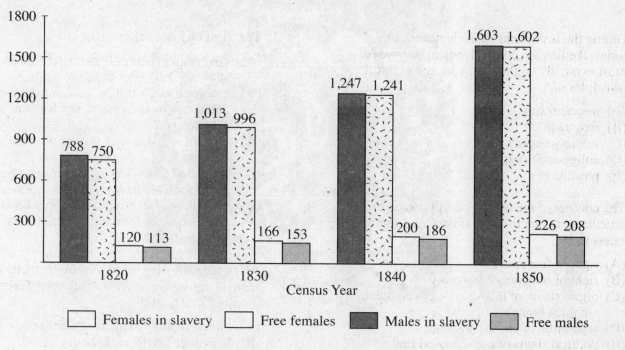

5. Which of the following statements about the period from 1820 to 1850 is supported by the diagram above?

(A) The percentage of the Black population held in slavery declined.
(B) The ratio of Black males to Black females remained fairly constant.
(C) Black males were more likely than Black females to be free.
(D) The number of Black females doubled every 20 years.
(E) The total Black population in each census exceeded two million.

GO ON TO THE NEXT PAGE

MAN·IS·BVT·A·WORM·

Punch Ltd.

6. The cartoon above illustrates popular reaction
   to publication of a theory by

   (A) Malthus
   (B) Darwin
   (C) Marx
   (D) Einstein
   (E) Freud

---

7. In the early years of the twentieth century, the
   majority of female workers employed outside
   of the home were

   (A) widowed
   (B) divorced
   (C) married with young children
   (D) married with grown children
   (E) young and unmarried

8. President Franklin D. Roosevelt attempted to
   "pack" the Supreme Court in 1937 for which
   of the following reasons?

   (A) He wanted to make sure that New Deal laws
       would be found constitutional.
   (B) He believed that additional conservative
       justices would balance the Court.
   (C) He owed favors to many political friends who
       were trained lawyers.
   (D) He wanted to increase minority representation
       on the Court.
   (E) He wanted socialists and communists to be
       represented on the Court.

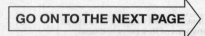
GO ON TO THE NEXT PAGE

By Permission of Chuck Asay and Creator's Syndicate, Inc.

9. The cartoon above makes which of the following points about federal aid policies in the years following the Second World War?

(A) The federal government has always been reluctant to offer financial aid to farmers.

(B) American farmers have never needed government support to maintain self-sufficiency.

(C) Much federal aid goes to individuals in forms other than welfare payments.

(D) Congress should cease paying both welfare and price supports.

(E) Price supports paid to farmers are not a significant percentage of the federal budget.

GO ON TO THE NEXT PAGE

10. The United States supported the Bay of Pigs invasion in 1961 in an attempt to overthrow

(A) Nikita Khrushchev
(B) Gamal Abdel Nasser
(C) Fidel Castro
(D) Chiang Kai-shek
(E) Ngo Dinh Diem

11. Single women and widows in the eighteenth-century British North American colonies had the legal right to

(A) hold political office
(B) serve as Protestant ministers
(C) vote
(D) own property
(E) serve on juries

12. Which of the following was most responsible for the repeal of the Stamp Act in 1766 ?

(A) The dumping of the East India Company's tea into Boston Harbor
(B) Petitions by the First Continental Congress to Parliament
(C) The boycott of British imports
(D) Acceptance by the Massachusetts colonists of alternate taxation
(E) Pressure on Parliament by the king

13. *Marbury* v. *Madison* was a significant turning point in the interpretation of the United States Constitution because it

(A) upheld the separation of church and state
(B) validated the principle of the free press
(C) established the practice of judicial review
(D) abolished the slave trade
(E) overturned the Alien and Sedition Acts

14. After the Civil War, sharecropping was an important element in the agricultural economy of which of the following regions?

(A) The Middle Atlantic states
(B) The South
(C) The Great Plains
(D) The West Coast
(E) New England

15. "Texas has been absorbed into the Union in the inevitable fulfillment of the general law which is rolling our population westward. . . . It was disintegrated from Mexico in the natural course of events, by a process perfectly legitimate on its own part, blameless on ours. . . . [Its] incorporation into the Union was not only inevitable, but the most natural, right and proper thing in the world."

The statement above is an expression of

(A) Social Darwinism
(B) antiabolitionism
(C) federalism
(D) Manifest Destiny
(E) self-determination

GO ON TO THE NEXT PAGE

Reprinted by permission of the New York Historical Society

16. The nineteenth-century cartoon above supports which of the following conclusions about the United States economy?

(A) The emergence of strong unions resulted in loss of productivity.

(B) The emergence of big government resulted in loss of liberties.

(C) Railroad corporations wielded tremendous power in American society.

(D) Southern planters wielded tremendous power in the Senate.

(E) Rapid urbanization led to unsanitary conditions in many cities.

GO ON TO THE NEXT PAGE

17. "There was never the least attention paid to what was cut up for sausage; there would come all the way back from Europe old sausage that had been rejected, and that was moldy and white.—it would be dosed with borax and glycerine, and dumped into the hoppers, and made over again for home consumption. . . . There would be meat stored in great piles in rooms; and the water from leaky roofs would drip over it, and thousands of rats would race about on it."

The passage above is most likely excerpted from

(A) John Steinbeck's *The Grapes of Wrath*
(B) Theodore Dreiser's *An American Tragedy*
(C) Jane Addams' *Twenty Years at Hull-House*
(D) Lincoln Steffens' *The Shame of the Cities*
(E) Upton Sinclair's *The Jungle*

MAJOR HOUSEHOLD EXPENDITURES,
1900 and 1928

1900	
2 Bicycles	$ 70
Wringer and washboard	$ 5
Brushes and brooms	$ 5
Sewing machine (mechanical)	$ 25
Total	$ 105
1928	
Automobile	$ 700
Radio	$ 75
Phonograph	$ 50
Washing machine	$ 150
Vacuum cleaner	$ 50
Sewing machine (electric)	$ 60
Other electrical equipment	$ 25
Telephone (year)	$ 35
Total	$1,145

18. The chart above shows the major household expenditures of a middle-class American family in 1900 and a similar family in 1928. Which of the following is an accurate statement supported by the chart?

(A) Families needed more mechanical help with housework in 1928 than they did in 1900 because they had less domestic help.
(B) Inflation caused a significant increase in the prices of most household goods by 1928.
(C) Many families moved from rural to urban areas between 1900 and 1930 in search of employment opportunities.
(D) By 1928 more consumer goods were available to families than had been available in 1900.
(E) Increased consumer spending was a major cause of the stock market crash of 1929.

GO ON TO THE NEXT PAGE

19. "Rosie the Riveter" was a nickname given during the Second World War to

(A) American women who did industrial work in the 1940's

(B) American women who cared for soldiers wounded in battle

(C) a machine that increased the speed of construction work

(D) a woman who was a popular radio talk-show host of the 1940's

(E) a woman who broadcast Japanese propaganda to American troops

GO ON TO THE NEXT PAGE

UPI/Corbis-Bettmann

20. The picture above illustrates efforts in the 1960's to organize
    a boycott that focused attention on the

    (A) long hours of grocery clerks and stock clerks
    (B) problems of Mississippi Valley fruit growers
    (C) labor shortages in produce transport companies
    (D) plight of migrant farmworkers
    (E) problems of West Coast wineries

GO ON TO THE NEXT PAGE

21. Which of the following statements best describes the response of Native Americans to the continued settlement of Europeans in North America during the eighteenth century?

 (A) Native Americans traded with the French and the English as a means of maintaining their autonomy.
 (B) Native Americans in the southern part of New France negotiated treaties with the French that allowed the peaceful expansion of the European timber trade.
 (C) Some Native Americans created a horse-based nomadic culture in the Northeast.
 (D) Native Americans in the Great Plains assimilated with the European settlers.
 (E) The Iroquois did not adopt European firearms and metal tools, in an effort to maintain their own traditions.

22. In the seventeenth century, the British colonies in the Chesapeake Bay region became economically viable due to the

 (A) adoption of representative government
 (B) introduction of tobacco cultivation
 (C) flourishing trade with American Indians
 (D) export of dried cod and whale tallow
 (E) cultivation of cotton

23. All of the following were aspects of the Constitution that was submitted to the states for ratification in 1787 EXCEPT

 (A) the ability to levy taxes
 (B) congressional authority to declare war
 (C) a two-term limit for Presidents
 (D) provision for impeachment of the President
 (E) provision for presidential State of the Union messages

GO ON TO THE NEXT PAGE

The St. Louis Art Museum. Gift Bank of America

24. The painting above, which shows an antebellum election site, supports which of the following statements?

   (A) Women were equal participants in the voting process.
   (B) The sale and provision of liquor was prohibited on election day.
   (C) Party workers had to remain at least 50 yards away from the polling place.
   (D) There were no property restrictions for male voters.
   (E) Elections were a welcome social event as well as a political obligation.

25. The introduction of canals, railroads, and new factory technology in the mid-nineteenth century affected which of the following regions LEAST?

   (A) New England
   (B) New York and Pennsylvania
   (C) New Jersey and Delaware
   (D) The South
   (E) The Midwest

GO ON TO THE NEXT PAGE

Questions 26-27 are based on the passage below.

"Unsanitary housing, poisonous sewage, contaminated water, infant mortality, the spread of contagion, adulterated food, impure milk, smoke-laden air, ill-ventilated factories . . . unwholesome crowding, prostitution and drunkenness are the enemies which the modern cities must face and overcome, would they survive. Logically their electorate should be made up of those who . . . have at least attempted to care for children, to clean houses, to prepare foods, to isolate the family from moral dangers. . . . To test the elector's fitness to deal with this situation by his ability to bear arms is absurd. . . . City housekeeping has failed partly because women, the traditional housekeepers, have not been consulted as to its multiform activities. The men have been carelessly indifferent to much of this civic housekeeping, as they have been carelessly indifferent to the details of the household."

Jane Addams, 1906.

26. Which of the following best reflects the main argument of the passage?

(A) Men should spend less time away from home and participate more fully in domestic life.
(B) Women should be able to vote in order to apply their proven housekeeping abilities to the civic sphere.
(C) Military solutions to social problems are ineffective because they ignore moral issues.
(D) Solving the problems of cities mostly depends on providing for poor children.
(E) Modern cities have been saved from ruin only by the involvement of women in civic issues.

27. The passage above suggests that Jane Addams would probably have supported all of the following EXCEPT

(A) military preparedness
(B) woman suffrage
(C) prohibition
(D) settlement houses
(E) the Pure Food and Drug Act

GO ON TO THE NEXT PAGE

PITTSBURG: A CITY ASHAMED

Culver Pictures, Inc.

28. The articles appearing in this 1905 issue of *McClure's Magazine* illustrate all of the following trends in the early twentieth-century United States EXCEPT:

(A) Popular magazines were beginning to turn their attention to issues of reform.

(B) Reform of municipal city governments was a growing concern.

(C) Exposure of monopolistic business practices was beginning to draw public attention.

(D) Scientific methods were increasingly called on to lend credibility to all sorts of theories.

(E) Reformers of both government and society enjoyed widespread support among leading industrialists.

GO ON TO THE NEXT PAGE

Questions 29-30 are based on the chart below.

IMMIGRATION TO THE UNITED STATES BY AREA OF ORIGIN

Year	All Countries	Europe	Asia	Americas	Africa	Australasia
1921	805,228	652,364	25,034	124,118	1,301	2,281
1922	309,556	216,385	14,263	77,448	520	915
1924	706,896	364,339	22,065	318,855	900	679
1925	294,314	148,366	3,578	141,496	412	462
1927	335,175	168,368	3,669	161,872	520	746
1928	307,255	158,513	3,380	144,281	475	606
1929	279,678	158,598	3,758	116,177	509	636

29. Which of the following areas of origin showed the greatest percentage decline in the number of immigrants to the United States between 1921 and 1929 ?

(A) Europe
(B) Asia
(C) The Americas
(D) Africa
(E) Australasia

30. Which of the following best accounts for the trend in immigration shown in the chart?

(A) Improved economic conditions in many areas of origin
(B) Warfare in several areas of the world during this period
(C) New United States immigration legislation
(D) Economic instability in the United States
(E) Increased immigration to other areas of North America

GO ON TO THE NEXT PAGE

31. In the seventeenth century, some Pueblo Indians of the desert Southwest adopted Christianity as

(A) an added dimension to their own religious culture, adding the Christian God as another deity
(B) evidence of an ancient European culture that they were willing to embrace
(C) a means of improving their agricultural practices
(D) a means of establishing greater equality within their community
(E) a means of direct communication with the afterlife through the practice of Christian prayer

32. Of the following, who challenged the religious establishment in Puritan New England?

(A) Cotton Mather
(B) Thomas Hutchinson
(C) Anne Hutchinson
(D) John Winthrop
(E) Abigail Adams

33. Henry Clay's "American System" included which of the following?

(A) A protective tariff that would fund internal improvements
(B) Restriction on the use of federal money for national defense
(C) Restriction on immigration from Asian countries
(D) Elimination of the national bank
(E) Protection of the property rights of Native Americans

34. In 1860 a southern writer, D. R. Hundley, wrote: "Know, then, that the Poor Whites of the South constitute a separate class to themselves; the Southern Yeomen are as distinct from them as the Southern Gentleman is from the Cotton Snob."

Which of the following characterizations would Hundley probably accept as best describing the southern yeoman?

(A) A class of White plantation employees who oversaw slave labor
(B) A group of landowners who generally owned more than 100 slaves and who formed the elite of southern society
(C) A group of independent farmers who owned small plots and few, if any, slaves
(D) A small group of farmers who believed that there were few, if any, class distinctions in the South
(E) A class of people known for their poor manners and lack of education

35. The Exclusion Act of 1882 prohibited the immigration of which of the following groups?

(A) Irish
(B) Mexicans
(C) Eastern European Jews
(D) Japanese
(E) Chinese

GO ON TO THE NEXT PAGE ➡

MONTHLY WAGES AND SEXUAL COMPOSITION OF THE WORKFORCE IN SELECTED TRADES IN NEW YORK CITY, 1850				
Trade	Average Male Wage	Average Female Wage	Percent Male	Percent Female
Clothing and tailors	$ 9.75	$ 6.99	48.5	51.5
Hats and millinery	27.51	17.14	43.5	56.5
Shoes and boots	24.32	10.43	75.2	24.8
Printing	36.28	14.48	71.3	28.7

36. Which of the following statements about the trades listed above is supported by the data in the table?

(A) The majority of female workers were in the hats and millinery trade.

(B) Both men and women received wages that were inadequate to support their families.

(C) In trades where women were in the majority, the difference between men's and women's wages was less than in trades where women were in the minority.

(D) The trades in which women were most highly represented had the lowest wages in the economy.

(E) The most skilled female workers were paid less than unskilled male workers.

GO ON TO THE NEXT PAGE

37. All of the following statements about the American home front during the Second World War are correct EXCEPT:

    (A) The government instituted direct price controls to halt inflation.
    (B) The Supreme Court upheld the forced relocation of Japanese Americans on the West Coast.
    (C) Black workers migrated in large numbers from the rural South to the industrial cities of the North and West.
    (D) Unemployment continued at Depression-era levels.
    (E) Business leaders served as heads of the federal war-mobilization programs.

38. Which of the following events of the civil rights movement best illustrates the concept of "non-violent civil disobedience"?

    (A) The *Brown* v. *The Board of Education of Topeka* case of 1954
    (B) The lunch-counter sit-ins of the early 1960's
    (C) The March on Washington, D.C., in 1963
    (D) The formation of the Black Panther party in 1966
    (E) The desegregation of Little Rock, Arkansas, Central High School

39. In the 1950's John Kenneth Galbraith's *The Affluent Society* and W. H. Whyte's *The Organization Man* were significant because they

    (A) criticized American conformity and the belief that economic growth would solve all problems
    (B) challenged the American view that the Soviet Union was responsible for the Cold War
    (C) advocated the nationalization of basic industries to increase production and profits
    (D) were novels describing life among the "beat generation"
    (E) urged a greater role for religion in American life and acceptance of Christian ethics by business executives

The Odd Couple

Reprinted by permission of Bill Mauldin and the Watkins/Loomis Agency.

40. Which of the following policies is the subject of the cartoon above?

    (A) Vietnamization
    (B) Containment
    (C) Détente
    (D) Interventionism
    (E) Isolationism

41. The Halfway Covenant adopted by many Puritan congregations in the late seventeenth century did which of the following?

    (A) Strengthened the Anglican church in New England
    (B) Undermined religious toleration in New England
    (C) Promoted Christianity among American Indians in New England
    (D) Eased the requirements for church membership
    (E) Encouraged belief in the doctrine of predestination

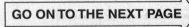
GO ON TO THE NEXT PAGE

42. At the time of the American Revolution, the most valuable cash crop produced in the southern states was

(A) cotton
(B) corn
(C) sugar
(D) wheat
(E) tobacco

43. The War of 1812 resulted in

(A) an upsurge of nationalism in the United States
(B) the acquisition of territories from Great Britain
(C) the strengthening of Napoleon in Europe
(D) the large-scale emigration of Europeans to the United States
(E) the elimination of United States shipping from European waters

44. Which of the following provides the best evidence of Lincoln's talents as a political leader?

(A) His success in getting his Reconstruction policies passed by Congress
(B) His skill in getting the South to acknowledge responsibility for the outbreak of the Civil War
(C) His success in securing adoption of the Fifteenth Amendment
(D) His ability to keep his party relatively united despite its internal conflicts
(E) His success in winning public support for a military draft

45. All of the following situations contributed to agrarian discontent in the late nineteenth century EXCEPT:

(A) Cotton averaged 5.8 cents a pound between 1894 and 1898, whereas it had been 15.1 cents a pound between 1870 and 1873.
(B) Short-haul railroad rates rose 60 percent in the 1890's.
(C) Farmers borrowed more heavily from banks than they had before the Civil War.
(D) European countries raised duties on agricultural products in the 1880's.
(E) The wheat harvest in Europe declined 30 percent in 1897.

46. At the beginning of the twentieth century, critics labeled individuals who exploited workers, charged high prices, and bribed public officials as

(A) robber barons
(B) free silverites
(C) knights of labor
(D) captains of industry
(E) muckrakers

GO ON TO THE NEXT PAGE

DISTRIBUTION OF TOTAL PERSONAL INCOME AMONG THE UNITED STATES POPULATION, 1950–1970

Year	Poorest Fifth	Second Poorest Fifth	Middle Fifth	Second Wealthiest Fifth	Wealthiest Fifth
1950	3.1%	10.5%	17.3%	24.1%	45.0%
1960	3.2%	10.6%	17.6%	24.7%	44.0%
1970	3.6%	10.3%	17.2%	24.7%	44.1%

47. The chart above supports which of the following statements?

(A) Federal antipoverty programs in the 1960's had little impact on the national distribution of income.

(B) Between 1950 and 1970, children tended to remain in the same socioeconomic groups as their parents.

(C) The wealthiest people earned about the same amount of money in 1970 as they earned in 1960.

(D) The increased number of women in the labor force in the 1970's had little effect on the amount of total family income.

(E) The number of people in the "poorest fifth" remained about the same from 1950 to 1970.

GO ON TO THE NEXT PAGE

48. "One who breaks an unjust law must do so openly, lovingly, and with a willingness to accept the penalty. I submit that an individual who breaks the law that conscience tells him is unjust, and who willingly accepts the penalty of imprisonment in order to arouse the conscience of the community over its injustice, is in reality expressing the highest respect for the law."

The quotation above most clearly expresses the views of

(A) Malcolm X
(B) Phyllis Schlafly
(C) Martin Luther King, Jr.
(D) Douglas MacArthur
(E) Barry Goldwater

49. Rachel Carson's book *Silent Spring* was a

(A) forestry manual
(B) description of deaf people's perception of the changing seasons
(C) protest against noise pollution
(D) protest against overuse of chemical insecticides
(E) protest against the Vietnam War

50. Which of the following was a consequence of President Lyndon B. Johnson's Great Society program?

(A) An end to the urban population decline in the East and Midwest
(B) Full employment until the end of the 1960's
(C) The near elimination of urban and rural poverty
(D) A major redistribution of the income tax burden
(E) An increase in federal spending on social services

51. "For we must consider that we shall be as a city upon a hill, the eyes of all people are upon us. So that if we shall deal falsely with our God in this work we shall have undertaken, and so cause Him to withdraw His present help from us, we shall be made a story and a by-word through the world."

The statement above was made by

(A) Jonathan Edwards preaching to a congregation during the Great Awakening
(B) John Winthrop defining the purpose of the Puritan colony
(C) Thomas Jefferson on the adoption of the Declaration of Independence
(D) William Penn defining the purpose of the Pennsylvania colony
(E) Benjamin Franklin gathering support for the American Revolution

52. Which of the following best characterizes the Anti-Federalists?

(A) They wanted a strong executive branch.
(B) They were loyal supporters of the Crown.
(C) They drew support primarily from rural areas.
(D) They favored universal suffrage.
(E) They favored rapid industrial development.

53. The Missouri Compromise was, in part, an effort to maintain the balance between the number of northerners and southerners in which of the following United States institutions?

(A) The Senate
(B) The House of Representatives
(C) Congress
(D) The Supreme Court
(E) The electoral college

GO ON TO THE NEXT PAGE

54. Which of the following is true of the Black Codes of the Reconstruction era?

(A) They promised every adult male former slave "forty acres and a mule."
(B) They were Andrew Johnson's response to criticism that he was not doing enough for former slaves.
(C) They were the result of joint actions by scalawags and carpetbaggers in the southern states.
(D) They were passed by the Radical Republicans in Congress to ensure the rights of former slaves.
(E) They were passed by Southern state legislatures to restrict the rights of former slaves.

55. Advocates of a free silver policy argued that the free coinage of silver would

(A) increase the supply of money and end economic depressions
(B) facilitate free trade between countries
(C) limit the market power of farmers
(D) stabilize the value of gold in relation to silver
(E) increase the value of the dollar in relation to currencies of foreign countries

56. Skilled male workers felt threatened by all of the following changes that occurred in the United States economy between 1890 and 1920 EXCEPT the

(A) arrival of large numbers of immigrants from southern Europe, eastern Europe, and Mexico
(B) introduction of "scientific management" to increase factory production and lower labor costs
(C) growing power of major corporations
(D) increasingly widespread distribution of inexpensive consumer goods
(E) growing presence of women workers in industry

57. Which of the following was demonstrated by the outcome of the presidential election of 1928 ?

(A) The nation had become convinced of the futility of Prohibition.
(B) "Republican prosperity" was a persuasive campaign slogan.
(C) Ethnic and religious differences among Americans exerted little influence on their voting behavior.
(D) Great numbers of ethnic minority-group voters switched from the Democratic to the Republican Party.
(E) The Ku Klux Klan was the commanding force in United States politics during the 1920's.

58. "[The American] is intensely and cocksurely moral, but his morality and his self-interest are crudely identical. He is emotional and easy to scare, but his imagination cannot grasp an abstraction. He is a violent nationalist and patriot, but he admires rogues in office and always beats the tax-collector if he can. He is violently jealous of what he conceives to be his rights, but brutally disregardful of the other fellow's."

The author of the quotation above is the noted journalist and satirist

(A) Dorothy Thompson
(B) Lillian Hellman
(C) H. L. Mencken
(D) Will Rogers
(E) Pearl Buck

GO ON TO THE NEXT PAGE

59. Which of the following contributed most to ending the post-Second World War economic boom?

  (A) Women leaving the workforce
  (B) Development of the computer
  (C) Consolidation of agriculture
  (D) A shift in population to the Sunbelt
  (E) The Arab oil embargo

60. The United States of the 1970's was characterized by an increase in all of the following EXCEPT

  (A) computer technology and marketing
  (B) an awareness of the rights of minorities
  (C) the migration of Americans from the Frostbelt to the Sunbelt
  (D) the strength of political party attachments
  (E) the number of multinational corporations

61. Colonists in eighteenth-century South Carolina benefited from the knowledge of Africans about the cultivation of

  (A) tobacco
  (B) rice
  (C) sugar
  (D) cotton
  (E) wheat

62. In the hundred years prior to 1776, which of the following had the LEAST influence on the emergence of the movement for independence in England's North American colonies?

  (A) The control of money bills by colonial legislatures
  (B) The long period of conflict between England and France
  (C) The models provided by the autonomous governments of other English colonies
  (D) The distance between England and its colonies
  (E) Constitutional developments in England

63. "To maintain the existing relations between the two races, inhabiting that section of the Union, is indispensable to the peace and happiness of both. It cannot be subverted without drenching the country in blood, and extirpating one or the other of the races."

The statement above was most likely made by which of the following?

  (A) John C. Calhoun to the United States Senate
  (B) Frederick Douglass to the Anti-Slavery Society
  (C) Daniel Webster to the South Carolina legislature
  (D) John Brown at Harpers Ferry
  (E) Abraham Lincoln in Springfield, Illinois

64. "In the late nineteenth century, the federal government followed a laissez-faire policy toward the economy."

A historian could argue against this thesis using all of the following pieces of evidence EXCEPT

  (A) tariff laws protecting various industries from European competition
  (B) laws granting land to the transcontinental railroad corporations
  (C) government policy toward the unemployed during the depression of the 1890's
  (D) the Bland-Allison Act of 1878 and the Sherman Silver Purchase Act of 1890
  (E) the Interstate Commerce Act of 1887

65. Booker T. Washington encouraged Black people to pursue all of the following EXCEPT

  (A) accommodation to White society
  (B) racial solidarity
  (C) industrial education
  (D) economic self-help
  (E) public political agitation

GO ON TO THE NEXT PAGE

66. "What we want to consider is, first, to make our employment more secure, and, secondly, to make wages more permanent. . . . I say the labor movement is a fixed fact. It has grown out of the necessities of the people, and, although some may desire to see it fail, still the labor movement will be found to have a strong lodgment in the hearts of the people; and we will go on until success has been achieved."

The quotation above best reflects the philosophy of which of the following organizations around 1900 ?

(A) Industrial Workers of the World
(B) National Labor Union
(C) American Federation of Labor
(D) Congress of Industrial Organizations
(E) Knights of Labor

67. Theodore Roosevelt issued his corollary to the Monroe Doctrine primarily because

(A) Japan's actions in Manchuria had violated the "open door"
(B) United States protection was needed by the colonies acquired in the Spanish-American War
(C) the Filipino people revolted against United States rule
(D) the financial difficulties of Caribbean nations threatened to bring about European intervention
(E) the declining toll revenue from the Panama Canal threatened Panamanian stability

68. "The problem lay buried, unspoken, for many years in the minds of American women. It was a strange stirring, a sense of dissatisfaction, a yearning that women suffered in the middle of the twentieth century in the United States. Each suburban wife struggled with it alone. As she made the beds, shopped for groceries, ate peanut butter sandwiches with her children, chauffeured Cub Scouts and Brownies, she was afraid to ask even of herself the silent question—'Is this all?'"

The passage above supports which of the following statements about women in the middle of the twentieth century?

(A) Women were no longer interested in political activities.
(B) Feminism tended to be a middle-class movement.
(C) Feminism renewed interest in religion among women.
(D) There were very few educational opportunities for women.
(E) Most women supported the feminist movement.

69. "Government is not the solution to our problems. Government is the problem."

The statement above was made by

(A) John F. Kennedy, asserting that the government did not do enough for the people
(B) Dwight D. Eisenhower, arguing that the government interfered with the military's operations
(C) Jimmy Carter, claiming that the government was inefficient and unfair
(D) Gerald Ford, charging that the government was corrupt
(E) Ronald Reagan, contending that the government had taken on functions properly belonging to the private sector

GO ON TO THE NEXT PAGE

"I DON'T KNOW WHY THEY DON'T SEEM TO HOLD US IN AWE THE WAY THEY USED TO"

©1987 HERBLOCK

From Herblock At Large (Pantheon, 1987)

70. Which of the following best summarizes the idea expressed in the 1987 cartoon above?

(A) In the 1980's, budget and trade deficits and scandal undermined the international standing of the United States.

(B) President Reagan expected that an international economic summit would enable the United States to solve its financial problems.

(C) In the 1980's, the United States could not look to its economic partners for help in solving its economic problems.

(D) The economic problems of the United States in the 1980's resulted from European economic policies.

(E) Had it not been for the Iran-Contra scandal, the United States could have solved its economic problems.

GO ON TO THE NEXT PAGE

71. "No man was a warmer wisher for reconciliation than myself, before the fatal nineteenth of April 1775, but the moment the event of that day was made known, I rejected the hardened, sullen tempered Pharaoh of England for ever; and disdain the wretch, that with the pretended title of FATHER OF HIS PEOPLE, can unfeelingly hear of their slaughter, and composedly sleep with their blood upon his soul."

    The passage above comes from

    (A) the Declaration of Independence
    (B) *The Federalist* papers
    (C) *Letters from a Farmer in Pennsylvania*
    (D) the Virginia Resolves against the Stamp Act
    (E) *Common Sense*

72. Alexander Hamilton's plan for stimulating economic growth in the United States included all of the following EXCEPT

    (A) acquisition of additional territory
    (B) a protective tariff
    (C) expansion of manufacturing
    (D) establishment of a national bank
    (E) federal assumption of debts incurred by states during the Revolutionary War

73. The first American party system, which developed in the 1790's, maintained party discipline at the federal level primarily by means of

    (A) caucuses
    (B) nominating conventions
    (C) rotation in office
    (D) restrictive primaries
    (E) "pork barrel" legislation

74. Which of the following was true of the Jacksonian Democrats in the 1830's?

    (A) They were the minority party in the nation.
    (B) They opposed a national bank.
    (C) They supported South Carolina's nullification of the protective tariff.
    (D) They were stronger in New England than in the West.
    (E) They generally repudiated the ideas of the Jeffersonian Republicans.

75. "We hold these truths to be self-evident: that all men and women are created equal. . . . The history of mankind is a history of repeated injuries and usurpations on the part of man toward woman, having in direct object the establishment of an absolute tyranny over her."

    The quotation above is excerpted from the

    (A) Seneca Falls Declaration of Sentiments and Resolutions
    (B) United States Declaration of Independence
    (C) United States Constitution
    (D) Declaration of Rights and Grievances
    (E) Equal Rights Amendment (ERA)

76. Which of the following is true of the Pullman strike of 1894 ?

    (A) It brought a substantial portion of American railroads to a standstill.
    (B) It started when Pullman workers were fired after the Haymarket riot.
    (C) It was caused by grievances about unsafe working conditions.
    (D) It ended when the government forced management to settle with the union.
    (E) It ended when the courts issued a blanket injunction against management.

GO ON TO THE NEXT PAGE

77. "We must be the great arsenal of democracy. For this is an emergency as serious as war itself. We must apply ourselves to our task with the same resolution, the same sense of urgency, the same spirit of patriotism, and sacrifice, as we would show were we at war."

The emergency to which the speaker refers was

(A) German U-boat attacks in 1917
(B) the Spanish Civil War in 1936
(C) German warfare against Britain in 1940
(D) the Berlin Blockade of 1948
(E) the Cuban missile crisis of 1962

78. The legislation passed between 1935 and 1937 dealing with the role of the United States in future wars seemed to reflect a belief that

(A) totalitarianism directly threatened the security of the United States
(B) the United States should quickly intervene in any future world wars
(C) the United States had made a mistake in not joining the League of Nations
(D) the United States should not have become involved in the First World War
(E) the United States should take a position of leadership in world affairs

79. Civil rights organizations in the 1950's and 1960's based their court suits primarily on the

(A) five freedoms of the First Amendment
(B) Fourteenth Amendment
(C) Thirteenth Amendment
(D) "necessary and proper" clause of the Constitution
(E) Preamble to the Constitution

80. The Nixon administration differed from previous administrations in adopting which of the following Vietnam War policies?

I. The bombing of North Vietnam
II. The use of American combat troops
III. The invasion of Cambodia
IV. The mining of North Vietnamese harbors

(A) I only
(B) I and III only
(C) II and III only
(D) II and IV only
(E) III and IV only

81. Which of the following political ideas or philosophies inspired the American revolutionaries of the eighteenth century?

(A) Progressivism
(B) Populism
(C) Manifest Destiny
(D) Republicanism
(E) The Social Gospel

82. The first major nineteenth-century political conflict over the issue of slavery was settled by the

(A) Alien and Sedition Acts
(B) Kentucky and Virginia Resolutions
(C) Missouri Compromise
(D) Kansas-Nebraska Act
(E) *Dred Scott* decision

GO ON TO THE NEXT PAGE

83. During the 1850's, Kansas became a significant issue for which of the following reasons?

   (A) The territory was an important way station in the Underground Railroad.
   (B) Northern and southern states vied to establish the first transcontinental railway through Kansas.
   (C) Kansas served as a center for the Peoples (Populist) Party's agitation against railroads and banks.
   (D) John Quincy Adams invoked the gag rule to prevent the discussion of slavery in the Senate.
   (E) It led to a divisive debate over the expansion of slavery into the territories.

84. Which of the following was a significant movement in American literature during the late nineteenth century?

   (A) Creationism
   (B) Modernism
   (C) Romanticism
   (D) Classicism
   (E) Realism

85. Edward Bellamy's *Looking Backward*, written in the 1880's, was a utopian reaction to which of the following?

   (A) The disillusionment with an increasingly competitive and industrial society
   (B) The plight of farmers who were driven off their land during the Great Depression
   (C) The disillusionment of the planter aristocracy in the post-Civil War era
   (D) The growing number of immigrants who regretted leaving their homes in Europe
   (E) Increasing concerns over the growth and power of labor unions in the railroad industry

86. The Harlem Renaissance refers to

   (A) Marcus Garvey's "back to Africa" crusade
   (B) the reemergence of the Ku Klux Klan as a force in American politics
   (C) writers and artists in New York who expressed pride in their African American culture
   (D) American expatriate writers living in Paris who wrote critically of American society
   (E) the political success of the Democratic Party in northern urban neighborhoods

87. The Federal Reserve Act of 1913 established a

   (A) single central bank like the Bank of England
   (B) method of insuring bank deposits against loss
   (C) system to guarantee the continued existence of the gold standard
   (D) system of local national banks
   (E) system of district banks coordinated by a central board

88. The Korean War and the Vietnam War differed in that only one involved

   (A) a formal declaration of war
   (B) a communist-led government
   (C) troops under United Nations auspices
   (D) Soviet arms support to one of the belligerents
   (E) United States air and ground forces

GO ON TO THE NEXT PAGE

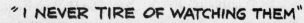

From Herblock On All Fronts (New American Library, 1980)

89. Which of the following best summarizes the idea expressed in the cartoon above?

(A) Most people are too dependent on computers in their daily lives.

(B) The amount of information available via computers is so overwhelming that people are no longer able to use the information effectively.

(C) Individual privacy is being threatened by the computerization of personal information.

(D) Many industries in the United States are threatened with significant layoffs as computers replace workers.

(E) People in the United States have been more reluctant to begin using computers than have people in other parts of the world.

GO ON TO THE NEXT PAGE

90. Which of the following is an accurate statement about the Equal Rights Amendment to the Constitution proposed in the 1970's?

    (A) It was opposed primarily by those who feared a loss of political power.
    (B) It guaranteed equal opportunity for women in the workplace.
    (C) It became a part of the Constitution in 1978.
    (D) It represented the first effort to enfranchise women.
    (E) It failed to gain the necessary votes for ratification within the constitutional time limit.

S T O P

IF YOU FINISH BEFORE TIME IS CALLED, YOU MAY CHECK YOUR WORK ON THIS TEST ONLY.
DO NOT TURN TO ANY OTHER TEST IN THIS BOOK.

How to Score the SAT Subject Test in United States History

When you take an actual SAT Subject Test in United States History, your answer sheet will be "read" by a scanning machine that will record your responses to each question. Then a computer will compare your answers with the correct answers and produce your raw score. You get one point for each correct answer. For each wrong answer, you lose one-quarter of a point. Questions you omit (and any for which you mark more than one answer) are not counted. This raw score is converted to a scaled score that is reported to you and to the colleges you specify.

Worksheet 1. Finding Your Raw Test Score

STEP 1: Table A on the following page lists the correct answers for all the questions on the Subject Test in United States History that is reproduced in this book. It also serves as a worksheet for you to calculate your raw score.

- Compare your answers with those given in the table.

- Put a check in the column marked "Right" if your answer is correct.

- Put a check in the column marked "Wrong" if your answer is incorrect.

- Leave both columns blank if you omitted the question.

STEP 2: Count the number of right answers.

Enter the total here: _____

STEP 3: Count the number of wrong answers.

Enter the total here: _____

STEP 4: Multiply the number of wrong answers by .250.

Enter the product here: _____

STEP 5: Subtract the result obtained in Step 4 from the total you obtained in Step 2.

Enter the result here: _____

STEP 6: Round the number obtained in Step 5 to the nearest whole number.

Enter the result here: _____

The number you obtained in Step 6 is your raw score.

Answers to Practice Test 3 for United States History

Table A
Answers to the Subject Test in United States History - Practice Test 3 and Percentage of Students Answering Each Question Correctly

Question Number	Correct Answer	Right	Wrong	Percentage of Students Answering the Question Correctly*	Question Number	Correct Answer	Right	Wrong	Percentage of Students Answering the Question Correctly*
1	A			71	26	B			53
2	C			85	27	A			83
3	B			89	28	E			36
4	C			64	29	B			57
5	B			92	30	C			60
6	B			80	31	A			31
7	E			62	32	C			43
8	A			77	33	A			43
9	C			74	34	C			38
10	C			77	35	E			42
11	D			72	36	C			46
12	C			61	37	D			64
13	C			61	38	B			64
14	B			77	39	A			32
15	D			80	40	C			29
16	C			74	41	D			37
17	E			69	42	E			54
18	D			83	43	A			52
19	A			69	44	D			37
20	D			53	45	E			33
21	A			41	46	A			57
22	B			55	47	A			32
23	C			71	48	C			48
24	E			90	49	D			30
25	D			56	50	E			57

Table A continued on next page

Table A continued from previous page

Question Number	Correct Answer	Right	Wrong	Percentage of Students Answering the Question Correctly*	Question Number	Correct Answer	Right	Wrong	Percentage of Students Answering the Question Correctly*
51	B			39	71	E			38
52	C			47	72	A			36
53	A			28	73	A			28
54	E			63	74	B			36
55	A			49	75	A			31
56	D			39	76	A			24
57	B			32	77	C			12
58	C			19	78	D			30
59	E			27	79	B			26
60	D			29	80	E			11
61	B			15	81	D			23
62	C			23	82	C			33
63	A			18	83	E			64
64	C			25	84	E			35
65	E			41	85	A			23
66	C			26	86	C			82
67	D			29	87	E			16
68	B			32	88	C			18
69	E			29	89	C			68
70	A			40	90	E			24

* These percentages are based on an analysis of the answer sheets of a representative sample of 8,509 students who took the original administration of this test and whose mean score was 534. They may be used as an indication of the relative difficulty of a particular question.

Finding Your Scaled Score

When you take SAT Subject Tests, the scores sent to the colleges you specify are reported on the College Board scale, which ranges from 200 to 800. You can convert your practice test raw score to a scaled score by using Table B. To find your scaled score, locate your raw score in the left-hand column of Table B; the corresponding score in the right-hand column is your scaled score. For example, a raw score of 39 on this particular edition of the SAT Subject Test in United States History corresponds to a scaled score of 560.

Raw scores are converted to scaled scores to ensure that a score earned on any one edition of a particular Subject Test is comparable to the same scaled score earned on any other edition of the same Subject Test. Because some editions of the tests may be slightly easier or more difficult than others, College Board scaled scores are adjusted so that they indicate the same level of performance regardless of the edition of the test taken and the ability of the group that takes it. Thus, for example, a score of 400 on one edition of a test taken at a particular administration indicates the same level of achievement as a score of 400 on a different edition of the test taken at a different administration.

When you take the SAT Subject Tests during a national administration, your scores are likely to differ somewhat from the scores you obtain on the tests in this book. People perform at different levels at different times for reasons unrelated to the tests themselves. The precision of any test is also limited because it represents only a sample of all the possible questions that could be asked.

Table B
Scaled Score Conversion Table
Subject Test in United States History - Practice Test 3

Raw Score	Scaled Score	Raw Score	Scaled Score	Raw Score	Scaled Score
90	800	52	630	14	430
89	800	51	630	13	430
88	800	50	620	12	420
87	800	49	620	11	420
86	800	48	610	10	410
85	800	47	610	9	410
84	800	46	600	8	400
83	800	45	600	7	400
82	800	44	590	6	390
81	800	43	590	5	390
80	800	42	580	4	380
79	800	41	580	3	380
78	790	40	570	2	370
77	780	39	560	1	370
76	780	38	560	0	360
75	770	37	550	−1	360
74	760	36	550	−2	350
73	750	35	540	−3	350
72	750	34	540	−4	340
71	740	33	530	−5	330
70	730	32	530	−6	330
69	730	31	520	−7	320
68	720	30	520	−8	310
67	710	29	510	−9	310
66	710	28	510	−10	300
65	700	27	500	−11	290
64	700	26	490	−12	290
63	690	25	490	−13	280
62	680	24	480	−14	270
61	680	23	480	−15	270
60	670	22	470	−16	260
59	670	21	470	−17	260
58	660	20	460	−18	250
57	660	19	460	−19	250
56	650	18	450	−20	240
55	650	17	450	−21	230
54	640	16	440	−22	230
53	640	15	440		

How Did You Do on the Subject Test in United States History?

After you score your test and analyze your performance, think about the following questions:

Did you run out of time before reaching the end of the test?

If so, you may need to pace yourself better. For example, maybe you spent too much time on one or two hard questions. A better approach might be to skip the ones you can't answer right away and try answering all the remaining questions on the test. Then if there's time, go back to the questions you skipped.

Did you take a long time reading the directions?

You will save time when you take the test by learning the directions to the Subject Test in United States History ahead of time. Each minute you spend reading directions during the test is a minute that you could use to answer questions.

How did you handle questions you were unsure of?

If you were able to eliminate one or more of the answer choices as wrong and guess from the remaining ones, your approach probably worked to your advantage. On the other hand, making haphazard guesses or omitting questions without trying to eliminate choices could cost you valuable points.

How difficult were the questions for you compared with other students who took the test?

Table A shows you how difficult the multiple-choice questions were for the group of students who took this test during its national administration. The right-hand column gives the percentage of students that answered each question correctly.

A question answered correctly by almost everyone in the group is obviously an easier question. For example, 85 percent of the students answered question 2 correctly. However, only 19 percent answered question 58 correctly.

Keep in mind that these percentages are based on just one group of students. They would probably be different with another group of students taking the test.

If you missed several easier questions, go back and try to find out why: Did the questions cover material you haven't yet reviewed? Did you misunderstand the directions?

Answer Explanations

For Practice Test 3

Question 1

Choice (A) is the correct answer. In the seventeenth and eighteenth centuries, the English colonial system was based largely on the principles of mercantilism, the theory that a nation's prosperity depends upon its supply of capital and the purpose of colonies is to enrich the home country. The English government implemented in its colonies such measures as the Navigation Acts, a series of acts intended to restrict England's carrying trade to English ships. Some of these acts enumerated colonial products, such as sugar, tobacco, indigo, rice, and molasses, that could only be shipped directly to England or to another English colony. These acts contributed to the unrest that led to the rebellion of the American colonies.

Question 2

Choice (C) is the correct answer. The term "separation of powers" refers to the framers' division of governmental authority among the legislative, executive, and judicial branches of the government. This division of authority allows each branch to check the actions of the others, more or less balancing the powers of each branch.

Question 3

Choice (B) is the correct answer. As a result of the enforcement of the Treaty of New Echota, Native American land in the East was exchanged for lands west of the Mississippi River. The Trail of Tears refers to the forced removal of the Cherokee tribe in 1838–39. Almost 17,000 tribe members were rounded up in camps and forced to relocate to the West. An estimated 4,000 Cherokees died during the relocation.

Question 4

Choice (C) is the correct answer. Harriet Beecher Stowe, the author of *Uncle Tom's Cabin*, advocated the abolition of slavery. She was not involved with prohibition.

Question 5

Choice (B) is the correct answer. The diagram indicates that the ratio of black males to black females remained fairly constant during the period from 1820 to 1850.

Question 6

Choice (B) is the correct answer. The cartoon's caption ("Man Is But a Worm") and the portrayal of human figures alongside monkeys and other animals refer to Darwin's theory of evolutionary progress through natural selection.

Question 7

Choice (E) is the correct answer. In the early twentieth century, young and unmarried women became more likely to work outside of the home. It was unusual for women who were married or had been married to work outside the home in the early years of the twentieth century.

Question 8

Choice (A) is the correct answer. President Franklin D. Roosevelt initiated the New Deal programs in 1933 to provide economic relief during the Great Depression, but in the following year the Supreme Court began to find significant parts of the New Deal unconstitutional. In 1937, Roosevelt proposed the Judiciary Reorganization Bill, also known as the Court-packing Bill, which would allow him to increase the number of Supreme Court judges. He proposed this measure in order to appoint justices who would uphold the New Deal legislation.

Question 9

Choice (C) is the correct answer. The cartoon depicts an individual portrayed as a farmer refusing welfare packets, while joyously accepting the same measures when they are called "price supports." This is a reference to the New Deal measures that guaranteed farmers a minimum price for their products in order to encourage the flow of production during the Great Depression.

Question 10

Choice (C) is the correct answer. In 1959, Fidel Castro overthrew the regime of Fulgencio Batista and oversaw Cuba's transformation into a Communist state. In January 1961, President Dwight D. Eisenhower broke diplomatic ties with Cuba and, in April, newly inaugurated President John F. Kennedy approved and enacted an invasion of Cuba. The Bay of Pigs invasion was undertaken in an attempt to overthrow Castro.

Question 11

Choice (D) is the correct answer. In colonial America, women could not hold political office, serve as clergy, vote, or serve as jurors, but single women and widows did have the right to own property.

Question 12

Choice (C) is the correct answer. In 1765, the British Parliament passed the Stamp Act, an act that implemented direct taxation of legal documents, permits, commercial contracts, newspapers, pamphlets, and playing cards in the American colonies by requiring that they carry a tax stamp. The Stamp Act was protested by the colonists, who refused to use the stamps and boycotted imports from British merchants and manufacturers.

Question 13

Choice (C) is the correct answer. The decision in *Marbury v. Madison* is significant because it asserted the principle of judicial review, or the power of the judiciary branch—in particular, the Supreme Court—to determine the constitutionality of legislation passed by Congress.

Question 14

Choice (B) is the correct answer. Sharecropping was a system that evolved after the abolition of slavery in the South. Former slaves used their crops to pay for their rent, while planters provided cash advances to secure labor for their lands. It was a system that provided a source of labor for planters and a meager source of income for poor laborers.

Question 15

Choice (D) is the correct answer. "Manifest Destiny," a term coined in the 1840s, refers to the belief that the United States has a destiny to expand its territorial borders and to spread its ideals of democracy and freedom. The quote discusses the annexation of Texas and expansion as a preordained ideal ("the most natural, right and proper thing in the world").

Question 16

Choice (C) is the correct answer. The cartoon depicts the growing power of railroads, represented by the figure of a steam engine. People watch fearfully as the giant figure symbolizing the railroad walks through a ravaged area carrying a club labeled "CAPITAL." The cartoon suggests that the financial interests of the railroads were taking precedence over all other cultural values.

Question 17

Choice (E) is the correct answer. *The Jungle*, a book written in 1906 by Upton Sinclair, was concerned with issues of food processing such as those listed in the passage. Sinclair, a socialist, wrote the book to elicit sympathy for workers but was ultimately successful in securing government legislation regarding food. The uproar caused by *The Jungle* aided the passage of the Meat Inspection Act and the Pure Food and Drug Act in 1906.

Question 18

Choice (D) is the correct answer. The chart indicates that by 1928 many consumer goods not available to middle-class American families in 1900—including automobiles, radios, vacuum cleaners, and telephones—had become available.

Question 19

Choice (A) is the correct answer. The nickname "Rosie the Riveter" referred to women who went to work in United States factories during the Second World War. Many women were employed by manufacturing plants to fill the positions left empty by men who were fighting in the war.

Question 20

Choice (D) is the correct answer. The picture depicts striking migrant workers. The captions in the placards held by the workers refer to the NFWA, the National Farm Workers Association, which was founded by César Chávez in 1962. In 1965, Chávez and the NFWA led a strike by California grape pickers and a boycott of California grapes.

Question 21

Choice (A) is the correct answer. In response to the continued settlement of Europeans in North America during the eighteenth century, Native Americans sought to establish trading relations with the French and the English.

Question 22

Choice (B) is the correct answer. The Chesapeake Bay colonies began to thrive economically only after the cultivation of tobacco as a cash crop.

Question 23

Choice (C) is the correct answer. The Twenty-second Amendment, proposed in 1947 and ratified in 1951, limits the president to two terms in office. The amendment was passed after President Franklin D. Roosevelt had been elected to a fourth term.

Question 24

Choice (E) is the correct answer. The painting depicts men socializing at an election site in the mid-nineteenth century.

Question 25

Choice (D) is the correct answer. New England, New York and Pennsylvania, New Jersey and Delaware, and the Midwest saw tremendous economic growth with the mid-nineteenth-century introduction of canals, railroads, and new factory technology. The South was the area that was least advanced in transportation and industry, and thus saw the least economic growth from the expansion in modes of transportation and industrial production.

Question 26

Choice (B) is the correct answer. The quotation implies that women, who have proven their abilities in the domestic sphere ("those who . . . have at least attempted to care for children, to clean houses, to prepare foods"), should be allowed to vote in order to extend their helpful influence into the political sphere ("civic housekeeping").

Question 27

Choice (A) is the correct answer. Jane Addams was a pacifist and the passage does not indicate her support for war. As her statement suggests ("To test the elector's fitness . . . by his ability to bear arms is absurd"), Addams thought society valued military prowess too highly. Moreover, choices (B), (C), (D), and (E) all describe reforms that Addams seems to think are necessary, given the information in the passage.

Question 28

Choice (E) is the correct answer. The articles in this issue of *McClure's Magazine* illustrate the nature and some of the tactics of Progressive reform. Progressives sought to reform municipal governments ("exposure of another type of municipal grafting") and business practices of monopoly ("famous oil crisis of 1878"), and to emphasize scientific investigations ("A powerful story, yet a scientific prediction"). Progressives also attempted to regulate business and therefore were not always looked on favorably by industrialists, so it is incorrect to suggest that the reformers enjoyed widespread support among industrialists.

Question 29

Choice (B) is the correct answer. Asia shows the sharpest drop in immigration during this period. The enforcement of the Chinese Exclusion Act coupled with the passage of the National Origins Act in 1924 resulted in a sharp decline in Asian immigration during this period.

Question 30

Choice (C) is the correct answer. The chart shows declining immigration due to the passage of the National Origins Act, which restricted immigration in 1924 by establishing a system of national quotas. The Act, which strengthened legislation passed in 1921 and virtually barred immigration from Asia, severely limited immigration from southern and eastern Europe.

Question 31

Choice (A) is the correct answer. Upon contact with Christianity, which had spread into South and Central America through the influence of the Spanish, some Pueblo Indians incorporated elements of Christianity into their own religious beliefs. This incorporation of Christian features into traditional belief systems occurred among native groups throughout the Americas.

Question 32

Choice (C) is the correct answer. This question is about dissent in seventeenth-century Puritan New England. Anne Hutchinson challenged the authority of the clergy. Choices (A) and (D) are incorrect, as Cotton Mather and John Winthrop were leading members of the Puritan clergy. Choices (B) and (E) are incorrect, as both Thomas Hutchinson and Abigail Adams lived during a later time period.

Question 33

Choice (A) is the correct answer. Henry Clay's "American System" was proposed during a period of heightened nationalism after the War of 1812. The American System was designed to promote national economic growth through high tariffs, internal improvements, western settlement, and reconciliation of regional differences. The other options were not aspects of Clay's system.

Question 34

Choice (C) is the correct answer. The quotation suggests that "yeomen" are neither "Poor Whites" nor "Southern Gentlemen." Choices (A), (B), (D), and (E) do not describe southern yeomen.

Question 35

Choice (E) is the correct answer. This question tests knowledge of immigration policy in the nineteenth century. The Exclusion Act of 1882 was passed as a reaction to Chinese immigration in the late nineteenth century. Many Chinese had come to the United States during the Gold Rush, and tended to work hard for low wages. When the United States economy suffered instability in the 1870s, Chinese immigrants were singled out.

Question 36

Choice (C) is the correct answer. The chart indicates that the gap between the wages of men and women was far smaller in clothing, tailoring, hats, and millinery—jobs in which women were in the majority. None of the other statements are supported by the data in the table.

Question 37

Choice (D) is the correct answer. Statement (D) is inaccurate. There was a sharp decrease in unemployment due to wartime industrial production. The need for workers was so great that thousands of women were employed in factories for the first time. All of the other statements are accurate.

Question 38

Choice (B) is the correct answer. Nonviolent civil disobedience is the protest act of breaking laws in a peaceful manner and without any harm to others. The lunch-counter sit-ins were such an example, as African American students entered restaurants and cafes that were segregated and sat in areas marked for "Whites only," despite the fact that there were laws supporting segregation. Choice (A) is incorrect. This was a Supreme Court ruling that overturned school segregation and was not a protest. Choices (C) and (D) are incorrect. They refer to protests and events that were legal. Choice (E) is incorrect. This is a reference to a government initiative that was implemented through the use of military force.

Question 39

Choice (A) is the correct answer. John Kenneth Galbraith and W. H. Whyte were two prominent social critics who criticized the American emphasis on materialism and conformity in the 1950s. The other choices do not describe Galbraith's and Whyte's books.

Question 40

Choice (C) is the correct answer. Détente was a policy of peaceful coexistence of the United States and the Soviet Union. The cartoon depicts the American eagle and the Russian bear and symbolizes the two countries in harmony and united as a family. Choice (A) is incorrect. Vietnamization referred to the escalating conflict in Vietnam and the cartoon indicates harmony. Choice (B) is incorrect. Containment was a policy that sought to check the spread of communism pitting the United States against the Soviet Union. Choice (D) is incorrect. It refers to intervention in the internal affairs of another country. Choice (E) is incorrect. Isolationism did not mean harmony and cooperation, but rather an effort to exclude the outside world.

Question 41

Choice (D) is the correct answer. The Halfway Covenant was adopted to address the problem of declining church membership in the late seventeenth century. Under this covenant, adults who had been baptized into the church as children but who had not yet experienced the conversion necessary for full membership could nonetheless have their children baptized. The other choices are incorrect.

Question 42

Choice (E) is the correct answer. Tobacco was the most valuable export crop that was produced in the South on the eve of the Revolution in the 1770s. Cotton, choice (A), did not surpass tobacco as the South's chief crop until the 1800s. Choices (B), (C), and (D) are incorrect.

Question 43

Choice (A) is the correct answer. The War of 1812 did lead to a rising spirit of nationalism. Choice (B) is incorrect. The war did not lead to the acquisition of territories. Choice (C) is incorrect. The war did not strengthen Napoleon. Choice (D) is incorrect. There was no large-scale emigration from Europe after the war. Choice (E) is incorrect. U.S. shipping and trade with Europe resumed after the war.

Question 44

Choice (D) is the correct answer. Lincoln displayed remarkable political skills in holding the Republican Party together during the Civil War period, as radicals and moderates contended to shape policy. The other choices are incorrect.

Question 45

Choice (E) is the correct answer. A declining wheat harvest in Europe did not contribute to agrarian discontent in the United States in the late nineteenth century. It helped to raise farm prices, relieving U.S. farmers. Each of the other choices did contribute to the economic depression suffered by American farmers in the 1890s.

Question 46

Choice (A) is the correct answer. Critics called wealthy industrialists who engaged in exploitative practices "robber barons." Choice (D) was not a term of criticism that was applied to these individuals, and choices (B), (C), and (E) are terms that applied to those who opposed the practices described in the question.

Question 47

Choice (A) is the correct answer. The chart shows that despite the passage of Great Society programs in the 1960s, the distribution of income remained relatively unchanged in 1970. One possible explanation may be due to the difficulty of promoting political and economic change through federal initiatives. Another reason may be due to the fact that in the 1970s technological change and economic growth had raised everyone's standard of living, minimizing the potential for wealth to be redistributed. The other statements are not supported by the information in the chart.

Question 48

Choice (C) is the correct answer. The quotation is an excerpt from the "Letter from a Birmingham Jail" by Martin Luther King, Jr., in which he expresses his philosophy of civil disobedience. The other choices are not correct.

Question 49

Choice (D) is the correct answer. This question concerns Rachel Carson's work on environmental pollution and its effects. Rachel Carson's book documented the harmful effects of chemicals. The other choices are incorrect.

Question 50

Choice (E) is the correct answer. This question asks about the effects of the Great Society programs. The programs, which included Head Start, Job Corps, and VISTA, did increase federal spending on social services. Choice (A) is incorrect. The Great Society programs did not lead to a decline in urban population. Choice (B) is incorrect. There was no full employment during this period. Choice (C) is incorrect. The Great Society programs did not eliminate poverty, although they made efforts to provide assistance to the poor. Choice (D) is incorrect. The programs did not change the income tax structure.

Question 51

Choice (B) is the correct answer. The quotation is an excerpt of John Winthrop's address to his Puritan congregation. The idea of "a city upon a hill," or a community that is an example to others, has been invoked by politicians, including Ronald Reagan, to describe the nation as a whole. The other choices are incorrect.

Question 52

Choice (C) is the correct answer. The Anti-Federalists, persons who opposed ratification of the U.S. Constitution in 1787–89, drew their support primarily from farmers in rural areas. Choice (A) is incorrect. The Anti-Federalists feared a strong central government. Choice (B) is incorrect. The Anti-Federalists were not supporters of the Crown. Choice (D) is incorrect. The Anti-Federalists did not favor universal suffrage. Choice (E) is incorrect. The Anti-Federalists were opposed to industrial development and favored an agrarian economy.

Question 53

Choice (A) is the correct answer. This question asks for an identification of one of the goals of the Missouri Compromise of 1820. The Compromise was an effort to maintain the balance between slave states and free states in the Senate, which in 1819 had senators from 11 free states and 11 slave states, by admitting Maine (free) and Missouri (slave) at the same time. Choices (B) and (C) are incorrect, as the Compromise did not change the House of Representatives. The other choices are incorrect, as the Compromise did not affect the balance in any of the other agencies of government.

Question 54

Choice (E) is the correct answer. This question asks about the purpose of the Black Codes. The Black Codes were laws passed by Southerners to restrict the freedom of former slaves. Choices (A) and (B) are incorrect, as the Black Codes restricted the rights of former slaves. Choice (C) is incorrect, as Southerners, not carpetbaggers, passed the Codes. Choice (D) is incorrect, as the measures passed by Radical Republicans were intended to help former slaves (or freed slaves) and the Black Codes had the opposite effect.

Question 55

Choice (A) is the correct answer. Advocates of free silver argued that the United States' tight domestic monetary policies were the cause of the economic depressions of the late nineteenth century. They believed that increasing the circulation of silver would help farmers by raising crop prices and allow farmers and others to pay their debts more easily. The other choices are incorrect.

Question 56

Choice (D) is the correct answer. Although consumerism began in the 1870s with catalog buying, it did not become widespread until the mid-twentieth century. Skilled male workers were not threatened by consumerism during this period. Each of the other choices reflects a specific threat to skilled male workers around the turn of the century.

Question 57

Choice (B) is the correct answer. In 1928, Republican Herbert Hoover, bolstered by years of economic prosperity under Republican administrations, defeated Alfred E. Smith, a Catholic who suffered from anti-Catholic prejudice.

Question 58

Choice (C) is the correct answer. The quote is an excerpt from the work of H. L. Mencken, a satirist and critic of American social and cultural weaknesses. As the quote suggests, Mencken was famous for exposing American pretensions and hypocrisy.

Question 59

Choice (E) is the correct answer. The question asks about the primary reason for the end of the post–Second World War boom. The 1973 oil embargo led to a huge increase in oil prices, inflation, and the end of the economic boom. The other choices are incorrect.

Question 60

Choice (D) is the correct answer. The election of 1972 was the first presidential election in which most of the Southern states broke ranks with the Democratic Party and voted Republican. This shift in allegiances contradicted traditional party affiliations and also changed Southern politics.

Question 61

Choice (B) is the correct answer. Colonists in South Carolina gained knowledge of rice cultivation from slaves from the "Rice Coast," the traditional rice-growing region of West Africa.

Question 62

Choice (C) is the correct answer. The colonists were not influenced by autonomous governments in other English colonies because there were no autonomous govern-ments in other English colonies. All the other choices refer to factors that contributed to the emergence of an independence movement.

Question 63

Choice (A) is the correct answer. This is an excerpt from an address by John C. Calhoun to the United States Senate. This speech reflects Calhoun's anti-abolitionist views.

Question 64

Choice (C) is the correct answer. The government provided no support for the unemployed during the 1890s. All other choices refer to intervention by the government to help particular interests and therefore could be used to disprove the statement that the government followed a laissez-faire, or "hands off," policy.

Question 65

Choice (E) is the correct answer. Booker T. Washington never advocated direct political activism for black people. Washington believed that black people would be best served by pursuing the goals listed in the other choices.

Question 66

Choice (C) is the correct answer. The quote represents the position of the American Federation of Labor, the sole unifying agency of the American labor movement in the early twentieth century.

Question 67

Choice (D) is the correct answer. Theodore Roosevelt responded to a crisis in the Caribbean, where the Dominican Republic stopped payments on its debts to various nations, by issuing a corollary to the Monroe Doctrine. This statement reasserted the intention of the United States to prevent European intervention in Latin America, as established by the Monroe Doctrine.

Question 68

Choice (B) is the correct answer. The passage is a quote from Betty Friedan and describes the frustrations of suburban middle-class women in the 1950s who generated the modern feminist movement. The other choices are not supported by the passage.

Question 69

Choice (E) is the correct answer. This statement expresses Ronald Reagan's policy of small government: cutting taxes, scaling back government intervention, and letting the market and the private sector attempt to solve domestic social problems. This attitude toward government is a hallmark of the Reagan Revolution.

Question 70

Choice (A) is the correct answer. The cartoon depicts the United States, symbolized by Ronald Reagan and Uncle Sam, afflicted by debt and scandals and no longer able to command respect from other nations.

Question 71

Choice (E) is the correct answer. This is an excerpt from Thomas Paine's *Common Sense*, a pamphlet published in January 1776 that sold 150,000 copies and helped inflame the American Revolution. Paine was referring to the day of fighting between colonists and British soldiers at Lexington and Concord, during which several colonists were killed.

Question 72

Choice (A) is the correct answer. Hamilton did not consider territorial acquisition as a primary factor in developing the economy and was a strong proponent of developing the manufacturing and mercantile base. The other choices represent aspects of his plan.

Question 73

Choice (A) is the correct answer. The caucus was the apparatus for selecting political candidates during this period. In every election from 1800 to 1824, members of Congress from each party met in a caucus to choose the party's candidates for president and vice president.

Question 74

Choice (B) is the correct answer. Jacksonian Democrats were vehemently opposed to a national bank, which they viewed as an instrument of mercantile interests. The other choices are inaccurate statements about the Jacksonian Democrats.

Question 75

Choice (A) is the correct answer. The quote is an excerpt from the Seneca Falls Declaration. This Declaration, which was drawn up at a meeting in Seneca Falls, New York, in 1848, uses the language and the logic of the Declaration of Independence to make the case for women's rights.

Question 76

Choice (A) is the correct answer. The Pullman strike was a major strike begun by Pullman rail workers who were angry about reduced wages. When sympathetic railway workers agreed to boycott all trains carrying Pullman cars, rail service was disrupted nationwide. Federal troops ended the strike and arrested the organizers.

Question 77

Choice (C) is the correct answer. This is a quote from Franklin D. Roosevelt's speech after Germany's attack on Britain in 1940, before the United States entered the Second World War. Roosevelt appealed to factory owners and workers to turn their efforts to weapons production to aid in the fight against Germany.

Question 78

Choice (D) is the correct answer. The neutrality acts passed between 1935 and 1937 sought to keep the United States out of the coming Second World War and were based on the belief that the United States' involvement in the First World War was a mistake. The other choices are incorrect.

Question 79

Choice (B) is the correct answer. Civil rights organizations used the "due process" and "equal protection" clause of the Fourteenth Amendment, which guarantees equal rights under the law to all Americans, to force changes in existing laws. In *Brown v. Board of Education of Topeka*, for example, the Supreme Court held that segregated schools were unconstitutional under the Fourteenth Amendment.

Question 80

Choice (E) is the correct answer. The invasion of Cambodia and the mining of North Vietnamese harbors were policies that were initiated by the Nixon administration. Previous administrations had sent thousands of combat troops to Vietnam and engaged in bombing the North.

Question 81

Choice (D) is the correct answer. The eighteenth-century revolutionaries were inspired by the principles of republicanism, which emphasized popular sovereignty, equality, and liberty. The other terms are all associated with later periods in American history.

Question 82

Choice (C) is the correct answer. The Missouri Compromise of 1820, which admitted Maine into the Union as a free state and Missouri as a slave state (but with some restrictions), solved the first major political conflict over slavery in the nineteenth century. The Missouri Compromise did not last; it was superceded by the Kansas-Nebraska Act of 1854. The other choices are incorrect.

Question 83

Choice (E) is the correct answer. The Kansas-Nebraska Act of 1854 allowed people in the territories of Kansas and Nebraska to decide for themselves whether to allow slavery. Rival groups of settlers, some pro-slavery and some anti-slavery, moved into Kansas and fought with one another to determine the future of the state. After seven years of well-publicized bitter conflict, Kansas entered the Union as a free state in January 1861. The conflict in Kansas reverberated throughout the country and set the stage for the Civil War.

Question 84

Choice (E) is the correct answer. This was a period when writers like William Dean Howells and Theodore Dreiser tried to portray the challenges posed by social and economic realities.

Question 85

Choice (A) is the correct answer. Edward Bellamy's novel imagines a plan for repairing the problems of industrial society. The novel's main character awakes in the year 2000 after 113 years of sleep and is pleased to find himself living in an organized utopian society under wise government control.

Question 86

Choice (C) is the correct answer. The term "Harlem Renaissance" refers to an outpouring of artistic and literary work by African American writers and artists centered in Harlem, in New York City, during the 1920s. The other choices are incorrect.

Question 87

Choice (E) is the correct answer. The Federal Reserve Act created a network of regional Federal Reserve banks. The Federal Reserve System includes 12 Federal Reserve banks, a governing board, and several thousand member banks.

Question 88

Choice (C) is the correct answer. The Korean War was supported by a United Nations resolution and involved United Nations troops. No U.N. troops participated in the Vietnam conflict. The other choices are incorrect.

Question 89

Choice (C) is the correct answer. The cartoon depicts Americans living in a fishbowl, symbolizing the loss of privacy that comes with the storing of personal information on computers. The 1978 cartoon reflects early fears about the security of computer technology. The other choices are incorrect.

Question 90

Choice (E) is the correct answer. The Equal Rights Amendment never gained sufficient votes for ratification. The amendment led to deep divisions within the feminist movement and was perceived by some opponents as a threat to family values.

United States History – Practice Test 4

Practice Helps

The test that follows is an actual, previously administered SAT Subject Test in United States History. To get an idea of what it's like to take this test, practice under conditions that are much like those of an actual test administration.

- Set aside an hour when you can take the test uninterrupted.

- Sit at a desk or table with no other books or papers. Dictionaries, other books, or notes are not allowed in the test room.

- Tear out an answer sheet from the back of this book and fill it in just as you would on the day of the test. One answer sheet can be used for up to three Subject Tests.

- Read the instructions that precede the practice test. During the actual administration, you will be asked to read them before answering test questions.

- Use a clock or kitchen timer to time yourself.

- After you finish the practice test, read the sections "How to Score the SAT Subject Test in United States History" and "How Did You Do on the Subject Test in United States History?"

- The appearance of the answer sheet in this book may differ from the answer sheet you see on test day.

UNITED STATES HISTORY TEST

The top portion of the page of the answer sheet that you will use to take the United States History Test must be filled in exactly as illustrated below. When your supervisor tells you to fill in the circle next to the name of the test you are about to take, mark your answer sheet as shown.

○ Literature	○ Mathematics Level 1	○ German	○ Chinese Listening	○ Japanese Listening
○ Biology E	○ Mathematics Level 2	○ Italian	○ French Listening	○ Korean Listening
○ Biology M	● U.S. History	○ Latin	○ German Listening	○ Spanish Listening
○ Chemistry	○ World History	○ Modern Hebrew		
○ Physics	○ French	○ Spanish	**Background Questions:** ① ② ③ ④ ⑤ ⑥ ⑦ ⑧ ⑨	

After filling in the circle next to the name of the test you are taking, locate the Background Questions section, which also appears at the top of your answer sheet (as shown above). This is where you will answer the following Background Questions on your answer sheet.

BACKGROUND QUESTIONS

Please answer the two questions below by filling in the appropriate circle in the Background Questions box on your answer sheet. <u>The information you provide is for statistical purposes only and will not affect your test score.</u>

Question I

How many semesters of United States History have you taken from grade 9 to the present? (If you are taking United States History this semester, count it as a full semester.) Fill in only <u>one</u> circle of circles 1-4.

- One semester or less   —Fill in circle 1.
- Two semesters   —Fill in circle 2.
- Three semesters   —Fill in circle 3.
- Four or more semesters   —Fill in circle 4.

Question II

Which, if any, of the following social studies courses have you taken from grade 9 to the present? (Fill in ALL circles that apply.)

- One or more semesters of government   —Fill in circle 5.
- One or more semesters of economics   —Fill in circle 6.
- One or more semesters of geography   —Fill in circle 7.
- One or more semesters of psychology   —Fill in circle 8.
- One or more semesters of sociology
  or anthropology   —Fill in circle 9.

If you have taken none of these social studies courses, leave the circles 5 through 9 blank.

When the supervisor gives the signal, turn the page and begin the United States History Test. There are 100 numbered circles on the answer sheet and 90 questions in the United States History Test. Therefore, use only circles 1 to 90 for recording your answers.

UNITED STATES HISTORY TEST

Directions: Each of the questions or incomplete statements below is followed by five suggested answers or completions. Select the one that is best in each case and then fill in the corresponding circle on the answer sheet.

1. Indentured servitude in the British colonies of North America was primarily a

   (A) method by which the colonies initially secured a workforce
   (B) device for preventing the emancipation of slaves
   (C) technique for regulating the size of the lower classes
   (D) means by which England rid itself of criminals
   (E) process by which young people learned skills

2. "My master used to ask us children, 'Do your folks pray at night?' We said 'No,' 'cause our folks had told us what to say. But the Lord have mercy, there was plenty of that going on. They'd pray, 'Lord, deliver us from under bondage.'"

   The statement above was probably made by a

   (A) Lowell mill worker who had escaped the poverty of a family farm
   (B) former indentured servant recalling praying for the end of the term of servitude
   (C) former slave criticizing the lack of religious worship in the quarters
   (D) former slave remembering the need to conceal one's thoughts under slavery
   (E) southern minister giving a sermon on prayer in the antebellum era

3. Which of the following was a major issue dividing the political parties during Andrew Jackson's presidency?

   (A) A national bank
   (B) Extension of the suffrage
   (C) Immigration
   (D) Military expenditures
   (E) Railroad construction

4. All of the following were true of the industrial working class of late-nineteenth-century America EXCEPT:

   (A) It was composed of native-born as well as immigrant workers.
   (B) Working-class neighborhoods were sometimes segregated ethnically.
   (C) Women and children frequently worked in factories.
   (D) Most workers belonged to unions.
   (E) Immigrants were hired primarily as unskilled and semiskilled workers.

5. The chief reason given by Woodrow Wilson for requesting a declaration of war against Germany in 1917 was the

   (A) refusal of Germany to accept the Fourteen Points as a basis for peace negotiations
   (B) need to establish a League of Nations after the war
   (C) resumption of unrestricted submarine warfare by Germany
   (D) economic rivalry between the United States and Germany
   (E) cultural ties between the United States and England

GO ON TO THE NEXT PAGE

6. "I have no doubt young criminals got their ideas of the romance of crime from moving pictures. I believe moving pictures are doing as much harm today as saloons did in the days of the open saloon, especially to the young. Movies are running day and night, Sunday and every other day, the year round, and in most jurisdictions without any regulation by censorship."

The speaker quoted above would most likely agree with which of the following statements?

(A) Blue laws should be repealed as unnecessary censorship.
(B) The content of movies needs to be monitored to prevent the corruption of youth.
(C) The censorship of technologies like radio and movies is not feasible.
(D) The culture of the 1920's was a vast improvement over the decadent "Gay Nineties."
(E) Outlawing movies would only cause a crime wave similar to that following Prohibition.

7. In the 50 years following the Second World War, inflation has meant a continuous increase in

(A) tax rates
(B) purchasing power
(C) exports
(D) prices
(E) stock market activity

8. Which of the following statements about social trends in the United States between 1945 and 1970 is INCORRECT?

(A) There was an overall increase in college enrollment.
(B) The proportion of blue-collar jobs in the economy decreased.
(C) Increasing numbers of African American children attended racially integrated schools.
(D) There was an exodus of population from the cities to the suburbs.
(E) More and more women abandoned paid employment in order to return to the home.

9. Which of the following was the stated reason for the Supreme Court ruling in the 1960's that prayer and formal religious instruction could not be required in public schools?

(A) Atheism and agnosticism had spread throughout American society.
(B) Church membership in America had declined rapidly.
(C) Prayer was no longer a significant way in which Americans expressed their religious faith.
(D) Prayer in public schools violated the principle of separation of church and state.
(E) Prayer in public schools encouraged the renewal of religious tests for public office.

GO ON TO THE NEXT PAGE

© 1991 The Pittsburgh Press

10. Which of the following best summarizes the idea expressed in the 1991 cartoon above?

   (A) Although the President claimed otherwise, the primary interest of the United States in the Persian Gulf War was access to oil.

   (B) The United States government was worried about the ecological impact of the oil spills that occurred during the Persian Gulf War.

   (C) The United States was justified in using military force because doing so was necessary to keep the price of oil low.

   (D) A glut of oil production in the Middle East was the main cause of the Persian Gulf War.

   (E) The United States should avoid involvement in disputes between governments in the Middle East.

GO ON TO THE NEXT PAGE

11. Which of the following actions would be INCONSISTENT with the English policy of mercantilism as it was applied to the North American colonies?

    (A) Requiring the colonists to export specified products only to England
    (B) Encouraging the colonies to produce articles that England otherwise would have to import from Europe
    (C) Encouraging the settlement of colonies suitable for the growing of tropical and semitropical staple crops
    (D) Encouraging the colonies to produce articles also produced in England
    (E) Prohibiting the importation of goods into the colonies except in English ships

12. The Great Awakening was a movement that

    (A) strengthened the position of the established clergy
    (B) appealed only to the lower classes
    (C) denied individual responsibility
    (D) excluded women and African Americans from religious services
    (E) emphasized inner experience as the principal way of discovering truth

13. In the first half of the nineteenth century, all of the following goals had widespread support among women reformers EXCEPT the

    (A) abolition of slavery
    (B) right of women to vote
    (C) liberalization of abortion laws
    (D) passage of temperance laws
    (E) right of married women to own property

14. In the United States all of the following changed in significant ways between 1850 and 1900 EXCEPT the

    (A) scale of business enterprise
    (B) election of women to national office
    (C) legal status of the African American population
    (D) technology of communication
    (E) religious affiliation of the total population

15. The Interstate Commerce Act of 1887 sought to prevent

    (A) discrimination by the railroads against small customers
    (B) publication of railroad rate schedules
    (C) transportation of children across state lines for immoral purposes
    (D) shipment across state lines of goods produced in sweatshops
    (E) use of the federal mails for the dissemination of birth control information

16. Which of the following statements best represents the nativist attitude toward the influx of immigrants around 1900 ?

    (A) Slavs and Italians will be assimilated as easily into the American way of life as were earlier immigrant groups.
    (B) Ellis Island should be enlarged to accommodate the huge influx of immigrants who do not speak English.
    (C) Immigrants will work for low wages and break strikes, which will hurt all American workers.
    (D) Native-born Americans should organize to help find jobs and homes for new immigrants so that they can become citizens as quickly as possible.
    (E) Political machines in the large cities must be responsible for providing immigrants with food, shelter, and jobs in return for their votes.

17. Which statement best describes the treatment of Black soldiers in the United States Army during the First World War?

    (A) Black soldiers were integrated into White units on a basis of full military equality.
    (B) Black soldiers served in segregated units often commanded by White officers.
    (C) Black Americans were drafted into the armed forces but not allowed to enlist.
    (D) Black Americans were not allowed in the armed forces but were encouraged to move to factory jobs.
    (E) Because Black leaders opposed the war, the government placed Black soldiers only in noncombat positions.

GO ON TO THE NEXT PAGE

18. Which of the following had the widest audience among Americans in the 1920's?

 (A) Jazz festivals
 (B) Professional football
 (C) Television
 (D) Movies
 (E) Circuses

19. The economic policies of the New Deal are best described as a

 (A) carefully designed plan to change the United States business system from capitalism to socialism
 (B) series of hastily conceived temporary measures that pulled the economy out of the Depression by the start of President Franklin D. Roosevelt's third term
 (C) mixture of partly effective short-run measures against the Depression and enduring changes in the role of the federal government
 (D) program designed to equalize income for all Americans
 (E) political response to the demand for federal deficit spending voiced by Democratic party platforms since the candidacy of Woodrow Wilson

20. Which of the following did most to broaden participation in the political process?

 (A) The success of the States' rights movement
 (B) The Supreme Court decision in the case of *Brown* v. *Board of Education of Topeka*
 (C) The election of Franklin D. Roosevelt
 (D) The decline of the Ku Klux Klan
 (E) The Voting Rights Act of 1965

21. In the past 50 years in the House of Representatives, which of the following issues would most likely have resulted in a vote along party lines?

 (A) Federal aid to education
 (B) Civil rights legislation
 (C) Election of the Speaker of the House
 (D) Appropriations for foreign aid
 (E) Agricultural subsidies

22. From the sixteenth through the eighteenth century, the cultural patterns of the American Indians of the western plains were most dramatically influenced by

 (A) major changes in ecological conditions
 (B) contact with tribes from eastern coastal areas
 (C) the adoption of European military weaponry
 (D) the adoption of European agricultural techniques
 (E) the introduction of the horse by Spanish explorers

23. Many Americans believed the Articles of Confederation had which of the following problems?

 (A) They gave insufficient power to the central government.
 (B) They did not provide for a national legislature.
 (C) They could not be amended.
 (D) They were too long and complicated for the average person to understand.
 (E) They lacked a Bill of Rights.

24. An important reason why Thomas Jefferson recommended the purchase of Louisiana from France was his wish to

 (A) stimulate American manufacturing
 (B) enhance the role of Congress in acquiring new territories
 (C) embarrass the Federalists
 (D) secure western territory to help fulfill his ideal of an agrarian republic
 (E) follow advice given to him by Alexander Hamilton

25. In his book *Walden*, Henry David Thoreau did which of the following?

 (A) Described the unspoiled innocence of the American West
 (B) Recorded his thoughts concerning the value of a life of simplicity and contemplation
 (C) Argued that such modern inventions as the telegraph and the railroad were bringing about a higher quality of cultural life in America
 (D) Offered his impressions of southern plantation life
 (E) Portrayed a fictional utopian community where all live in peace and harmony

GO ON TO THE NEXT PAGE

26. The primary reason the United States advanced the Open Door policy in 1899 was to

(A) consolidate good relations between the United States and European countries holding leases in China

(B) encourage Asian nations to protect Chinese interests

(C) expand the effort of European nations to Westernize China

(D) protect United States missionaries in China

(E) protect United States trading opportunities in China

27. A major difference between the Ku Klux Klan of the Reconstruction period and the Klan of the 1920's was that the Klan of the 1920's

(A) was hostile toward immigrants, non-Protestants, and African Americans

(B) was not particularly hostile toward African Americans

(C) expressed hostility only toward African Americans

(D) practiced vigilantism

(E) was confined to the South in its activities and membership

28. Which of the following contributed LEAST to the Great Depression?

(A) Weaknesses in the banking system

(B) Inflationary wage settlements

(C) The depressed agricultural sector

(D) Production in excess of consumption

(E) The stock market crash

29. Prior to its declaration of war in December 1941, the United States government gave help to the Allies by

(A) supplying war materials to the rebel forces in the Spanish Civil War

(B) placing an embargo on the export of oil and metal to Fascist Italy

(C) providing Lend-Lease aid

(D) denying aid to the Soviet Union

(E) encouraging the efforts of the America First Committee

30. Senator I: This amendment removes the incentive system from industry.

Senator II: This amendment will abolish capitalism.

Senator III: This amendment helps the worst elements in the country at the expense of the best elements in the country.

This discussion would most likely have taken place during the debate on which of the following constitutional amendments?

(A) Granting the vote to women

(B) Extending due process of law to all citizens

(C) Instituting direct election of senators

(D) Creating a federal income tax

(E) Abolishing slavery and indentured servitude

GO ON TO THE NEXT PAGE

Hy Rosen, in Albany *Times-Union*

31. Which of the following international incidents is the subject of the cartoon above?

    (A) The Soviet invasion of Finland in 1939
    (B) The Soviet blockade of Berlin in 1948
    (C) The Hungarian Revolution of 1956
    (D) The U-2 affair of 1960
    (E) The Cuban missile crisis of 1962

GO ON TO THE NEXT PAGE

32. Highly developed astronomy, mathematics, calendar systems, and agricultural techniques characterized the pre-Columbian cultures of

   (A) Mesoamerica
   (B) the Great Plains
   (C) the Eastern Woodlands
   (D) California
   (E) the Subarctic

33. The first decade of the English settlement at Jamestown is most notable for the

   (A) discovery of gold and precious metals
   (B) successful cultivation and export of tobacco
   (C) violent struggles between English and Spanish forces
   (D) harmonious relations between the native inhabitants and settlers
   (E) high mortality rate among the settlers

34. A principal consequence of the Northwest Ordinance of 1787 was that it

   (A) terminated the earlier system of land surveying established by the federal government for the territories
   (B) established a procedure for bringing new states into the Union as the equals of the older states
   (C) stimulated the formation of the first political parties organized on a national basis
   (D) encouraged the drafting of a new treaty with England on the disposition of the western territories
   (E) strengthened the role of the thirteen original states in Congress

35. As chief justice of the Supreme Court, John Marshall issued significant opinions on all of the following EXCEPT

   (A) judicial review
   (B) federal *versus* state power
   (C) the sanctity of contracts
   (D) the rights of slaves as persons
   (E) congressional control of interstate commerce

36. Of the following, which author was the first to create a western hero?

   (A) Mark Twain
   (B) Edgar Allan Poe
   (C) James Fenimore Cooper
   (D) Helen Hunt Jackson
   (E) Willa Cather

37. "If the Creator had separated Texas from the Union by mountain barriers, the Alps or the Andes, there might be plausible objections; but He has planed down the whole [Mississippi] Valley including Texas, and united every atom of the soil and every drop of the water of the mighty whole. He has linked their rivers with the great Mississippi, and marked and united the whole for the dominion of one government, the residence of one people."

   This quotation from the 1840's can be viewed as an expression of

   (A) the New Nationalism
   (B) popular sovereignty
   (C) Manifest Destiny
   (D) the Good Neighbor policy
   (E) the frontier thesis

38. At the start of the Civil War, the North had all of the following advantages EXCEPT

   (A) better military leaders
   (B) a more extensive railroad network
   (C) a larger population
   (D) more heavy industry
   (E) more abundant food resources

39. "Let it be understood that we cannot go outside of this alternative: liberty, inequality, survival of the fittest; not-liberty, equality, survival of the unfittest. The former carries society forward and favors all its best members; the latter carries society downward and favors all its worst members."

   These sentiments are most characteristic of

   (A) the Social Gospel
   (B) Social Darwinism
   (C) Socialism
   (D) Progressivism
   (E) Neoorthodoxy

GO ON TO THE NEXT PAGE

40. The participation of women in the labor force between 1880 and 1930 rose primarily because

(A) most married women sought employment outside the home
(B) new jobs for women were created in offices, stores, and factories
(C) domestic service jobs increased
(D) discrimination against women in professions such as medicine and law declined
(E) equal pay acts encouraged more women to enter the workforce

41. All of the following accurately characterize the United States during the Second World War EXCEPT:

(A) Some consumer goods were rationed.
(B) Women entered the paid workforce in record numbers.
(C) Southerners migrated to industrial cities in increased numbers.
(D) The size and power of the federal government increased.
(E) The gross national product and wage levels declined.

42. During the period from 1492 to 1700, French activity in the Americas was primarily directed toward

(A) establishing trade with American Indians
(B) plundering American Indian settlements for gold and silver
(C) conquering Spanish and English colonies
(D) encouraging the growth of permanent settlements
(E) discovering a new route to Africa

43. During the years 1565-1763, Spanish Florida was important to Spain for which of the following reasons?

(A) It was a major source of valuable tropical produce.
(B) It was the center of the Catholic mission system in the New World.
(C) It retarded English colonial expansion southward from the Carolinas.
(D) It helped supply Spain with precious metals.
(E) It shielded converted Catholic Indians from Protestant missionaries.

44. Colonists supported the American Revolution for all of the following reasons EXCEPT

(A) the desire to preserve their local autonomy and way of life from British interference
(B) strong resentment against the quartering of British troops in colonial homes
(C) the desire for greater political participation in policies affecting the colonies
(D) a strong interest in achieving a more even distribution of income among the colonists
(E) a conviction that British ministers and other government officials were a corrupting influence on the colonists

45. The Supreme Court's dependency on the President to enforce its decisions is demonstrated by President Andrew Jackson's refusal to uphold

(A) the right of antislavery societies to send abolitionist publications through the mail
(B) land claims of the Cherokee in Georgia
(C) women's right to vote
(D) a slave's right to freedom after being in free territory
(E) payments made in paper money for public lands

GO ON TO THE NEXT PAGE

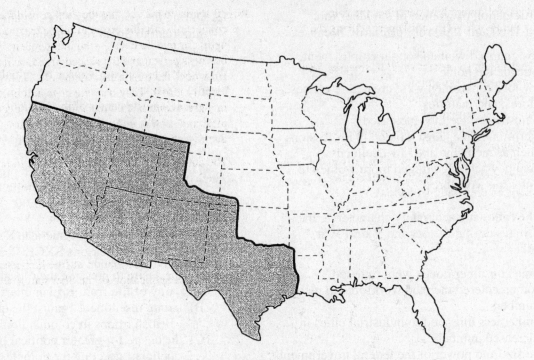

46. The entire shaded area in the map above was

    (A) ceded by Spain to the United States
    (B) once part of Mexico
    (C) claimed by the Confederacy
    (D) claimed by the Bear Flag Republic
    (E) known as the Gadsden Purchase

GO ON TO THE NEXT PAGE ⟶

47. Which of the following best describes the role played by the People's (Populist) party during the 1890's?

   (A) An instrument to protect small businesses from governmental regulation

   (B) An organization foreshadowing the subsequent socialist movement

   (C) A vehicle for agrarian protest against the economic system

   (D) The political arm of the new labor movement

   (E) The medium through which urban ethnic groups entered national politics

48. "It seems to me . . . that the vital consideration connected with this problem of the trust is its effect upon our middle class — the independent, individual business person and the skilled artisan and mechanic. How does the trust affect them? . . . Their personal identity is lost. They become cogs and little wheels in a great complicated machine . . . . I favor complete and prompt annihilation of the trust — with due regard for property rights, of course."

The author of this statement would be likely to favor which of the following measures?

   (A) Nationalization of industry

   (B) A 100 percent inheritance tax

   (C) The rapid diffusion of mass-production techniques

   (D) Extensive distribution of free homestead land

   (E) Strict application of the Sherman Act

GO ON TO THE NEXT PAGE

Puck/Rothco Cartoons

49. The cartoon above is making the point that Woodrow Wilson

(A) was the heir to the Populist tradition
(B) was the last in a line of reform-minded Presidents that included William Howard Taft and Theodore Roosevelt
(C) had a political philosophy that combined the tenets of the Republican and Progressive (Bull Moose) parties
(D) owed his election to the presidency in 1912 to the split in the Republican party
(E) owed his reelection to the presidency in 1916 to crossover votes by Republicans

GO ON TO THE NEXT PAGE

50. The primary purpose of the National Origins Act of 1924 was to

   (A) enumerate the populations of ethnic groups in the United States
   (B) limit immigration to the United States
   (C) help preserve American Indian culture
   (D) fund archaeological expeditions
   (E) support historical and genealogical research

51. Under Franklin D. Roosevelt's Good Neighbor policy, the United States stated its intention to refrain from intervening in the affairs of

   (A) Latin America
   (B) Europe
   (C) Canada
   (D) China
   (E) Japan

52. President Truman's foreign policy after the Second World War had as its expressed aim

   (A) preventive war
   (B) atomic proliferation
   (C) liberation of peoples under communist rule
   (D) massive retaliation against Soviet aggression
   (E) containment of international communism

53. The intellectual justification for revolutionary action contained in the Declaration of Independence was derived most directly from the work of

   (A) Rousseau
   (B) Locke
   (C) Montesquieu
   (D) Hobbes
   (E) Voltaire

GO ON TO THE NEXT PAGE

SLAVE IMPORTATIONS, 1500–1810

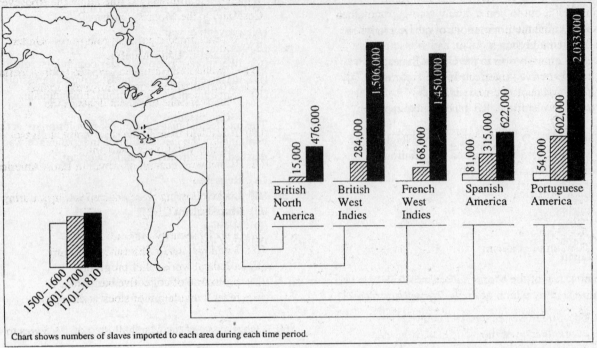

Chart shows numbers of slaves imported to each area during each time period.

Philip Curtin, *The Atlantic Slave Trade: A Census.*
Copyright © 1972 The University of Wisconsin Press.

54. The chart above lends support to which of the following
    statements about slave importations between 1500 and 1810 ?

    (A) Sugar-growing regions imported more slaves than did any
        other region.
    (B) The British imported more slaves to mainland colonies than
        to island colonies.
    (C) The British monopolized the African slave trade in the
        eighteenth century.
    (D) The importation of slaves decreased in proportion to the
        increase in native-born slave populations.
    (E) The importation of slaves increased at the same rate in each
        region represented.

55. "What then is the American, this new man? . . .
I could point out to you a family whose grandfather
was an Englishman, whose wife was Dutch, whose
son married a French woman, and whose present
four sons have now four wives of different nations.
He is an American who, leaving behind him all his
ancient prejudices and manners, receives new ones
from the new mode of life he has embraced. . . . "

Which of the following is being described in this
statement by an eighteenth-century observer of
American life?

(A) Social stratification
(B) Nativism
(C) Anglicization
(D) Acculturation
(E) Denominationalism

56. The meaning of the Monroe Doctrine of 1823 is best
summarized by which of the following statements?

(A) The United States would not permit the
continuance of the African slave trade.
(B) The United States proclaimed its right to
interfere in the internal affairs of neighboring
nations.
(C) The United States would fight the creation of
new colonies in the Western Hemisphere,
although it would not interfere with existing
ones.
(D) The United States would insist on a policy of
equal treatment in trade with the Far East.
(E) The United States would not extend diplomatic
recognition to any foreign government that
came to power by force.

57. All of the following are correct statements about
religious thought and expression in the nineteenth
century EXCEPT:

(A) The religions of American Indians emphasized
the sanctity of nature.
(B) The religion of slaves drew heavily on the Old
Testament story of the Exodus.
(C) Catholic priests worked to establish parochial
schools for the education of parish children.
(D) Deism and freethinking attracted wider support
among Protestants than did evangelicalism.
(E) Most Protestant denominations supported the
development of the temperance movement.

58. Which of the following is true about the Roosevelt
Corollary to the Monroe Doctrine?

(A) It proclaimed a policing role for the United
States in Latin America.
(B) It prohibited European loans to Latin America.
(C) It permitted temporary European armed
interventions to collect debts in the
Caribbean.
(D) It resulted from Japanese attempts to lease
territory in Lower California.
(E) It met with general approval in Latin America.

59. All of the following were enacted into law during
the New Deal EXCEPT

(A) a social security program
(B) a national health insurance program
(C) a federal work-relief program
(D) protection of collective bargaining
(E) federal regulation of stock exchanges

60. One purpose of the Marshall Plan of 1948 was to

(A) rebuild European economies through a joint
recovery program
(B) aid the depressed agricultural economies of
Latin American nations
(C) aid communist nations that would agree to
embrace democracy
(D) give military aid to those nations resisting
communist subversion
(E) help the peoples of Asia establish heavy
industries

61. The decline of sharecropping and of the crop-lien
system in the South after 1940 was due primarily to
which of the following?

(A) The New Deal's establishment of an agricul-
tural credit system for sharecroppers
(B) The political and social gains achieved by
Black people through the civil rights
movement
(C) The rise in cotton prices that freed sharecroppers
from debt
(D) The closing of many southern banks during the
Depression of the 1930's
(E) The increase in mechanization and the declining
demand for cotton

GO ON TO THE NEXT PAGE

62. Economic inequality in colonial North America was greatest

(A) in the Carolina backcountry
(B) in inland towns
(C) in seaboard cities
(D) among the Pennsylvania Dutch
(E) in the Shenandoah Valley

63. All of the following were basic to seventeenth-century New England Puritanism EXCEPT

(A) belief in the innate goodness of human nature
(B) belief in the general principles of Calvinism
(C) intolerance of outspoken religious dissenters
(D) the necessity for a trained and educated ministry
(E) the duty of merchants to sell wares at a just price

64. As a diplomat during the American Revolution, Benjamin Franklin played a part in which of the following?

(A) Preventing the French government from joining with the British against the United States
(B) Bringing Spain into the Revolutionary War on the side of the United States
(C) Concluding a peace between Britain and France, thereby ending the war in Europe
(D) Concluding an alliance between France and the United States
(E) Preserving French neutrality during the war

65. All of the following were among the causes of the War of 1812 EXCEPT

(A) British Orders-in-Council
(B) British monopoly of the Atlantic slave trade
(C) British violations of United States territorial waters
(D) British impressment of United States seamen
(E) the desire of some United States citizens to annex Canada

66. Which of the following was NOT prominently advocated during the reform era of the 1830's and 1840's?

(A) Trust-busting
(B) Temperance
(C) Abolitionism
(D) Free public education
(E) Utopian communitarianism

67. Which of the following most accurately characterizes the slave system in the South between 1820 and 1860 ?

(A) Slaves were so restricted that they were unable to develop their own social life and culture.
(B) The high mortality and low birthrates of the slaves necessitated large slave importations.
(C) Slaves were assisted in their work by substantial numbers of White wage earners, most of whom were foreign immigrants.
(D) Slaves worked in a wide variety of skilled and unskilled occupations.
(E) Slave owners had little incentive to keep their slaves healthy.

68. The first free immigrants whose right of entry into the United States was curtailed by federal legislation were

(A) Africans
(B) Asians
(C) Latin Americans
(D) Eastern and Southern Europeans
(E) Western and Northern Europeans

69. The rapid rise in labor union membership in the late 1930's was mainly a result of the

(A) spread of assembly-line production
(B) merger of the AFL and the CIO
(C) opposition of labor to Franklin D. Roosevelt's New Deal policies
(D) organizing efforts of the Knights of Labor
(E) passage of the Wagner Act

GO ON TO THE NEXT PAGE

THE SHIFTING FRONT IN KOREA*

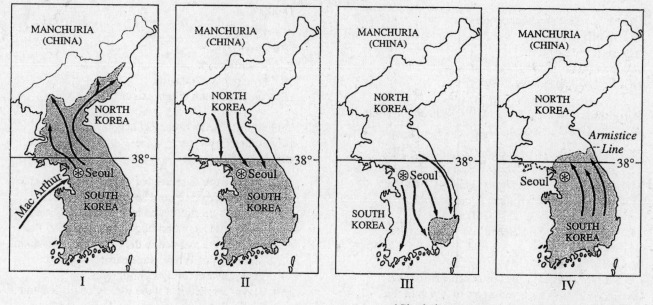

*Shaded areas represent position of UN forces.

70. Which of the following is the correct chronological sequence of
    the maps above?

    (A) I, II, IV, III
    (B) I, III, IV, II
    (C) II, III, I, IV
    (D) III, II, I, IV
    (E) IV, II, III, I

GO ON TO THE NEXT PAGE

BIRTHS PER THOUSAND WOMEN
AGED 15–44

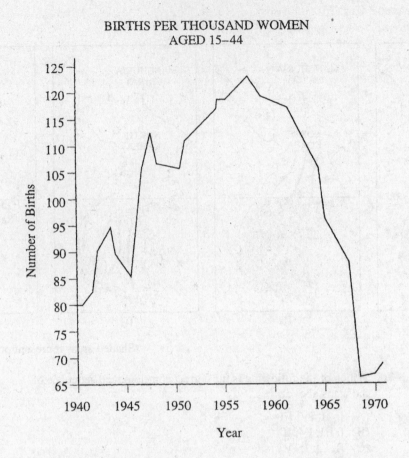

71. Which of the following statements is consistent with the data in the graph above?

(A) The number of women having children rose during the Depression.

(B) The wide availability of contraceptives led to a sharp decline in the birthrate during the 1960's.

(C) Between 1955 and 1960 the United States had more women aged 15 to 44 than at any other time.

(D) The number of single women having babies peaked in the 1960's.

(E) The birthrate rose consistently between 1945 and 1960.

GO ON TO THE NEXT PAGE

72. In the 1700's the southern Appalachian region was distinguished by

    (A) reliance on plantation agriculture
    (B) the absence of indentured servitude
    (C) numerous textile mills
    (D) large numbers of Scots-Irish and German settlers
    (E) high population densities

73. Anti-Federalist objections to ratification of the Constitution expressed all of the following fears EXCEPT:

    (A) Congress would levy heavy taxes.
    (B) The government would raise a standing army.
    (C) The Bill of Rights was too broad.
    (D) The President would have almost as much power as a king.
    (E) State governments would wither away.

74. A broad discussion of the significance of the Missouri Compromise, the Tariff of 1833, and the Compromise of 1850 would necessarily mention which of the following?

    (A) National debt
    (B) Religious conflict
    (C) The suffrage
    (D) The Monroe Doctrine
    (E) Sectional conflict

75. The Radical Republicans of America's post-Civil War period were radical in the sense that they favored

    (A) civil and political rights for Black people
    (B) the Reconstruction policies of President Andrew Johnson
    (C) nationalization of the railroad and coal industries
    (D) a government representing economic interests rather than geographical units
    (E) a guaranteed minimum income for former slaves

76. When American reformers in the late nineteenth century claimed that "the tariff is the mother of trusts," they were arguing

    (A) for a protective tariff and for an improvement in business ethics
    (B) for a protective tariff and against monopolies
    (C) for lower tariffs and against monopolies
    (D) against monopolies and against the sales tax
    (E) against monopolies and against taxes on exports

77. Which of the following events best supports a "class conflict" interpretation of American history?

    (A) The nationwide railroad strike of 1877
    (B) The Nullification crisis
    (C) The rise of the Know-Nothing party
    (D) The Supreme Court's decision in *Plessy* v. *Ferguson*
    (E) Theodore Roosevelt's "taking" of the Panama Canal Zone

78. The year 1890 is significant in the history of the American West because the

    (A) last major gold strike occurred in the Black Hills
    (B) last massacre of American Indians occurred at Sand Creek
    (C) most devastating blizzard ever to hit the Great Plains ended the long cattle drives
    (D) transcontinental railroad was officially completed
    (E) federal Census Office reported that a frontier line no longer existed

79. Organized labor opposed which of the following laws?

    (A) The Social Security Act
    (B) The Wagner Act
    (C) The Fair Labor Standards Act
    (D) The Taft-Hartley Act
    (E) The Employment Act of 1946

GO ON TO THE NEXT PAGE

80. During the 1930's, which of the following was a fundamental political change that occurred among Black Americans?

   (A) A shift of Black voters from the two major parties to the minor parties
   (B) A shift of Black voters from the Republican party to the Democratic party
   (C) A great increase in the proportion of Black people who registered to vote
   (D) An increase in the importance of the Black vote in local elections in the South
   (E) A decrease in the participation of Black voters in federal elections

81. The United Nations was designed to maintain peace in the post-Second World War period through the implementation of

   (A) principles of free trade
   (B) bipolarity
   (C) collective security
   (D) bilateral treaties
   (E) regional pacts

82. Which of the following congressional actions resulted from an alleged attack on United States warships by North Vietnamese gunboats in 1964 ?

   (A) A declaration of war against North Vietnam
   (B) Passage of the War Powers Act
   (C) Authorization for air attacks against selected targets in China as well as in North Vietnam
   (D) A resolution urging the President to withdraw United States naval forces from Southeast Asian waters
   (E) The Tonkin Gulf Resolution

83. In the early decades of the republic, the intentions and expectations of the authors of the United States Constitution were most fully realized in the

   (A) respective roles of the executive and the legislative branches in conducting foreign policy
   (B) extensive role of the executive branch in drafting legislation
   (C) method of electing vice presidents
   (D) formation of political parties
   (E) elimination of property qualifications for voting

84. As Secretary of the Treasury, Alexander Hamilton did which of the following?

   (A) Sought to avoid a centralized banking system that could control the nation's currency
   (B) Sought to link the interests of the national government and monied people
   (C) Proposed to tax domestic manufactures to discourage the growth of factory towns
   (D) Proposed to require the state governments to pay off the national debt
   (E) Proposed to give away western land to small farmers to encourage settlement

85. One of the goals of the Populist movement was

   (A) government control of railroads
   (B) collective ownership of farms
   (C) a strengthened electoral college
   (D) legislation to raise tariffs
   (E) abolition of income taxes

86. In *How the Other Half Lives*, Jacob Riis revealed the plight of

   (A) Black sharecroppers in the Deep South
   (B) Chinese workers in the railroad gangs of the West
   (C) European immigrants in the tenements of New York City
   (D) young boys in the Pennsylvania coal mines
   (E) American Indians in the Southwest

87. All of the following statements about the American economy during the First World War are correct EXCEPT:

   (A) Government boards were organized to manage crucial sectors of the economy.
   (B) Members of minority groups, especially Black people, moved into northern industrial cities to work in war factories.
   (C) The number of unionized workers increased.
   (D) The federal government expanded its prosecution of antitrust suits against large corporations.
   (E) Taxes were increased for corporations and wealthy individuals to help finance the war.

GO ON TO THE NEXT PAGE

88. At the Yalta Conference in February 1945, Franklin D. Roosevelt's options were limited most seriously by which of the following?

    (A) Winston Churchill's suspicions of Roosevelt's motives and friendship
    (B) The poor health of Joseph Stalin
    (C) The rising tide of criticism of Roosevelt's leadership at home
    (D) The presence of Soviet troops in the Far East
    (E) The presence of Soviet troops in Poland

89. The American counterculture of the 1960's opposed

    (A) left-wing ideals of the 1930's and 1940's
    (B) modernist art and literature
    (C) the conservation movement
    (D) the materialism of American society
    (E) trade unionism

90. In the United States, the largest growth in population during the 1970's occurred in which of the following?

    (A) The Northeast Corridor from Boston to Washington, D.C.
    (B) States below the 37th parallel from Virginia to California
    (C) States of the upper Midwest from Ohio to Minnesota
    (D) The most heavily populated states, including New York, Pennsylvania, Illinois, and California
    (E) The regions concentrating on mature industries such as steel, automobiles, and major appliances

STOP
**IF YOU FINISH BEFORE TIME IS CALLED, YOU MAY CHECK YOUR WORK ON THIS TEST ONLY.
DO NOT TURN TO ANY OTHER TEST IN THIS BOOK.**

How to Score the SAT Subject Test in United States History

When you take an actual SAT Subject Test in United States History, your answer sheet will be "read" by a scanning machine that will record your responses to each question. Then a computer will compare your answers with the correct answers and produce your raw score. You get one point for each correct answer. For each wrong answer, you lose one-quarter of a point. Questions you omit (and any for which you mark more than one answer) are not counted. This raw score is converted to a scaled score that is reported to you and to the colleges you specify.

Worksheet 1. Finding Your Raw Test Score

STEP 1: Table A on the following page lists the correct answers for all the questions on the SAT Subject Test in United States History that is reproduced in this book. It also serves as a worksheet for you to calculate your raw score.

- Compare your answers with those given in the table.

- Put a check in the column marked "Right" if your answer is correct.

- Put a check in the column marked "Wrong" if your answer is incorrect.

- Leave both columns blank if you omitted the question.

STEP 2: Count the number of right answers.

Enter the total here: _____

STEP 3: Count the number of wrong answers.

Enter the total here: _____

STEP 4: Multiply the number of wrong answers by .250.

Enter the product here: _____

STEP 5: Subtract the result obtained in Step 4 from the total you obtained in Step 2.

Enter the result here: _____

STEP 6: Round the number obtained in Step 5 to the nearest whole number.

Enter the result here: _____

The number you obtained in Step 6 is your raw score.

Answers to Practice Test 4 for United States History

Table A
Answers to the Subject Test in United States History – Practice Test 4 and Percentage of Students Answering
Each Question Correctly

Question Number	Correct Answer	Right	Wrong	Percentage of Students Answering the Question Correctly*	Question Number	Correct Answer	Right	Wrong	Percentage of Students Answering the Question Correctly*
1	A			66	26	E			73
2	D			85	27	A			59
3	A			69	28	B			33
4	D			71	29	C			73
5	C			74	30	D			74
6	B			95	31	E			69
7	D			78	32	A			70
8	E			63	33	E			45
9	D			96	34	B			45
10	A			90	35	D			45
11	D			68	36	C			45
12	E			54	37	C			65
13	C			68	38	A			57
14	B			76	39	B			69
15	A			65	40	B			51
16	C			86	41	E			54
17	B			83	42	A			47
18	D			35	43	C			51
19	C			58	44	D			62
20	E			79	45	B			56
21	C			59	46	B			61
22	E			56	47	C			26
23	A			54	48	E			42
24	D			67	49	D			49
25	B			57	50	B			53

Table A continued on next page

Table A continued from previous page

Question Number	Correct Answer	Right	Wrong	Percentage of Students Answering the Question Correctly*	Question Number	Correct Answer	Right	Wrong	Percentage of Students Answering the Question Correctly*
51	A			61	71	B			56
52	E			54	72	D			28
53	B			57	73	C			47
54	A			58	74	E			64
55	D			40	75	A			43
56	C			45	76	C			40
57	D			51	77	A			31
58	A			65	78	E			22
59	B			34	79	D			34
60	A			37	80	B			40
61	E			41	81	C			45
62	C			32	82	E			42
63	A			34	83	A			37
64	D			61	84	B			31
65	B			32	85	A			27
66	A			34	86	C			44
67	D			33	87	D			37
68	B			35	88	E			36
69	E			19	89	D			51
70	C			36	90	B			24

* These percentages are based on an analysis of the answer sheets of a representative sample of 2,993 students who took the original administration of this test and whose mean score was 556. They may be used as an indication of the relative difficulty of a particular question.

Finding Your Scaled Score

When you take SAT Subject Tests, the scores sent to the colleges you specify are reported on the College Board scale, which ranges from 200 to 800. You can convert your practice test raw score to a scaled score by using Table B. To find your scaled score, locate your raw score in the left-hand column of Table B; the corresponding score in the right-hand column is your scaled score. For example, a raw score of 60 on this particular edition of the SAT Subject Test in United States History corresponds to a scaled score of 680.

Raw scores are converted to scaled scores to ensure that a score earned on any one edition of a particular Subject Test is comparable to the same scaled score earned on any other edition of the same Subject Test. Because some editions of tests may be slightly easier or more difficult than others, College Board scaled scores are adjusted so that they indicate the same level of performance regardless of the edition of the test taken and the ability of the group that takes it. Thus, for example, a score of 400 on one edition of a test taken at a particular administration indicates the same level of achievement as a score of 400 on a different edition of the test taken at a different administration.

When you take the SAT Subject Tests during a national administration, your scores are likely to differ somewhat from the scores you obtain on the tests in this book. People perform at different levels at different times for reasons unrelated to the tests themselves. The precision of any test is also limited because it represents only a sample of all the possible questions that could be asked.

Table B
Scaled Score Conversion Table
Subject Test in United States History – Practice Test 4

Raw Score	Scaled Score	Raw Score	Scaled Score	Raw Score	Scaled Score
90	800	52	630	14	420
89	800	51	630	13	420
88	800	50	620	12	410
87	800	49	610	11	410
86	800	48	610	10	400
85	800	47	600	9	400
84	800	46	600	8	390
83	800	45	590	7	390
82	800	44	580	6	380
81	800	43	580	5	380
80	790	42	570	4	370
79	790	41	570	3	370
78	780	40	560	2	360
77	780	39	560	1	360
76	770	38	550	0	350
75	770	37	540	−1	350
74	760	36	540	−2	340
73	760	35	530	−3	340
72	750	34	530	−4	330
71	740	33	520	−5	330
70	740	32	520	−6	320
69	730	31	510	−7	320
68	730	30	510	−8	310
67	720	29	500	−9	310
66	720	28	490	−10	300
65	710	27	490	−11	300
64	700	26	480	−12	290
63	700	25	480	−13	280
62	690	24	470	−14	280
61	690	23	470	−15	270
60	680	22	460	−16	270
59	670	21	460	−17	260
58	670	20	450	−18	250
57	660	19	450	−19	250
56	660	18	440	−20	240
55	650	17	440	−21	230
54	640	16	430	−22	230
53	640	15	430		

How Did You Do on the Subject Test in United States History?

After you score your test and analyze your performance, think about the following questions:

Did you run out of time before reaching the end of the test?

If so, you may need to pace yourself better. For example, maybe you spent too much time on one or two hard questions. A better approach might be to skip the ones you can't answer right away and try answering all the remaining questions on the test. Then if there's time, go back to the questions you skipped.

Did you take a long time reading the directions?

You will save time when you take the test by learning the directions to the Subject Test in United States History ahead of time. Each minute you spend reading directions during the test is a minute that you could use to answer questions.

How did you handle questions you were unsure of?

If you were able to eliminate one or more of the answer choices as wrong and guess from the remaining ones, your approach probably worked to your advantage. On the other hand, making haphazard guesses or omitting questions without trying to eliminate choices could cost you valuable points.

How difficult were the questions for you compared with other students who took the test?

Table A shows you how difficult the multiple-choice questions were for the group of students who took this test during its national administration. The right-hand column gives the percentage of students that answered each question correctly.

A question answered correctly by almost everyone in the group is obviously an easier question. For example, 96 percent of the students answered question 9 correctly. However, only 19 percent answered question 69 correctly.

Keep in mind that these percentages are based on just one group of students. They would probably be different with another group of students taking the test.

If you missed several easier questions, go back and try to find out why: Did the questions cover material you haven't yet reviewed? Did you misunderstand the directions?

Answer Explanations

Practice Test 4

Question 1

Choice (A) is the correct answer. In colonial America, one of the biggest problems faced by large landowners was the need of laborers to work their land. Indentured servitude was a method by which these landowners paid for the passage of young men and women from Europe in return for their labor for a fixed period of time.

Question 2

Choice (D) is the correct answer. Most American slave owners feared any kind of thinking, religious or political, on the part of their slaves and would punish slaves for having any ideas of their own. Slaves had learned to keep their thoughts—and their prayers—concealed from their owners. This quotation is evidently from a former slave who had learned this lesson even as a young child.

Question 3

Choice (A) is the correct answer. One of the major issues between political parties during Andrew Jackson's presidency was the national bank. Jackson and the Jacksonian Democrats were against a bank that had control over public (government) finances and little regulation by the government. The National Republicans wanted the charter for the bank renewed. The issue led to the end of the national bank. Voting rights for anyone except white adult males, immigration to the United States, military expenditures, and railroad construction did not become major political issues until after Jackson's presidency.

Question 4

Choice (D) is the correct answer. Of all the choices, this statement is the only one that is not true. Although labor unions emerged during the second half of the nineteenth century, only a small percentage of workers belonged to unions.

Question 5

Choice (C) is the correct answer. Although Germany had slowed its submarine warfare after the sinking of the *Lusitania*, it reinstated unrestricted submarine warfare not only against British ships, but also against American merchant ships.

Question 6

Choice (B) is the correct answer. The speaker states that young people who have entered a life of crime were persuaded to do so by the romanticized portrayal of crime in the movies. The speaker would certainly agree that the content of movies needs to be monitored and censored to protect young people from such undesirable influence.

Question 7

Choice (D) is the correct answer. Although the economic factors mentioned in the other choices—tax rates, purchasing power, exports, and stock market activity—also increased during the last half of the twentieth century, inflation refers to the general rise in the prices of consumer goods.

Question 8

Choice (E) is the correct answer. The statement in choice (E) is not true. In fact, the opposite is true. After the Second World War, more and more American women entered the workforce.

Question 9

Choice (D) is the correct answer. The Supreme Court would base its ruling on constitutional law, not on religious trends of Americans. One of the fundamental principles of the Constitution is the separation of church and state. The Supreme Court ruled that prayer and religious instruction—aspects of "church"—could not be required by public schools—an aspect of "state."

Question 10

Choice (A) is the correct answer. In the cartoon the speaker is from the United States White House; the implication is that the speaker is the president. Oil is dripping off the other side of the globe; nothing else, such as people, foreign government buildings, or war machinery (tanks, jets), is depicted. Although the president is saying that the Persian Gulf War is not about oil, the *only* thing pictured in the Persian Gulf area of the globe is oil.

Question 11

Choice (D) is the correct answer. Under mercantilism, England would not want competition for articles produced in England, even from articles produced in its own colonies. Such competition would not benefit England. All of the activities mentioned in choices (A), (B), (C), and (E) ensured that colonial economic activities would benefit England, which was the purpose of mercantilism.

Question 12

Choice (E) is the correct answer. The Great Awakening was a religious movement by revivalists who preached that the individual must make a personal commitment to Christ, that the individual was responsible. The movement weakened the established colonial clergy (A), appealed to all classes of people (B), and welcomed women and African Americans (D).

Question 13

Choice (C) is the correct answer. In the first half of the nineteenth century, there were no laws regarding abortion. All of the other movements—abolition of slavery, women's suffrage, temperance laws, and property ownership—were widely supported by women reformers.

Question 14

Choice (B) is the correct answer. In the last half of the nineteenth century, most states did not allow women to vote, much less to run for office, despite the movement for women's rights during this time. Significant changes did occur in all of the other areas—business, legal status of African Americans (men), communication technology, and the diversification of religious affiliation.

Question 15

Choice (A) is the correct answer. The Interstate Commerce Act of 1887 was one of the first attempts by the federal government to regulate commerce. It required railroads to publish their rate schedules (prices for passengers and freight) so that railroads could not charge small shippers higher prices than they charged the larger companies. The activities mentioned in choices (C), (D), and (E) were not yet issues in the United States.

Question 16

Choice (C) is the correct answer. Nativists were native-born American citizens who viewed new immigrants as a threat to the American way of life. Included in this anti-immigrant view was the belief that immigrants would take away jobs from American workers. With these views, nativists were unlikely to help immigrants or to view them in any favorable way.

Question 17

Choice (B) is the correct answer. Although African American men were both drafted and allowed to enlist during the First World War, they were assigned to segregated units commanded by white officers. Progress toward racial desegregation of the United States military did not begin until 1948, after the Second World War.

Question 18

Choice (D) is the correct answer. Although the 1920s was known as the "Jazz Age," festivals were little known. Television was still in experimental stages, and professional football was only beginning. Although circuses were still popular, especially in rural areas, the moving pictures—and the new "talkies"—appealed to vast urban audiences.

Question 19

Choice (C) is the correct answer. Becoming president for the first of his four terms in 1933, Franklin Delano Roosevelt instituted the New Deal, a series of federal programs intended to pull the United States out of the Great Depression. Although short-lived, many of the measures were effective in providing employment and relief to millions of Americans. The New Deal also permanently extended the federal government's role in regulating business, industry, commerce, banking, and labor.

Question 20

Choice (E) is the correct answer. Although the States' rights movement (A) and the presidency of Franklin D. Roosevelt (C) created interest on the part of voters, neither extended political participation to disenfranchised sectors of the American population. Certainly, the Supreme Court ruling in *Brown v. Board of Education of Topeka* (B) and the decline of the Ku Klux Klan (D) helped African Americans gain momentum in the Civil Rights Movement but, again, neither extended political participation. The Civil Rights Act of 1965 did away with practices, such as literacy tests, that made voting by some people almost impossible, thereby ensuring participation in the political process, through voting, of African Americans and other minority groups.

Question 21

Choice (C) is the correct answer. During the last 50 years, members of opposing political parties have been on the same side of the issues listed in choices (A), (B), (D), and (E), and members of the same political party have opposed each other on these same issues. The Speaker of the House is elected by the members of the House and is the most likely issue to be voted on according to party affiliation. Usually, the Speaker is a member of the majority party.

Question 22

Choice (E) is the correct answer. Before the eighteenth century, the most dramatic influence on the culture of the American Plains Indians was the introduction of the horse by Spanish explorers. The horse increased their mobility so that they could more easily follow the herds of buffalo on which their lives depended. It also increased their ability to make war on neighboring tribes and to expand their control over vast areas.

Question 23

Choice (A) is the correct answer. The major problem with the Articles of Confederation was the insufficient power of the central government. Although the new government could deal with foreign countries and settle disputes between or among states, it had very few powers. Most of the powers of government remained with the states. Basically, the Articles created a very loose confederation of very independent states.

Question 24

Choice (D) is the correct answer. Thomas Jefferson's ideal nation was an agrarian republic. He did not push for the purchase of the Louisiana Territory to embarrass the Federalists (C), whom he said all lived in cities, or to follow the advice of Alexander Hamilton (E), his political opponent, or to stimulate manufacturing (A), which he despised. Instead, he advocated the purchase in order to mold the United States into his ideal.

Question 25

Choice (B) is the correct answer. In *Walden*, Thoreau recounts his experiences during his two years living in near seclusion in the woods of Massachusetts, not the American West (A) or a Southern plantation (C). Thoreau also expounded on his philosophy of individualism and living simply in harmony with nature, away from the noisy, industrialized, and densely populated cities.

Question 26

Choice (E) is the correct answer. Although the United States might have stated other reasons for the Open Door Policy of 1899, its primary interest was economic—to protect U.S. trading opportunities in China and to prevent European and Asian countries from taking over all Chinese trade.

Question 27

Choice (A) is the correct answer. In the 1920s, the Ku Klux Klan began to target anyone who was not a white, Protestant, native-born American—African Americans, Jews, immigrants, union workers, Catholics. As during the Reconstruction period, the Klan used vigilante tactics, not only in the South, but also in northern, midwestern, and western states.

Question 28

Choice (B) is the correct answer. Inflationary wages were nonexistent before the 1930s. On the other hand, all of the factors mentioned in the other choices—a nonregulated banking system, low farm prices, overproduction of manufactured goods, and the stock market crash—did contribute to the Great Depression.

Question 29

Choice (C) is the correct answer. Before it entered the Second World War, the neutral United States used the lend-lease policy to provide war materials, food, and other necessities to the Allied forces, without requiring the Allied nations to pay for those goods.

Question 30

Choice (D) is the correct answer. Many viewed a tax on individual and corporate income as an end to capitalism and free enterprise. Choice (A) is incorrect. Women's suffrage was not associated with the economic issue discussed. Choice (B) is incorrect. Due process of law protected all citizens, the best and the worst, and had no direct effect on the economic system of the country. Choice (C) is incorrect. The method of electing senators would have no direct effect on the economy. Choice (E) is incorrect. Abolishing slavery and indentured servitude was not considered a threat to industrial capitalism.

Question 31

Choice (E) is the correct answer. The political cartoon requires the reader to recognize Nikita Khrushchev, premier of the USSR, disguised as Napoleon Bonaparte, retreating on a horse made of missiles. In the background is Fidel Castro, leader of Cuba, dressed as a peasant and waving the Cuban flag. With the word "retreat" at the top, the cartoon refers to the withdrawal of Soviet missiles from Cuba in 1962. The other choices are incorrect because neither Cuba nor Fidel Castro had anything to do with these other events.

Question 32

Choice (A) is the correct answer. The technological and agricultural advances mentioned in this question were accomplishments of the Maya, Toltec, and Aztec who had empires throughout Mesoamerica (in Mexico and upper Central America) before the arrival of Spanish explorers. Although the Native Americans of the Eastern Woodlands had an advanced agricultural economy and some large cities, the peoples who populated the areas mentioned in the other choices did not have highly developed systems of astronomy, mathematics, or calendars.

Question 33

Choice (E) is the correct answer. Although Jamestown was the first permanent English settlement in North America, nearly two-thirds of the first settlers died from disease (dysentery and typhoid fever) during the first year. At first, Native Americans were helpful; however, they soon began making war on the English settlers (D). Neither gold nor other precious metals were found here, as they had been in Mexico (A), and the cultivation and export of tobacco did not occur until more settlers and supplies arrived and the colony had been made a royal colony (B). Although the Spanish had claimed the land that would later become known as Florida, they had no interest in this area of North America (C).

Question 34

Choice (B) is the correct answer. The Northwest Ordinance of 1787 set the guidelines for the government of the area known as the Northwest Territory and specified that the area would make up from three to five states. The Ordinance also set the minimum adult male population for each of these areas to become a territory and eventually a state, outlawed slavery, and granted its citizens the same rights as other American citizens had. Most important, these newly organized states would have the same status as the older states of the Union.

Question 35

Choice (D) is the correct answer. John Marshall, Chief Justice of the Supreme Court from 1801 to 1833, led the Court in making numerous rulings that firmly established the Court's power of judicial review (*Marbury v. Madison*), strengthened the power of the federal government over the states, and affirmed congressional control of both the sanctity of contracts and interstate commerce. The question of a slave's rights did not come before the Supreme Court until 1857 in *Dred Scott v. Sandford*.

Question 36

Choice (C) is the correct answer. In the five novels that compose *The Leatherstocking Tales*, published between 1823 and 1841, Cooper portrays Natty Bumppo, the hero, as a noble frontiersman caught between two worlds—the natural, unsettled wilderness and the developing, growing settlements of the young nation. Although Twain and Cather both created western heroes and heroines, their works came much later. Poe wrote poetry and short stories of the macabre. Jackson's works focused on the cruel and unjust treatment of Native Americans.

Question 37

Choice (C) is the correct answer. This quotation supports the idea of Manifest Destiny—that the expansion of the United States to include not only Texas but all of the lands leading to the Pacific Ocean was not only inevitable but also divinely ordained.

Question 38

Choice (A) is the correct answer. Although the Union dominated the Confederacy in terms of railroads, population, industry, resources, wealth, and military force, the South had Robert E. Lee, a military genius, as leader of Virginia's military forces and eventually as chief of all the Confederate forces. The South also had a number of talented and highly trained military officers. The Union army had little effective military leadership until Lincoln appointed Ulysses S. Grant as military commander in 1864.

Question 39

Choice (B) is the correct answer. This quotation reflects the concept of Social Darwinism, which held that government should not interfere in human interactions because political power and economic dominance would naturally fall to "the fittest."

Question 40

Choice (B) is the correct answer. From 1880 through 1930, the growth of business and industry provided opportunities for women as office workers, store clerks, and factory workers. The other choices are incorrect. During this period, most married women were homemakers or worked in the home; women did not receive equal pay; and women faced increased restrictions on entering professions such as medicine and law.

Question 41

Choice (E) is the correct answer. Rather than declining, both production and wages in the United States increased during the Second World War. Domestic factories and industries became "war" factories and industries, and workers were needed and paid to perform the jobs. Because of the war effort, some goods, such as gasoline and food, were rationed; women performed jobs once held only by men; Southerners, especially African Americans, migrated north in search of jobs and a better life; and the federal government became stronger and bigger.

Question 42

Choice (A) is the correct answer. The main interest of France in establishing settlements in the Americas was trade with American Indians. In exchange for furs, especially beaver, the French gave metal products (pots and tools), decorated blankets, glass beads, and other goods that the native peoples did not make for themselves. The French established only a few permanent settlements, mostly along the St. Lawrence River and at the mouth of the Mississippi River, where there was easy access to shipping ports.

Question 43

Choice (C) is the correct answer. To maintain its hold in the Americas, Spain needed Florida to prevent English colonial expansion into the area south of the Carolinas. Florida was neither a source of precious metals or tropical produce, nor a center of Catholicism.

Question 44

Choice (D) is the correct answer. The colonists were not interested in achieving an even distribution of income. Instead, they supported the idea of independence from England because they wanted more say in how they were governed and in preserving their way of life.

Question 45

Choice (B) is the correct answer. The state of Georgia had taken land owned by the Cherokee under a treaty with the United States. The Cherokee appealed to the Supreme Court, which ruled in their favor. However, Georgia ignored the ruling and continued to take the land. Jackson, as president, did not intervene to enforce the Supreme Court's decision, and the Cherokee were forced to leave their lands in Georgia and move to the Oklahoma Territory.

Question 46

Choice (B) is the correct answer. The area shaded in the map was once part of Mexico. Although all of the land had once been part of the Spanish Empire, none of this area was ceded by Spain to the United States (A), and only Texas was part of the Confederacy (C). The Bear Flag Republic included only a small area in northern California (D), and the Gadsden Purchase included a small portion in southern Arizona and New Mexico (E).

Question 47

Choice (C) is the correct answer. The Populist Party of the 1890s, supported by southern and western farmers, called for measures, such as abolishing the national banking system and nationalizing the railroads, to help them out of financial difficulties.

Question 48

Choice (E) is the correct answer. Large trusts or monopolies were combinations of companies that gained control of the market and forced out any competition. The Sherman Antitrust Act of 1890 made such monopolies illegal.

Question 49

Choice (D) is the correct answer. The cartoon requires the reader to recognize the symbols of the political parties in the 1912 election: the elephant symbolizes the Republican Party, the bull moose symbolizes the Progressive Party, and the donkey, ridden by Wilson, represents the Democratic Party. The mathematic division sign between the elephant and bull moose means "the Republican Party divided (or split) by the Progressive Party," and the equal sign means that this split resulted in the election of the Democratic Party's candidate, Woodrow Wilson.

Question 50

Choice (B) is the correct answer. According to the National Origins Act of 1924, the number of immigrants from a certain country allowed into the United States was based on the proportion of the U.S. population with the number of people from that country already living in the United States in 1890. This Act was passed in order to exclude or minimize immigrants from different racial, ethnic, or religious backgrounds.

Question 51

Choice (A) is the correct answer. In general, the Good Neighbor policy under Franklin D. Roosevelt meant that the United States would no longer interfere in Latin American countries. Previously, the United States had used economic, political, and military force in various Latin American countries in order to protect American business interests in those countries.

Question 52

Choice (E) is the correct answer. To counteract the spread of communism, President Truman proposed the Truman Doctrine in 1947, by which the United States would aid any country threatened by communist takeover.

Question 53

Choice (B) is the correct answer. The principles of government embodied in the Declaration of Independence and the U.S. Constitution are directly based on the political theories of John Locke. According to Locke's theory, government derived its power from the people who were governed, not by divine right; government had an obligation to protect the people's natural and property rights; and government that failed in this protection should be abolished.

Question 54

Choice (A) is the correct answer. According to the chart, the highest numbers of slaves were imported to the British West Indies, French West Indies, and Portuguese America, all sugar-growing areas. British colonies in North America imported the fewest number of slaves (B), and the Portuguese imported the highest number of slaves during all three periods (C). The information provided in the chart is insufficient to support the statements in choices (D) and (E).

Question 55

Choice (D) is the correct answer. The statement focuses on the eighteenth-century cultural diversity of American families, which, in this quotation, are a mixture of English, Dutch, French, and other backgrounds. The statement does not mention social status (A) or religious faith (E). By implication, the statement indicates that the American family is opposite of the concepts of nativism (B) and Anglicization (C).

Question 56

Choice (C) is the correct answer. According to the Monroe Doctrine, first proposed by James Monroe in 1823, the United States would not allow any European powers to establish new colonies on the American continents or to attempt to regain control of colonies that had won their independence.

Question 57

Choice (D) is the correct answer. In the United States during the nineteenth century, the tenets of evangelicalism—that the individual must make a personal religious commitment and that the Bible is the authoritative source of religious knowledge—were widely supported by Protestant churches and continue to be represented in most Protestant denominations.

Question 58

Choice (A) is the correct answer. Proposed by Theodore Roosevelt in 1904, the Roosevelt Corollary extended the Monroe Doctrine (which was meant to prevent European expansion in Latin America) and stated that the United States could intervene in the affairs of Latin American countries.

Question 59

Choice (B) is the correct answer. Under the New Deal in the 1930s, laws to establish a social security program, set up a federal work-relief program, protect collective bargaining, and regulate stock exchanges were all enacted. A law to establish a national health insurance program was not enacted until 1966.

Question 60

Choice (A) is the correct answer. Under the Marshall Plan, the United States would provide financial aid to rebuild the economy, agriculture, and industry of European countries, including Germany, that had been ravaged by the Second World War.

Question 61

Choice (E) is the correct answer. After 1940, the increase in farming mechanization, such as cotton-picking machines, and a decrease in the cotton market meant that farmers no longer needed sharecroppers to help produce their crops.

Question 62

Choice (C) is the correct answer. In most areas of colonial America, such as inland towns and farming backcountries, the people tended to be fairly equal economically. In the seaboard cities, however, export merchants became quite wealthy and composed an economic upper class. These wealthy merchants represented only a small percentage of the population of these cities, but they owned much of the total wealth. Their wealth was far greater than that of the middle class, which was composed of artisans and shopkeepers, and even greater than that of those who worked for wages.

Question 63

Choice (A) is the correct answer. Rather than innate goodness of human nature, one of the principles of Puritanism is the basic sinfulness of human nature. Although Puritans believed that one's eternal fate was predetermined and could not be known for certain, they also believed that a person's conversion might indicate that he or she was chosen by God for salvation.

Question 64

Choice (D) is the correct answer. Shortly after the Revolutionary War began in 1776, Franklin was able to convince the king of France to provide financial aid to the United States. Less than two years later, in February 1778, Franklin was able to establish an economic and military alliance between France and the United States.

Question 65

Choice (B) is the correct answer. The slave trade had been outlawed by both Great Britain and the United States before the War of 1812. The United States entered a war against Great Britain because Great Britain had prohibited neutral countries from trading with France, with which it was at war (A), violated U.S. territorial waters by attacking and boarding American ships to look for deserters (C), and forced American sailors into military service (D). Some U.S. citizens also wanted to make Canada part of the United States (E).

Question 66

Choice (A) is the correct answer. Trusts, or monopolies, did not become a factor in the American economy until the late nineteenth century. However, temperance, abolitionism, and free public education were widely supported by various segments of the American population. Utopian communitarianism resulted in communities such as the Oneida Community, where there was no government or any other restraints on individual behavior.

Question 67

Choice (D) is the correct answer. In the four decades before the American Civil War, most slaves worked as field laborers on the plantations, but many also worked as housemaids, seamstresses, carpenters, blacksmiths, cooks, midwives, nurses, and gardeners. Even within the restricted environment, slaves developed their own social lives (A), and their population in the American South grew at a normal rate, so importation, which had been outlawed in 1808, was not necessary (B). Because plantation owners depended almost entirely on slave labor (C), they had great incentive to keep the slaves healthy (E).

Question 68

Choice (B) is the correct answer. With the enactment of the Chinese Exclusion Act of 1882, passed in response to growing feelings of nativism, Congress limited the number of new Chinese immigrants to almost none.

Question 69

Choice (E) is the correct answer. The National Labor Relations Act (NLRA), also known as the Wagner Act, was passed by Congress in 1935. Its purpose was to govern relations between laborers and management in businesses involved in interstate commerce. The NLRA, along with other laws that supported workers, such as the Fair Labor Standards Act, was part of Roosevelt's Second New Deal.

Question 70

Choice (C) is the correct answer. On June 25, 1950, fighting between North and South Korean troops broke out along the 38th parallel (Map II). Within three days, the North Koreans had taken Seoul and advanced quickly, taking all but a small area surrounding Pusan (Map III). United Nations troops led by General Douglas MacArthur pushed the North Koreans back all the way to the Chinese border (Map I). China sent troops to help the North Koreans retake the area that included Seoul, but an armistice between the U.N., China, and North Korea was signed, setting the North–South border at the 38th parallel (Map IV).

Question 71

Choice (B) is the correct answer. From about 1962 to 1968, the number of births sharply dropped from about 117 to about 66 per 1,000 women. Although it is not shown, the wide availability of contraceptives during this time period would be consistent with the drop in number of births.

Question 72

Choice (D) is the correct answer. Attracted by cheap land and relative freedom of religion, thousands of Germans and Scots-Irish immigrated to the Middle Colonies and settled in the Appalachian frontier of western Pennsylvania, Maryland, Virginia, and the Carolinas.

Question 73

Choice (C) is the correct answer. The Anti-Federalists opposed the ratification of the new United States Constitution because it did not have a Bill of Rights. Despite the long and hard debate over this issue, each of the 13 states finally ratified the Constitution between 1787 and 1790. In 1791, the first 10 amendments to the Constitution were ratified and became the Bill of Rights.

Question 74

Choice (E) is the correct answer. The Missouri Compromise, the Tariff of 1833, and the Compromise of 1850 all centered on the slavery issue, which divided the United States along sectional lines—North, South, and West. The Missouri Compromise dealt with the admission of new states as slave states or free states; the Tariff of 1833 dealt with high taxes on manufactured goods imported by Southern (slave) states; and the Compromise of 1850 dealt with the lands obtained from Mexico after the Mexican War and their admission as slave or free states.

Question 75

Choice (A) is the correct answer. After the Civil War, the Radical Republicans favored punitive measures against the former Confederate states and leaders, and equal rights for former slaves. They opposed President Andrew Johnson's Reconstruction policy (B) because they believed it was not punitive enough against the Southern states and did not grant civil and political rights to black Americans.

Question 76

Choice (C) is the correct answer. The late nineteenth century was the time of big business trusts, or monopolies, which knocked out competition from small businesses and controlled prices of goods. High tariffs, or taxes on imported goods, favored monopolies because they reduced competition from foreign businesses. Progressive reformers sought lower tariffs and the end of trusts.

Question 77

Choice (A) is the correct answer. The railroad strike of 1877 started out as a local strike against a single railroad, but grew to involve workers and railroads across the country. The railroad workers represented the poor working class, who worked in dangerous conditions for low wages and no benefits. The railroads represented the wealthy owners.

Question 78

Choice (E) is the correct answer. By 1890, the American frontier, in the common meaning of the word, no longer existed. The country from the Atlantic to the Pacific was settled, crisscrossed with railroads, spotted with booming towns, and most of the territories of the American West had been admitted as states into the Union. All parts of the country were linked geographically, economically, and politically.

Question 79

Choice (D) is the correct answer. The Labor-Management Relations Act of 1947, also known as the Taft-Hartley Act, was unfavorable toward organized labor. It amended the National Labor Relations Act by limiting and regulating union activities, especially with regard to the right of workers not to belong to a union or to participate in collective bargaining. The acts mentioned in the other choices were all favorable to workers and were generally supported by organized labor.

Question 80

Choice (B) is the correct answer. Since Reconstruction, black voters had supported the Republican Party, the party of Abraham Lincoln. During the 1930s, however, large numbers of black voters switched to the Democratic Party. This shift occurred as a result of the devastating effects of the Great Depression on the black population, the increased involvement of black workers in labor unions, and the Republican Party's recruitment of Southern segregationists.

Question 81

Choice (C) is the correct answer. According to the doctrine of collective security, the nations of the world could unite into a federation that could protect its member countries and smaller countries against aggression by other countries. After the First World War, this idea took shape as the League of Nations, whose purpose was to prevent another world war. The League of Nations failed, unable to prevent the Second World War. At the end of the Second World War, the United Nations was created to achieve collective security.

Question 82

Choice (E) is the correct answer. In response to alleged attacks on U.S. naval ships that were in North Vietnam's territorial waters, Congress passed the Tonkin Gulf Resolution. The Resolution granted President Lyndon Johnson war-making powers and, in effect, represented Congressional approval of U.S. involvement in the Vietnam War.

Question 83

Choice (A) is the correct answer. Several events during the first few decades of the republic proved that the executive and legislative branches of the government could function in their respective roles in making and carrying out foreign policy. With the Louisiana Purchase, the War of 1812, and the proclamation of the Monroe Doctrine, the United States proved itself to be a strong, independent nation in its dealings with the other nations of the world.

Question 84

Choice (B) is the correct answer. As part of his plan to organize the finances and solve the money problems of the new nation, Secretary of the Treasury Alexander Hamilton proposed a national bank that would hold the government's money and back its currency. The bank would be regulated by the government but would be privately financed and owned by wealthy financiers. This plan would have permanently tied the government to the bank's owners.

Question 85

Choice (A) is the correct answer. The Populist movement, which had its roots in farmers' alliances and eventually formed the People's Party, embraced several reforms that would help farmers, including government control of the railroads to lower shipping costs for farmers.

Question 86

Choice (C) is the correct answer. In *How the Other Half Lives*, Riis documented the conditions of tenements, schools, and neighborhoods of immigrants in New York City and was instrumental in bringing about needed reforms in the congested parts of the city.

Question 87

Choice (D) is the correct answer. Although the federal government increased its control over big business through banking reforms, lower tariffs, and stricter antitrust laws, most of the big trusts and monopolies had already been "busted" before the First World War.

Question 88

Choice (E) is the correct answer. By the time Roosevelt, Winston Churchill, and Joseph Stalin met at Yalta in February 1945, the Soviet Union had taken over Poland.

Question 89

Choice (D) is the correct answer. Members of the American counterculture of the 1960s, sometimes called hippies, protested against many aspects of American society, including its materialism. Many members of the counterculture believed that Americans should be more concerned with the environment, civil rights, women's rights, and world peace than with material indulgences.

Question 90

Choice (B) is the correct answer. During the 1970s, the greatest population growth occurred in the Sunbelt, the states south of the 37th parallel. This growth was a result of population migrations from the North and Northeast as well as immigration from Latin American and Asian countries.

CollegeBoard

SAT Subject Tests™

COMPLETE MARK ● EXAMPLES OF INCOMPLETE MARKS Ⓐ ⊗ ⊖ Ⓟ

You must use a No. 2 pencil and marks must be complete. Do not use a mechanical pencil. It is very important that you fill in the entire circle darkly and completely. If you change your response, erase as completely as possible. Incomplete marks or erasures may affect your score.

---

1 Your Name:
(Print)

_____ Last _____ First _____ M.I.

I agree to the conditions on the front and back of the SAT Subject Tests™ book. I also agree with the SAT Test Security and Fairness policies and understand that any violation of these policies will result in score cancellation and may result in reporting of certain violations to law enforcement.

Signature: _____ Today's Date: ___/___/___
                                          MM DD YY

Home Address: _____
(Print)   Number and Street   City   State/Country   Zip Code

Phone: ( ) Test Center: _____
                    (Print)   City   State/Country

---

2 YOUR NAME

Last Name (First 6 Letters) First Name (First 4 Letters) Mid. Init.

3 DATE OF BIRTH

MONTH DAY YEAR

○ Jan
○ Feb
○ Mar
○ Apr
○ May
○ Jun
○ Jul
○ Aug
○ Sep
○ Oct
○ Nov
○ Dec

4 REGISTRATION NUMBER
(Copy from Admission Ticket.)

Important: Fill in items 8 and 9 exactly as shown on the back of test book.

7 TEST BOOK SERIAL NUMBER
(Copy from front of test book.)

8 BOOK CODE
(Copy and grid as on back of test book.)

9 BOOK ID
(Copy from back of test book.)

PLEASE MAKE SURE to fill in these fields completely and correctly. If they are not correct, we won't be able to score your test(s)!

5 ZIP CODE

6 TEST CENTER
(Supplied by Test Center Supervisor.)

FOR OFFICIAL USE ONLY
⓪ ① ② ③ ④ ⑤ ⑥
⓪ ① ② ③ ④ ⑤ ⑥
⓪ ① ② ③ ④ ⑤ ⑥

103648-77191 · NS1114C1085 · Printed in U.S.A.

194415-001   1 2 3 4 5 A B C D E   Printed in the USA   ISD11312   783175

PLEASE DO NOT WRITE IN THIS AREA

SERIAL #

COMPLETE MARK ●	EXAMPLES OF INCOMPLETE MARKS Ⓐ ⊗ ⊕ Ⓓ ⊝ ⊘ ⬤ ⊛	You must use a No. 2 pencil and marks must be complete. Do not use a mechanical pencil. It is very important that you fill in the entire circle darkly and completely. If you change your response, erase as completely as possible. Incomplete marks or erasures may affect your score.

- ○ Literature
- ○ Biology E
- ○ Biology M
- ○ Chemistry
- ○ Physics

- ○ Mathematics Level 1
- ○ Mathematics Level 2
- ○ U.S. History
- ○ World History
- ○ French

- ○ German
- ○ Italian
- ○ Latin
- ○ Modern Hebrew
- ○ Spanish

- ○ Chinese Listening
- ○ French Listening
- ○ German Listening

- ○ Japanese Listening
- ○ Korean Listening
- ○ Spanish Listening

Background Questions: ① ② ③ ④ ⑤ ⑥ ⑦ ⑧ ⑨

1 Ⓐ Ⓑ Ⓒ Ⓓ Ⓔ	26 Ⓐ Ⓑ Ⓒ Ⓓ Ⓔ	51 Ⓐ Ⓑ Ⓒ Ⓓ Ⓔ	76 Ⓐ Ⓑ Ⓒ Ⓓ Ⓔ
2 Ⓐ Ⓑ Ⓒ Ⓓ Ⓔ	27 Ⓐ Ⓑ Ⓒ Ⓓ Ⓔ	52 Ⓐ Ⓑ Ⓒ Ⓓ Ⓔ	77 Ⓐ Ⓑ Ⓒ Ⓓ Ⓔ
3 Ⓐ Ⓑ Ⓒ Ⓓ Ⓔ	28 Ⓐ Ⓑ Ⓒ Ⓓ Ⓔ	53 Ⓐ Ⓑ Ⓒ Ⓓ Ⓔ	78 Ⓐ Ⓑ Ⓒ Ⓓ Ⓔ
4 Ⓐ Ⓑ Ⓒ Ⓓ Ⓔ	29 Ⓐ Ⓑ Ⓒ Ⓓ Ⓔ	54 Ⓐ Ⓑ Ⓒ Ⓓ Ⓔ	79 Ⓐ Ⓑ Ⓒ Ⓓ Ⓔ
5 Ⓐ Ⓑ Ⓒ Ⓓ Ⓔ	30 Ⓐ Ⓑ Ⓒ Ⓓ Ⓔ	55 Ⓐ Ⓑ Ⓒ Ⓓ Ⓔ	80 Ⓐ Ⓑ Ⓒ Ⓓ Ⓔ
6 Ⓐ Ⓑ Ⓒ Ⓓ Ⓔ	31 Ⓐ Ⓑ Ⓒ Ⓓ Ⓔ	56 Ⓐ Ⓑ Ⓒ Ⓓ Ⓔ	81 Ⓐ Ⓑ Ⓒ Ⓓ Ⓔ
7 Ⓐ Ⓑ Ⓒ Ⓓ Ⓔ	32 Ⓐ Ⓑ Ⓒ Ⓓ Ⓔ	57 Ⓐ Ⓑ Ⓒ Ⓓ Ⓔ	82 Ⓐ Ⓑ Ⓒ Ⓓ Ⓔ
8 Ⓐ Ⓑ Ⓒ Ⓓ Ⓔ	33 Ⓐ Ⓑ Ⓒ Ⓓ Ⓔ	58 Ⓐ Ⓑ Ⓒ Ⓓ Ⓔ	83 Ⓐ Ⓑ Ⓒ Ⓓ Ⓔ
9 Ⓐ Ⓑ Ⓒ Ⓓ Ⓔ	34 Ⓐ Ⓑ Ⓒ Ⓓ Ⓔ	59 Ⓐ Ⓑ Ⓒ Ⓓ Ⓔ	84 Ⓐ Ⓑ Ⓒ Ⓓ Ⓔ
10 Ⓐ Ⓑ Ⓒ Ⓓ Ⓔ	35 Ⓐ Ⓑ Ⓒ Ⓓ Ⓔ	60 Ⓐ Ⓑ Ⓒ Ⓓ Ⓔ	85 Ⓐ Ⓑ Ⓒ Ⓓ Ⓔ
11 Ⓐ Ⓑ Ⓒ Ⓓ Ⓔ	36 Ⓐ Ⓑ Ⓒ Ⓓ Ⓔ	61 Ⓐ Ⓑ Ⓒ Ⓓ Ⓔ	86 Ⓐ Ⓑ Ⓒ Ⓓ Ⓔ
12 Ⓐ Ⓑ Ⓒ Ⓓ Ⓔ	37 Ⓐ Ⓑ Ⓒ Ⓓ Ⓔ	62 Ⓐ Ⓑ Ⓒ Ⓓ Ⓔ	87 Ⓐ Ⓑ Ⓒ Ⓓ Ⓔ
13 Ⓐ Ⓑ Ⓒ Ⓓ Ⓔ	38 Ⓐ Ⓑ Ⓒ Ⓓ Ⓔ	63 Ⓐ Ⓑ Ⓒ Ⓓ Ⓔ	88 Ⓐ Ⓑ Ⓒ Ⓓ Ⓔ
14 Ⓐ Ⓑ Ⓒ Ⓓ Ⓔ	39 Ⓐ Ⓑ Ⓒ Ⓓ Ⓔ	64 Ⓐ Ⓑ Ⓒ Ⓓ Ⓔ	89 Ⓐ Ⓑ Ⓒ Ⓓ Ⓔ
15 Ⓐ Ⓑ Ⓒ Ⓓ Ⓔ	40 Ⓐ Ⓑ Ⓒ Ⓓ Ⓔ	65 Ⓐ Ⓑ Ⓒ Ⓓ Ⓔ	90 Ⓐ Ⓑ Ⓒ Ⓓ Ⓔ
16 Ⓐ Ⓑ Ⓒ Ⓓ Ⓔ	41 Ⓐ Ⓑ Ⓒ Ⓓ Ⓔ	66 Ⓐ Ⓑ Ⓒ Ⓓ Ⓔ	91 Ⓐ Ⓑ Ⓒ Ⓓ Ⓔ
17 Ⓐ Ⓑ Ⓒ Ⓓ Ⓔ	42 Ⓐ Ⓑ Ⓒ Ⓓ Ⓔ	67 Ⓐ Ⓑ Ⓒ Ⓓ Ⓔ	92 Ⓐ Ⓑ Ⓒ Ⓓ Ⓔ
18 Ⓐ Ⓑ Ⓒ Ⓓ Ⓔ	43 Ⓐ Ⓑ Ⓒ Ⓓ Ⓔ	68 Ⓐ Ⓑ Ⓒ Ⓓ Ⓔ	93 Ⓐ Ⓑ Ⓒ Ⓓ Ⓔ
19 Ⓐ Ⓑ Ⓒ Ⓓ Ⓔ	44 Ⓐ Ⓑ Ⓒ Ⓓ Ⓔ	69 Ⓐ Ⓑ Ⓒ Ⓓ Ⓔ	94 Ⓐ Ⓑ Ⓒ Ⓓ Ⓔ
20 Ⓐ Ⓑ Ⓒ Ⓓ Ⓔ	45 Ⓐ Ⓑ Ⓒ Ⓓ Ⓔ	70 Ⓐ Ⓑ Ⓒ Ⓓ Ⓔ	95 Ⓐ Ⓑ Ⓒ Ⓓ Ⓔ
21 Ⓐ Ⓑ Ⓒ Ⓓ Ⓔ	46 Ⓐ Ⓑ Ⓒ Ⓓ Ⓔ	71 Ⓐ Ⓑ Ⓒ Ⓓ Ⓔ	96 Ⓐ Ⓑ Ⓒ Ⓓ Ⓔ
22 Ⓐ Ⓑ Ⓒ Ⓓ Ⓔ	47 Ⓐ Ⓑ Ⓒ Ⓓ Ⓔ	72 Ⓐ Ⓑ Ⓒ Ⓓ Ⓔ	97 Ⓐ Ⓑ Ⓒ Ⓓ Ⓔ
23 Ⓐ Ⓑ Ⓒ Ⓓ Ⓔ	48 Ⓐ Ⓑ Ⓒ Ⓓ Ⓔ	73 Ⓐ Ⓑ Ⓒ Ⓓ Ⓔ	98 Ⓐ Ⓑ Ⓒ Ⓓ Ⓔ
24 Ⓐ Ⓑ Ⓒ Ⓓ Ⓔ	49 Ⓐ Ⓑ Ⓒ Ⓓ Ⓔ	74 Ⓐ Ⓑ Ⓒ Ⓓ Ⓔ	99 Ⓐ Ⓑ Ⓒ Ⓓ Ⓔ
25 Ⓐ Ⓑ Ⓒ Ⓓ Ⓔ	50 Ⓐ Ⓑ Ⓒ Ⓓ Ⓔ	75 Ⓐ Ⓑ Ⓒ Ⓓ Ⓔ	100 Ⓐ Ⓑ Ⓒ Ⓓ Ⓔ

PLEASE MAKE SURE to fill in these fields completely and correctly. If they are not correct, we won't be able to score your test(s)!

7 TEST BOOK SERIAL NUMBER (Copy from front of test book.)

8 BOOK CODE (Copy and grid as on back of test book.)

9 BOOK ID (Copy from back of test book.)

Quality Assurance Mark ●

Chemistry   *Fill in circle CE only if II is correct explanation of I.

	I	II	CE*		I	II	CE*
101	Ⓣ Ⓕ	Ⓣ Ⓕ	○	109	Ⓣ Ⓕ	Ⓣ Ⓕ	○
102	Ⓣ Ⓕ	Ⓣ Ⓕ	○	110	Ⓣ Ⓕ	Ⓣ Ⓕ	○
103	Ⓣ Ⓕ	Ⓣ Ⓕ	○	111	Ⓣ Ⓕ	Ⓣ Ⓕ	○
104	Ⓣ Ⓕ	Ⓣ Ⓕ	○	112	Ⓣ Ⓕ	Ⓣ Ⓕ	○
105	Ⓣ Ⓕ	Ⓣ Ⓕ	○	113	Ⓣ Ⓕ	Ⓣ Ⓕ	○
106	Ⓣ Ⓕ	Ⓣ Ⓕ	○	114	Ⓣ Ⓕ	Ⓣ Ⓕ	○
107	Ⓣ Ⓕ	Ⓣ Ⓕ	○	115	Ⓣ Ⓕ	Ⓣ Ⓕ	○
108	Ⓣ Ⓕ	Ⓣ Ⓕ	○				

FOR OFFICIAL USE ONLY				
R/C	W/S1	FS/S2	CS/S3	WS

CERTIFICATION STATEMENT   Copy the statement below and sign your name as you would an official document.

I hereby agree to the conditions set forth online at sat.collegeboard.org and in any paper registration materials given to me and certify that I am the person whose name, address and signature appear on this answer sheet.

Signature _____   Date _____

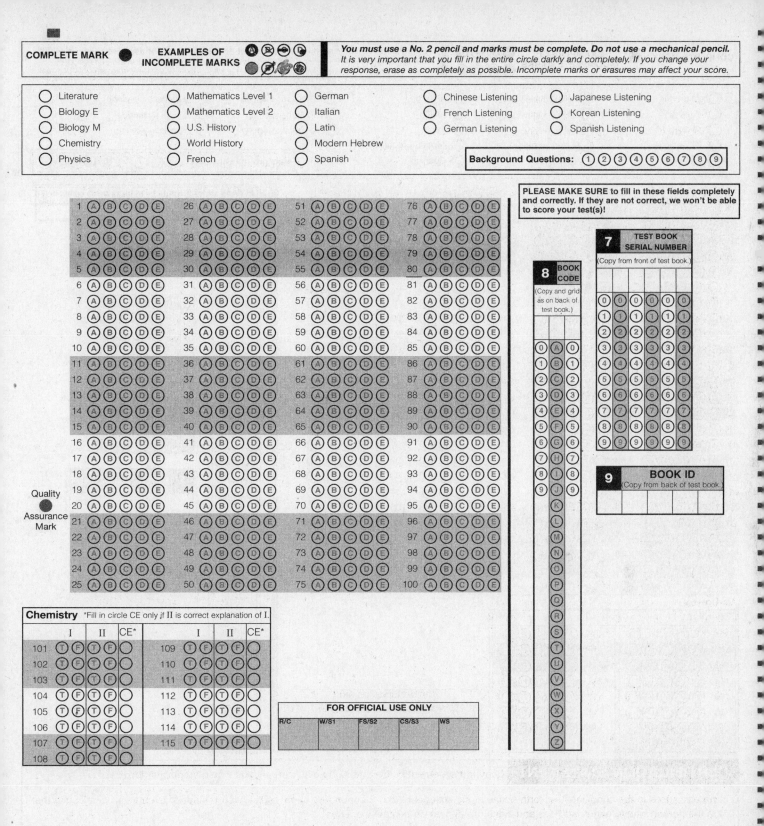

COMPLETE MARK ●	EXAMPLES OF INCOMPLETE MARKS Ⓐ ⊗ ⊕ Ⓓ ◑ Ⓒ̸ ⬤ Ⓐ	You must use a No. 2 pencil and marks must be complete. Do not use a mechanical pencil. It is very important that you fill in the entire circle darkly and completely. If you change your response, erase as completely as possible. Incomplete marks or erasures may affect your score.

○ Literature
○ Biology E
○ Biology M
○ Chemistry
○ Physics

○ Mathematics Level 1
○ Mathematics Level 2
○ U.S. History
○ World History
○ French

○ German
○ Italian
○ Latin
○ Modern Hebrew
○ Spanish

○ Chinese Listening
○ French Listening
○ German Listening

○ Japanese Listening
○ Korean Listening
○ Spanish Listening

Background Questions: ① ② ③ ④ ⑤ ⑥ ⑦ ⑧ ⑨

1–100 answer grid, each item A B C D E (questions 1 through 100)

PLEASE MAKE SURE to fill in these fields completely and correctly. If they are not correct, we won't be able to score your test(s)!

8 BOOK CODE (Copy and grid as on back of test book.)

Column: 0 1 2 3 4 5 6 7 8 9
Column: A B C D E F G H I J K L M N O P Q R S T U V W X Y Z
Column: 0 1 2 3 4 5 6 7 8 9

7 TEST BOOK SERIAL NUMBER (Copy from front of test book.)

0 1 2 3 4 5 6 7 8 9 (six columns)

9 BOOK ID (Copy from back of test book.)

● Quality Assurance Mark

Chemistry *Fill in circle CE only if II is correct explanation of I.

	I	II	CE*		I	II	CE*
101	T F	T F	○	109	T F	T F	○
102	T F	T F	○	110	T F	T F	○
103	T F	T F	○	111	T F	T F	○
104	T F	T F	○	112	T F	T F	○
105	T F	T F	○	113	T F	T F	○
106	T F	T F	○	114	T F	T F	○
107	T F	T F	○	115	T F	T F	○
108	T F	T F	○				

FOR OFFICIAL USE ONLY				
R/C	W/S1	FS/S2	CS/S3	WS

Page 4

SAT Subject Tests™

1 Your Name:
(Print)

_____ _____ _____
Last   First   M.I.

I agree to the conditions on the front and back of the SAT Subject Tests™ book. I also agree with the SAT Test Security and Fairness policies and understand that any violation of these policies will result in score cancellation and may result in reporting of certain violations to law enforcement.

Signature: _____   Today's Date: ___/___/___
                                                                      MM   DD   YY

Home Address: _____
(Print)   Number and Street   City   State/Country   Zip Code

Phone: (____)   Test Center: _____
                       (Print)   City   State/Country

2 YOUR NAME
Last Name (First 6 Letters)   First Name (First 4 Letters)   Mid. Init.

3 DATE OF BIRTH
MONTH   DAY   YEAR
○ Jan
○ Feb
○ Mar
○ Apr
○ May
○ Jun
○ Jul
○ Aug
○ Sep
○ Oct
○ Nov
○ Dec

4 REGISTRATION NUMBER
(Copy from Admission Ticket.)

Important: Fill in items 8 and 9 exactly as shown on the back of test book.

7 TEST BOOK SERIAL NUMBER
(Copy from front of test book.)

8 BOOK CODE
(Copy and grid as on back of test book.)

9 BOOK ID
(Copy from back of test book.)

PLEASE MAKE SURE to fill in these fields completely and correctly. If they are not correct, we won't be able to score your test(s)!

5 ZIP CODE

6 TEST CENTER
(Supplied by Test Center Supervisor.)

FOR OFFICIAL USE ONLY

PLEASE DO NOT WRITE IN THIS AREA   SERIAL #

○ Literature
○ Biology E
○ Biology M
○ Chemistry
○ Physics

○ Mathematics Level 1
○ Mathematics Level 2
○ U.S. History
○ World History
○ French

○ German
○ Italian
○ Latin
○ Modern Hebrew
○ Spanish

○ Chinese Listening
○ French Listening
○ German Listening

○ Japanese Listening
○ Korean Listening
○ Spanish Listening

Background Questions: ① ② ③ ④ ⑤ ⑥ ⑦ ⑧ ⑨

1–100 answer grid, each A B C D E

PLEASE MAKE SURE to fill in these fields completely and correctly. If they are not correct, we won't be able to score your test(s)!

7 TEST BOOK SERIAL NUMBER (Copy from front of test book.)

8 BOOK CODE (Copy and grid as on back of test book.)

9 BOOK ID (Copy from back of test book.)

Quality Assurance Mark

Chemistry *Fill in circle CE only if II is correct explanation of I.

	I	II	CE*			I	II	CE*
101	T F	T F	○		109	T F	T F	○
102	T F	T F	○		110	T F	T F	○
103	T F	T F	○		111	T F	T F	○
104	T F	T F	○		112	T F	T F	○
105	T F	T F	○		113	T F	T F	○
106	T F	T F	○		114	T F	T F	○
107	T F	T F	○		115	T F	T F	○
108	T F	T F	○					

FOR OFFICIAL USE ONLY

R/C	W/S1	FS/S2	CS/S3	WS

CERTIFICATION STATEMENT Copy the statement below and sign your name as you would an official document.

I hereby agree to the conditions set forth online at sat.collegeboard.org and in any paper registration materials given to me and certify that I am the person whose name, address and signature appear on this answer sheet.

Signature _____   Date _____

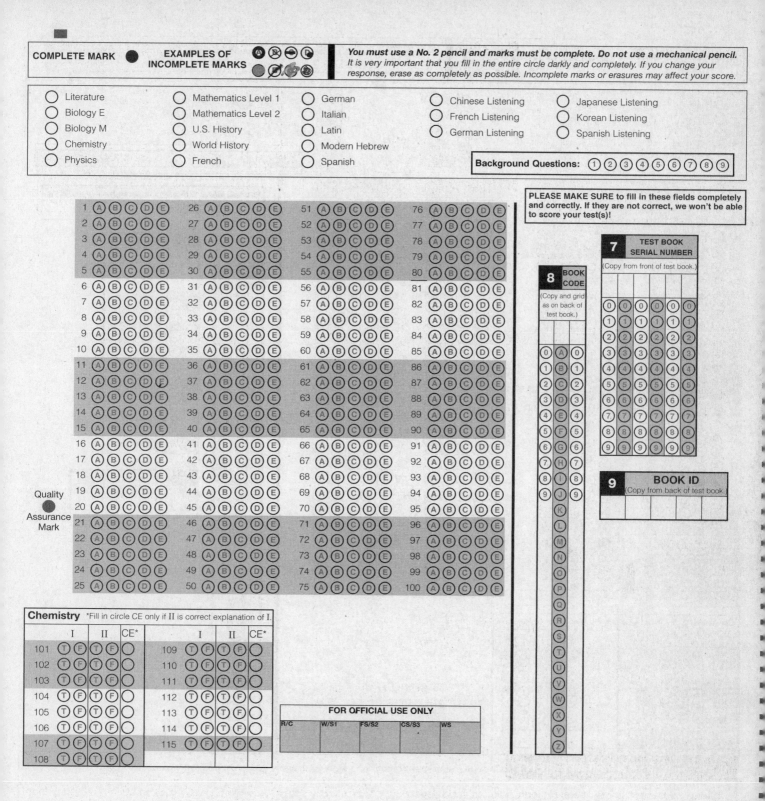

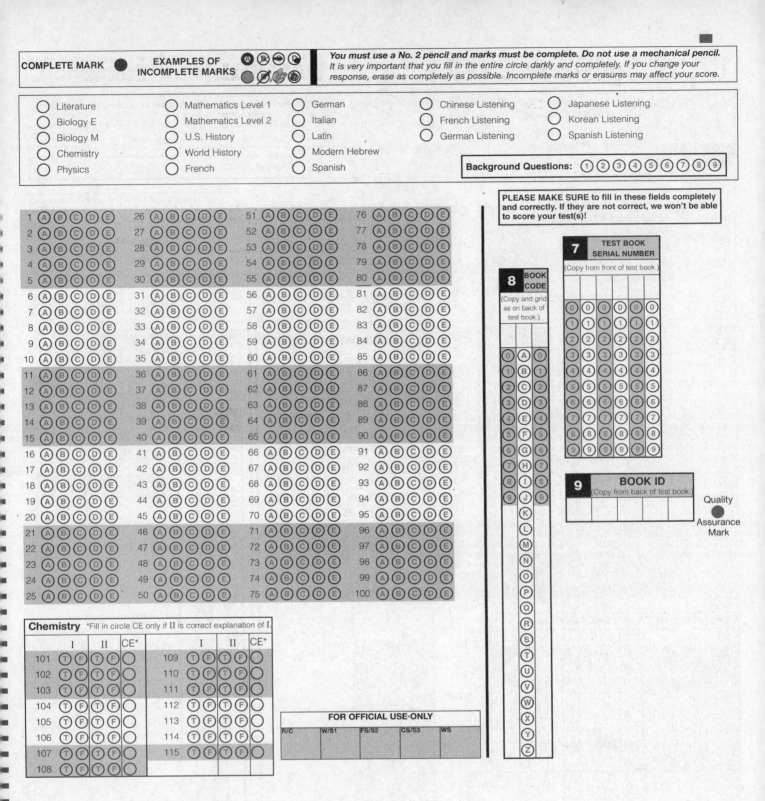

○ Literature
○ Biology E
○ Biology M
○ Chemistry
○ Physics

○ Mathematics Level 1
○ Mathematics Level 2
○ U.S. History
○ World History
○ French

○ German
○ Italian
○ Latin
○ Modern Hebrew
○ Spanish

○ Chinese Listening
○ French Listening
○ German Listening

○ Japanese Listening
○ Korean Listening
○ Spanish Listening

Background Questions: ① ② ③ ④ ⑤ ⑥ ⑦ ⑧ ⑨

PLEASE MAKE SURE to fill in these fields completely and correctly. If they are not correct, we won't be able to score your test(s)!

7 TEST BOOK SERIAL NUMBER (Copy from front of test book.)

8 BOOK CODE (Copy and grid as on back of test book.)

9 BOOK ID (Copy from back of test book.)

Quality Assurance Mark

Chemistry *Fill in circle CE only if II is correct explanation of I.

	I	II	CE*		I	II	CE*
101	T F	T F	○	109	T F	T F	○
102	T F	T F	○	110	T F	T F	○
103	T F	T F	○	111	T F	T F	○
104	T F	T F	○	112	T F	T F	○
105	T F	T F	○	113	T F	T F	○
106	T F	T F	○	114	T F	T F	○
107	T F	T F	○	115	T F	T F	○
108	T F	T F	○				

FOR OFFICIAL USE ONLY

R/C	W/S1	FS/S2	CS/S3	WS

Page 4

PLEASE DO NOT WRITE IN THIS AREA

SERIAL #

CollegeBoard

SAT Subject Tests™

COMPLETE MARK ●	EXAMPLES OF INCOMPLETE MARKS

You must use a No. 2 pencil and marks must be complete. Do not use a mechanical pencil. *It is very important that you fill in the entire circle darkly and completely. If you change your response, erase as completely as possible. Incomplete marks or erasures may affect your score.*

1 Your Name:
(Print)

Last   First   M.I.

I agree to the conditions on the front and back of the SAT Subject Tests™ book. I also agree with the SAT Test Security and Fairness policies and understand that any violation of these policies will result in score cancellation and may result in reporting of certain violations to law enforcement.

Signature:

Today's Date: ___/___/___
MM   DD   YY

Home Address:
(Print)

Number and Street   City   State/Country   Zip Code

Phone: (   )

Test Center:
(Print)   City   State/Country

2 YOUR NAME

Last Name (First 6 Letters) | First Name (First 4 Letters) | Mid. Init.

3 DATE OF BIRTH

MONTH	DAY	YEAR

Jan, Feb, Mar, Apr, May, Jun, Jul, Aug, Sep, Oct, Nov, Dec

4 REGISTRATION NUMBER
(Copy from Admission Ticket.)

Important: Fill in items 8 and 9 exactly as shown on the back of test book.

7 TEST BOOK SERIAL NUMBER
(Copy from front of test book.)

8 BOOK CODE
(Copy and grid as on back of test book.)

9 BOOK ID
(Copy from back of test book.)

5 ZIP CODE

6 TEST CENTER
(Supplied by Test Center Supervisor.)

PLEASE MAKE SURE to fill in these fields completely and correctly. If they are not correct, we won't be able to score your test(s)!

FOR OFFICIAL USE ONLY

103648-77191 • NS1114C1085 • Printed in U.S.A.

194415-001   1 2 3 4 5 A B C D E   Printed in the USA   ISD11312   783175

PLEASE DO NOT WRITE IN THIS AREA

SERIAL #

○ Literature
○ Biology E
○ Biology M
○ Chemistry
○ Physics

○ Mathematics Level 1
○ Mathematics Level 2
○ U.S. History
○ World History
○ French

○ German
○ Italian
○ Latin
○ Modern Hebrew
○ Spanish

○ Chinese Listening
○ French Listening
○ German Listening

○ Japanese Listening
○ Korean Listening
○ Spanish Listening

Background Questions: ① ② ③ ④ ⑤ ⑥ ⑦ ⑧ ⑨

1 Ⓐ Ⓑ Ⓒ Ⓓ Ⓔ   26 Ⓐ Ⓑ Ⓒ Ⓓ Ⓔ   51 Ⓐ Ⓑ Ⓒ Ⓓ Ⓔ   76 Ⓐ Ⓑ Ⓒ Ⓓ Ⓔ
2 Ⓐ Ⓑ Ⓒ Ⓓ Ⓔ   27 Ⓐ Ⓑ Ⓒ Ⓓ Ⓔ   52 Ⓐ Ⓑ Ⓒ Ⓓ Ⓔ   77 Ⓐ Ⓑ Ⓒ Ⓓ Ⓔ
3 Ⓐ Ⓑ Ⓒ Ⓓ Ⓔ   28 Ⓐ Ⓑ Ⓒ Ⓓ Ⓔ   53 Ⓐ Ⓑ Ⓒ Ⓓ Ⓔ   78 Ⓐ Ⓑ Ⓒ Ⓓ Ⓔ
4 Ⓐ Ⓑ Ⓒ Ⓓ Ⓔ   29 Ⓐ Ⓑ Ⓒ Ⓓ Ⓔ   54 Ⓐ Ⓑ Ⓒ Ⓓ Ⓔ   79 Ⓐ Ⓑ Ⓒ Ⓓ Ⓔ
5 Ⓐ Ⓑ Ⓒ Ⓓ Ⓔ   30 Ⓐ Ⓑ Ⓒ Ⓓ Ⓔ   55 Ⓐ Ⓑ Ⓒ Ⓓ Ⓔ   80 Ⓐ Ⓑ Ⓒ Ⓓ Ⓔ
6 Ⓐ Ⓑ Ⓒ Ⓓ Ⓔ   31 Ⓐ Ⓑ Ⓒ Ⓓ Ⓔ   56 Ⓐ Ⓑ Ⓒ Ⓓ Ⓔ   81 Ⓐ Ⓑ Ⓒ Ⓓ Ⓔ
7 Ⓐ Ⓑ Ⓒ Ⓓ Ⓔ   32 Ⓐ Ⓑ Ⓒ Ⓓ Ⓔ   57 Ⓐ Ⓑ Ⓒ Ⓓ Ⓔ   82 Ⓐ Ⓑ Ⓒ Ⓓ Ⓔ
8 Ⓐ Ⓑ Ⓒ Ⓓ Ⓔ   33 Ⓐ Ⓑ Ⓒ Ⓓ Ⓔ   58 Ⓐ Ⓑ Ⓒ Ⓓ Ⓔ   83 Ⓐ Ⓑ Ⓒ Ⓓ Ⓔ
9 Ⓐ Ⓑ Ⓒ Ⓓ Ⓔ   34 Ⓐ Ⓑ Ⓒ Ⓓ Ⓔ   59 Ⓐ Ⓑ Ⓒ Ⓓ Ⓔ   84 Ⓐ Ⓑ Ⓒ Ⓓ Ⓔ
10 Ⓐ Ⓑ Ⓒ Ⓓ Ⓔ   35 Ⓐ Ⓑ Ⓒ Ⓓ Ⓔ   60 Ⓐ Ⓑ Ⓒ Ⓓ Ⓔ   85 Ⓐ Ⓑ Ⓒ Ⓓ Ⓔ
11 Ⓐ Ⓑ Ⓒ Ⓓ Ⓔ   36 Ⓐ Ⓑ Ⓒ Ⓓ Ⓔ   61 Ⓐ Ⓑ Ⓒ Ⓓ Ⓔ   86 Ⓐ Ⓑ Ⓒ Ⓓ Ⓔ
12 Ⓐ Ⓑ Ⓒ Ⓓ Ⓔ   37 Ⓐ Ⓑ Ⓒ Ⓓ Ⓔ   62 Ⓐ Ⓑ Ⓒ Ⓓ Ⓔ   87 Ⓐ Ⓑ Ⓒ Ⓓ Ⓔ
13 Ⓐ Ⓑ Ⓒ Ⓓ Ⓔ   38 Ⓐ Ⓑ Ⓒ Ⓓ Ⓔ   63 Ⓐ Ⓑ Ⓒ Ⓓ Ⓔ   88 Ⓐ Ⓑ Ⓒ Ⓓ Ⓔ
14 Ⓐ Ⓑ Ⓒ Ⓓ Ⓔ   39 Ⓐ Ⓑ Ⓒ Ⓓ Ⓔ   64 Ⓐ Ⓑ Ⓒ Ⓓ Ⓔ   89 Ⓐ Ⓑ Ⓒ Ⓓ Ⓔ
15 Ⓐ Ⓑ Ⓒ Ⓓ Ⓔ   40 Ⓐ Ⓑ Ⓒ Ⓓ Ⓔ   65 Ⓐ Ⓑ Ⓒ Ⓓ Ⓔ   90 Ⓐ Ⓑ Ⓒ Ⓓ Ⓔ
16 Ⓐ Ⓑ Ⓒ Ⓓ Ⓔ   41 Ⓐ Ⓑ Ⓒ Ⓓ Ⓔ   66 Ⓐ Ⓑ Ⓒ Ⓓ Ⓔ   91 Ⓐ Ⓑ Ⓒ Ⓓ Ⓔ
17 Ⓐ Ⓑ Ⓒ Ⓓ Ⓔ   42 Ⓐ Ⓑ Ⓒ Ⓓ Ⓔ   67 Ⓐ Ⓑ Ⓒ Ⓓ Ⓔ   92 Ⓐ Ⓑ Ⓒ Ⓓ Ⓔ
18 Ⓐ Ⓑ Ⓒ Ⓓ Ⓔ   43 Ⓐ Ⓑ Ⓒ Ⓓ Ⓔ   68 Ⓐ Ⓑ Ⓒ Ⓓ Ⓔ   93 Ⓐ Ⓑ Ⓒ Ⓓ Ⓔ
19 Ⓐ Ⓑ Ⓒ Ⓓ Ⓔ   44 Ⓐ Ⓑ Ⓒ Ⓓ Ⓔ   69 Ⓐ Ⓑ Ⓒ Ⓓ Ⓔ   94 Ⓐ Ⓑ Ⓒ Ⓓ Ⓔ
20 Ⓐ Ⓑ Ⓒ Ⓓ Ⓔ   45 Ⓐ Ⓑ Ⓒ Ⓓ Ⓔ   70 Ⓐ Ⓑ Ⓒ Ⓓ Ⓔ   95 Ⓐ Ⓑ Ⓒ Ⓓ Ⓔ
21 Ⓐ Ⓑ Ⓒ Ⓓ Ⓔ   46 Ⓐ Ⓑ Ⓒ Ⓓ Ⓔ   71 Ⓐ Ⓑ Ⓒ Ⓓ Ⓔ   96 Ⓐ Ⓑ Ⓒ Ⓓ Ⓔ
22 Ⓐ Ⓑ Ⓒ Ⓓ Ⓔ   47 Ⓐ Ⓑ Ⓒ Ⓓ Ⓔ   72 Ⓐ Ⓑ Ⓒ Ⓓ Ⓔ   97 Ⓐ Ⓑ Ⓒ Ⓓ Ⓔ
23 Ⓐ Ⓑ Ⓒ Ⓓ Ⓔ   48 Ⓐ Ⓑ Ⓒ Ⓓ Ⓔ   73 Ⓐ Ⓑ Ⓒ Ⓓ Ⓔ   98 Ⓐ Ⓑ Ⓒ Ⓓ Ⓔ
24 Ⓐ Ⓑ Ⓒ Ⓓ Ⓔ   49 Ⓐ Ⓑ Ⓒ Ⓓ Ⓔ   74 Ⓐ Ⓑ Ⓒ Ⓓ Ⓔ   99 Ⓐ Ⓑ Ⓒ Ⓓ Ⓔ
25 Ⓐ Ⓑ Ⓒ Ⓓ Ⓔ   50 Ⓐ Ⓑ Ⓒ Ⓓ Ⓔ   75 Ⓐ Ⓑ Ⓒ Ⓓ Ⓔ   100 Ⓐ Ⓑ Ⓒ Ⓓ Ⓔ

PLEASE MAKE SURE to fill in these fields completely and correctly. If they are not correct, we won't be able to score your test(s)!

7 TEST BOOK SERIAL NUMBER (Copy from front of test book.)

8 BOOK CODE (Copy and grid as on back of test book.)

9 BOOK ID (Copy from back of test book.)

Quality Assurance Mark

Chemistry *Fill in circle CE only if II is correct explanation of I.

	I	II	CE*		I	II	CE*
101	Ⓣ Ⓕ	Ⓣ Ⓕ	○	109	Ⓣ Ⓕ	Ⓣ Ⓕ	○
102	Ⓣ Ⓕ	Ⓣ Ⓕ	○	110	Ⓣ Ⓕ	Ⓣ Ⓕ	○
103	Ⓣ Ⓕ	Ⓣ Ⓕ	○	111	Ⓣ Ⓕ	Ⓣ Ⓕ	○
104	Ⓣ Ⓕ	Ⓣ Ⓕ	○	112	Ⓣ Ⓕ	Ⓣ Ⓕ	○
105	Ⓣ Ⓕ	Ⓣ Ⓕ	○	113	Ⓣ Ⓕ	Ⓣ Ⓕ	○
106	Ⓣ Ⓕ	Ⓣ Ⓕ	○	114	Ⓣ Ⓕ	Ⓣ Ⓕ	○
107	Ⓣ Ⓕ	Ⓣ Ⓕ	○	115	Ⓣ Ⓕ	Ⓣ Ⓕ	○
108	Ⓣ Ⓕ	Ⓣ Ⓕ	○				

FOR OFFICIAL USE ONLY				
R/C	W/S1	FS/S2	CS/S3	WS

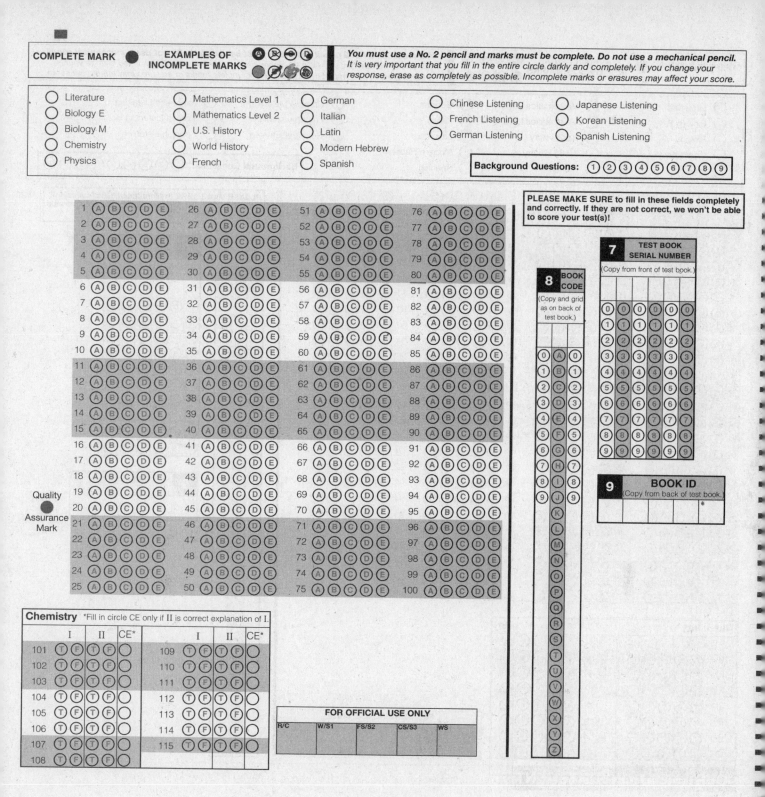

COMPLETE MARK ● EXAMPLES OF INCOMPLETE MARKS

You must use a No. 2 pencil and marks must be complete. Do not use a mechanical pencil. It is very important that you fill in the entire circle darkly and completely. If you change your response, erase as completely as possible. Incomplete marks or erasures may affect your score.

○ Literature
○ Biology E
○ Biology M
○ Chemistry
○ Physics

○ Mathematics Level 1
○ Mathematics Level 2
○ U.S. History
○ World History
○ French

○ German
○ Italian
○ Latin
○ Modern Hebrew
○ Spanish

○ Chinese Listening
○ French Listening
○ German Listening

○ Japanese Listening
○ Korean Listening
○ Spanish Listening

Background Questions: ① ② ③ ④ ⑤ ⑥ ⑦ ⑧ ⑨

PLEASE MAKE SURE to fill in these fields completely and correctly. If they are not correct, we won't be able to score your test(s)!

7 TEST BOOK SERIAL NUMBER
(Copy from front of test book.)

8 BOOK CODE
(Copy and grid as on back of test book.)

9 BOOK ID
(Copy from back of test book.)

Quality Assurance Mark ●

Chemistry *Fill in circle CE only if II is correct explanation of I.

FOR OFFICIAL USE ONLY

R/C	W/S1	FS/S2	CS/S3	WS

Page 3

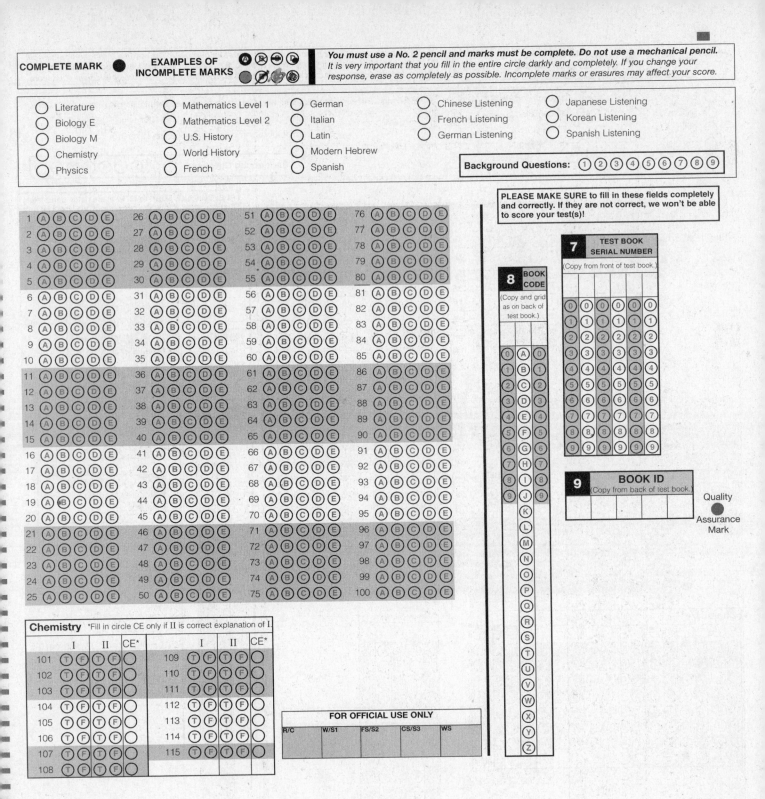

COMPLETE MARK ● **EXAMPLES OF INCOMPLETE MARKS** Ⓐ Ⓑ Ⓒ Ⓓ ● Ⓐ Ⓑ Ⓒ Ⓓ

You must use a No. 2 pencil and marks must be complete. Do not use a mechanical pencil. It is very important that you fill in the entire circle darkly and completely. If you change your response, erase as completely as possible. Incomplete marks or erasures may affect your score.

- ○ Literature
- ○ Biology E
- ○ Biology M
- ○ Chemistry
- ○ Physics
- ○ Mathematics Level 1
- ○ Mathematics Level 2
- ○ U.S. History
- ○ World History
- ○ French
- ○ German
- ○ Italian
- ○ Latin
- ○ Modern Hebrew
- ○ Spanish
- ○ Chinese Listening
- ○ French Listening
- ○ German Listening
- ○ Japanese Listening
- ○ Korean Listening
- ○ Spanish Listening

Background Questions: ① ② ③ ④ ⑤ ⑥ ⑦ ⑧ ⑨

PLEASE MAKE SURE to fill in these fields completely and correctly. If they are not correct, we won't be able to score your test(s)!

7 TEST BOOK SERIAL NUMBER (Copy from front of test book.)

8 BOOK CODE (Copy and grid as on back of test book.)

9 BOOK ID (Copy from back of test book.)

Quality Assurance Mark

Chemistry *Fill in circle CE only if II is correct explanation of I.

	I	II	CE*		I	II	CE*
101	T F	T F	○	109	T F	T F	○
102	T F	T F	○	110	T F	T F	○
103	T F	T F	○	111	T F	T F	○
104	T F	T F	○	112	T F	T F	○
105	T F	T F	○	113	T F	T F	○
106	T F	T F	○	114	T F	T F	○
107	T F	T F	○	115	T F	T F	○
108	T F	T F	○				

FOR OFFICIAL USE ONLY

R/C	W/S1	FS/S2	CS/S3	WS

Page 4

CollegeBoard

SAT Subject Tests™

COMPLETE MARK ●	EXAMPLES OF INCOMPLETE MARKS	Ⓐ ⊗ ⊝ Ⓓ ⊜ ∅ ⊘

You must use a No. 2 pencil and marks must be complete. Do not use a mechanical pencil. It is very important that you fill in the entire circle darkly and completely. If you change your response, erase as completely as possible. Incomplete marks or erasures may affect your score.

1 **Your Name:**
(Print)

Last _____ First _____ M.I. ___

I agree to the conditions on the front and back of the SAT Subject Tests™ book. I also agree with the SAT Test Security and Fairness policies and understand that any violation of these policies will result in score cancellation and may result in reporting of certain violations to law enforcement.

Signature: _____ Today's Date: __ / __ / __
MM DD YY

Home Address:
(Print)
Number and Street _____ City _____ State/Country ___ Zip Code

Phone: (   ) _____ **Test Center:**
(Print) _____ City _____ State/Country

2 YOUR NAME

Last Name (First 6 Letters) | First Name (First 4 Letters) | Mid. Init.

3 DATE OF BIRTH

MONTH	DAY	YEAR
Jan Feb Mar Apr May Jun Jul Aug Sep Oct Nov Dec		

4 REGISTRATION NUMBER
(Copy from Admission Ticket.)

Important: Fill in items 8 and 9 exactly as shown on the back of test book.

7 TEST BOOK SERIAL NUMBER
(Copy from front of test book.)

5 ZIP CODE

6 TEST CENTER
(Supplied by Test Center Supervisor.)

8 BOOK CODE
(Copy and grid as on back of test book.)

9 BOOK ID
(Copy from back of test book.)

PLEASE MAKE SURE to fill in these fields completely and correctly. If they are not correct, we won't be able to score your test(s)!

FOR OFFICIAL USE ONLY

0 1 2 3 4 5 6
0 1 2 3 4 5 6
0 1 2 3 4 5 6

103648-77191 • NS1114C1085 • Printed in U.S.A.

194415-001   1 2 3 4 5 A B C D E   Printed in the USA   ISD11312   783175

PLEASE DO NOT WRITE IN THIS AREA   **SERIAL #**

○ Literature
○ Biology E
○ Biology M
○ Chemistry
○ Physics

○ Mathematics Level 1
○ Mathematics Level 2
○ U.S. History
○ World History
○ French

○ German
○ Italian
○ Latin
○ Modern Hebrew
○ Spanish

○ Chinese Listening
○ French Listening
○ German Listening

○ Japanese Listening
○ Korean Listening
○ Spanish Listening

Background Questions: ① ② ③ ④ ⑤ ⑥ ⑦ ⑧ ⑨

1. Ⓐ Ⓑ Ⓒ Ⓓ Ⓔ
2. Ⓐ Ⓑ Ⓒ Ⓓ Ⓔ
3. Ⓐ Ⓑ Ⓒ Ⓓ Ⓔ
4. Ⓐ Ⓑ Ⓒ Ⓓ Ⓔ
5. Ⓐ Ⓑ Ⓒ Ⓓ Ⓔ
6. Ⓐ Ⓑ Ⓒ Ⓓ Ⓔ
7. Ⓐ Ⓑ Ⓒ Ⓓ Ⓔ
8. Ⓐ Ⓑ Ⓒ Ⓓ Ⓔ
9. Ⓐ Ⓑ Ⓒ Ⓓ Ⓔ
10. Ⓐ Ⓑ Ⓒ Ⓓ Ⓔ
11. Ⓐ Ⓑ Ⓒ Ⓓ Ⓔ
12. Ⓐ Ⓑ Ⓒ Ⓓ Ⓔ
13. Ⓐ Ⓑ Ⓒ Ⓓ Ⓔ
14. Ⓐ Ⓑ Ⓒ Ⓓ Ⓔ
15. Ⓐ Ⓑ Ⓒ Ⓓ Ⓔ
16. Ⓐ Ⓑ Ⓒ Ⓓ Ⓔ
17. Ⓐ Ⓑ Ⓒ Ⓓ Ⓔ
18. Ⓐ Ⓑ Ⓒ Ⓓ Ⓔ
19. Ⓐ Ⓑ Ⓒ Ⓓ Ⓔ
20. Ⓐ Ⓑ Ⓒ Ⓓ Ⓔ
21. Ⓐ Ⓑ Ⓒ Ⓓ Ⓔ
22. Ⓐ Ⓑ Ⓒ Ⓓ Ⓔ
23. Ⓐ Ⓑ Ⓒ Ⓓ Ⓔ
24. Ⓐ Ⓑ Ⓒ Ⓓ Ⓔ
25. Ⓐ Ⓑ Ⓒ Ⓓ Ⓔ

26. Ⓐ Ⓑ Ⓒ Ⓓ Ⓔ
27. Ⓐ Ⓑ Ⓒ Ⓓ Ⓔ
28. Ⓐ Ⓑ Ⓒ Ⓓ Ⓔ
29. Ⓐ Ⓑ Ⓒ Ⓓ Ⓔ
30. Ⓐ Ⓑ Ⓒ Ⓓ Ⓔ
31. Ⓐ Ⓑ Ⓒ Ⓓ Ⓔ
32. Ⓐ Ⓑ Ⓒ Ⓓ Ⓔ
33. Ⓐ Ⓑ Ⓒ Ⓓ Ⓔ
34. Ⓐ Ⓑ Ⓒ Ⓓ Ⓔ
35. Ⓐ Ⓑ Ⓒ Ⓓ Ⓔ
36. Ⓐ Ⓑ Ⓒ Ⓓ Ⓔ
37. Ⓐ Ⓑ Ⓒ Ⓓ Ⓔ
38. Ⓐ Ⓑ Ⓒ Ⓓ Ⓔ
39. Ⓐ Ⓑ Ⓒ Ⓓ Ⓔ
40. Ⓐ Ⓑ Ⓒ Ⓓ Ⓔ
41. Ⓐ Ⓑ Ⓒ Ⓓ Ⓔ
42. Ⓐ Ⓑ Ⓒ Ⓓ Ⓔ
43. Ⓐ Ⓑ Ⓒ Ⓓ Ⓔ
44. Ⓐ Ⓑ Ⓒ Ⓓ Ⓔ
45. Ⓐ Ⓑ Ⓒ Ⓓ Ⓔ
46. Ⓐ Ⓑ Ⓒ Ⓓ Ⓔ
47. Ⓐ Ⓑ Ⓒ Ⓓ Ⓔ
48. Ⓐ Ⓑ Ⓒ Ⓓ Ⓔ
49. Ⓐ Ⓑ Ⓒ Ⓓ Ⓔ
50. Ⓐ Ⓑ Ⓒ Ⓓ Ⓔ

51. Ⓐ Ⓑ Ⓒ Ⓓ Ⓔ
52. Ⓐ Ⓑ Ⓒ Ⓓ Ⓔ
53. Ⓐ Ⓑ Ⓒ Ⓓ Ⓔ
54. Ⓐ Ⓑ Ⓒ Ⓓ Ⓔ
55. Ⓐ Ⓑ Ⓒ Ⓓ Ⓔ
56. Ⓐ Ⓑ Ⓒ Ⓓ Ⓔ
57. Ⓐ Ⓑ Ⓒ Ⓓ Ⓔ
58. Ⓐ Ⓑ Ⓒ Ⓓ Ⓔ
59. Ⓐ Ⓑ Ⓒ Ⓓ Ⓔ
60. Ⓐ Ⓑ Ⓒ Ⓓ Ⓔ
61. Ⓐ Ⓑ Ⓒ Ⓓ Ⓔ
62. Ⓐ Ⓑ Ⓒ Ⓓ Ⓔ
63. Ⓐ Ⓑ Ⓒ Ⓓ Ⓔ
64. Ⓐ Ⓑ Ⓒ Ⓓ Ⓔ
65. Ⓐ Ⓑ Ⓒ Ⓓ Ⓔ
66. Ⓐ Ⓑ Ⓒ Ⓓ Ⓔ
67. Ⓐ Ⓑ Ⓒ Ⓓ Ⓔ
68. Ⓐ Ⓑ Ⓒ Ⓓ Ⓔ
69. Ⓐ Ⓑ Ⓒ Ⓓ Ⓔ
70. Ⓐ Ⓑ Ⓒ Ⓓ Ⓔ
71. Ⓐ Ⓑ Ⓒ Ⓓ Ⓔ
72. Ⓐ Ⓑ Ⓒ Ⓓ Ⓔ
73. Ⓐ Ⓑ Ⓒ Ⓓ Ⓔ
74. Ⓐ Ⓑ Ⓒ Ⓓ Ⓔ
75. Ⓐ Ⓑ Ⓒ Ⓓ Ⓔ

76. Ⓐ Ⓑ Ⓒ Ⓓ Ⓔ
77. Ⓐ Ⓑ Ⓒ Ⓓ Ⓔ
78. Ⓐ Ⓑ Ⓒ Ⓓ Ⓔ
79. Ⓐ Ⓑ Ⓒ Ⓓ Ⓔ
80. Ⓐ Ⓑ Ⓒ Ⓓ Ⓔ
81. Ⓐ Ⓑ Ⓒ Ⓓ Ⓔ
82. Ⓐ Ⓑ Ⓒ Ⓓ Ⓔ
83. Ⓐ Ⓑ Ⓒ Ⓓ Ⓔ
84. Ⓐ Ⓑ Ⓒ Ⓓ Ⓔ
85. Ⓐ Ⓑ Ⓒ Ⓓ Ⓔ
86. Ⓐ Ⓑ Ⓒ Ⓓ Ⓔ
87. Ⓐ Ⓑ Ⓒ Ⓓ Ⓔ
88. Ⓐ Ⓑ Ⓒ Ⓓ Ⓔ
89. Ⓐ Ⓑ Ⓒ Ⓓ Ⓔ
90. Ⓐ Ⓑ Ⓒ Ⓓ Ⓔ
91. Ⓐ Ⓑ Ⓒ Ⓓ Ⓔ
92. Ⓐ Ⓑ Ⓒ Ⓓ Ⓔ
93. Ⓐ Ⓑ Ⓒ Ⓓ Ⓔ
94. Ⓐ Ⓑ Ⓒ Ⓓ Ⓔ
95. Ⓐ Ⓑ Ⓒ Ⓓ Ⓔ
96. Ⓐ Ⓑ Ⓒ Ⓓ Ⓔ
97. Ⓐ Ⓑ Ⓒ Ⓓ Ⓔ
98. Ⓐ Ⓑ Ⓒ Ⓓ Ⓔ
99. Ⓐ Ⓑ Ⓒ Ⓓ Ⓔ
100. Ⓐ Ⓑ Ⓒ Ⓓ Ⓔ

PLEASE MAKE SURE to fill in these fields completely and correctly. If they are not correct, we won't be able to score your test(s)!

7 TEST BOOK SERIAL NUMBER (Copy from front of test book.)

8 BOOK CODE (Copy and grid as on back of test book.)

0 / 0 A 0
1 / 1 B 1
2 / 2 C 2
3 / 3 D 3
4 / 4 E 4
5 / 5 F 5
6 / 6 G 6
7 / 7 H 7
8 / 8 I 8
9 / 9 J 9
K
L
M
N
O
P
Q
R
S
T
U
V
W
X
Y
Z

9 BOOK ID (Copy from back of test book.)

● Quality
● Assurance Mark

Chemistry *Fill in circle CE only if II is correct explanation of I.

	I	II	CE*		I	II	CE*
101	Ⓣ Ⓕ	Ⓣ Ⓕ	○	109	Ⓣ Ⓕ	Ⓣ Ⓕ	○
102	Ⓣ Ⓕ	Ⓣ Ⓕ	○	110	Ⓣ Ⓕ	Ⓣ Ⓕ	○
103	Ⓣ Ⓕ	Ⓣ Ⓕ	○	111	Ⓣ Ⓕ	Ⓣ Ⓕ	○
104	Ⓣ Ⓕ	Ⓣ Ⓕ	○	112	Ⓣ Ⓕ	Ⓣ Ⓕ	○
105	Ⓣ Ⓕ	Ⓣ Ⓕ	○	113	Ⓣ Ⓕ	Ⓣ Ⓕ	○
106	Ⓣ Ⓕ	Ⓣ Ⓕ	○	114	Ⓣ Ⓕ	Ⓣ Ⓕ	○
107	Ⓣ Ⓕ	Ⓣ Ⓕ	○	115	Ⓣ Ⓕ	Ⓣ Ⓕ	○
108	Ⓣ Ⓕ	Ⓣ Ⓕ	○				

FOR OFFICIAL USE ONLY				
R/C	W/S1	FS/S2	CS/S3	WS

CERTIFICATION STATEMENT Copy the statement below and sign your name as you would an official document.

I hereby agree to the conditions set forth online at sat.collegeboard.org and in any paper registration materials given to me and certify that I am the person whose name, address and signature appear on this answer sheet.

Signature _____

Date _____

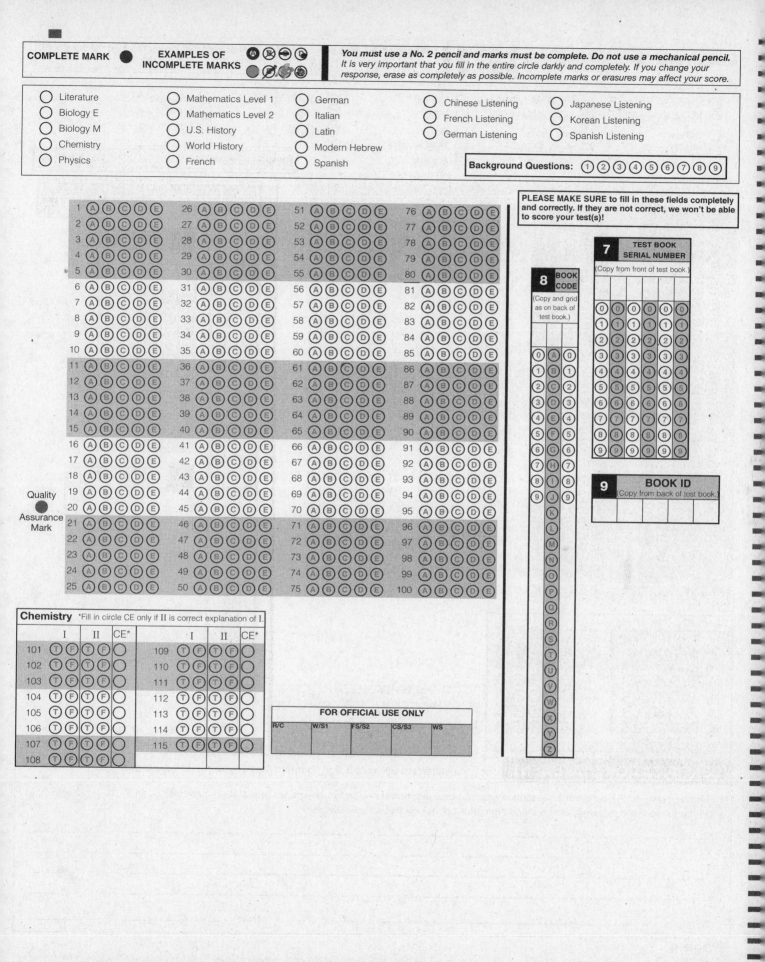

COMPLETE MARK ● **EXAMPLES OF INCOMPLETE MARKS**

You must use a No. 2 pencil and marks must be complete. Do not use a mechanical pencil. It is very important that you fill in the entire circle darkly and completely. If you change your response, erase as completely as possible. Incomplete marks or erasures may affect your score.

○ Literature
○ Biology E
○ Biology M
○ Chemistry
○ Physics

○ Mathematics Level 1
○ Mathematics Level 2
○ U.S. History
○ World History
○ French

○ German
○ Italian
○ Latin
○ Modern Hebrew
○ Spanish

○ Chinese Listening
○ French Listening
○ German Listening

○ Japanese Listening
○ Korean Listening
○ Spanish Listening

Background Questions: ① ② ③ ④ ⑤ ⑥ ⑦ ⑧ ⑨

Quality Assurance Mark ●

PLEASE MAKE SURE to fill in these fields completely and correctly. If they are not correct, we won't be able to score your test(s)!

7 TEST BOOK SERIAL NUMBER (Copy from front of test book.)

8 BOOK CODE (Copy and grid as on back of test book.)

9 BOOK ID (Copy from back of test book.)

Chemistry *Fill in circle CE only if II is correct explanation of I.

	I	II	CE*		I	II	CE*
101	T F	T F	○	109	T F	T F	○
102	T F	T F	○	110	T F	T F	○
103	T F	T F	○	111	T F	T F	○
104	T F	T F	○	112	T F	T F	○
105	T F	T F	○	113	T F	T F	○
106	T F	T F	○	114	T F	T F	○
107	T F	T F	○	115	T F	T F	○
108	T F	T F	○				

FOR OFFICIAL USE ONLY

R/C	W/S1	FS/S2	CS/S3	WS

Page 3

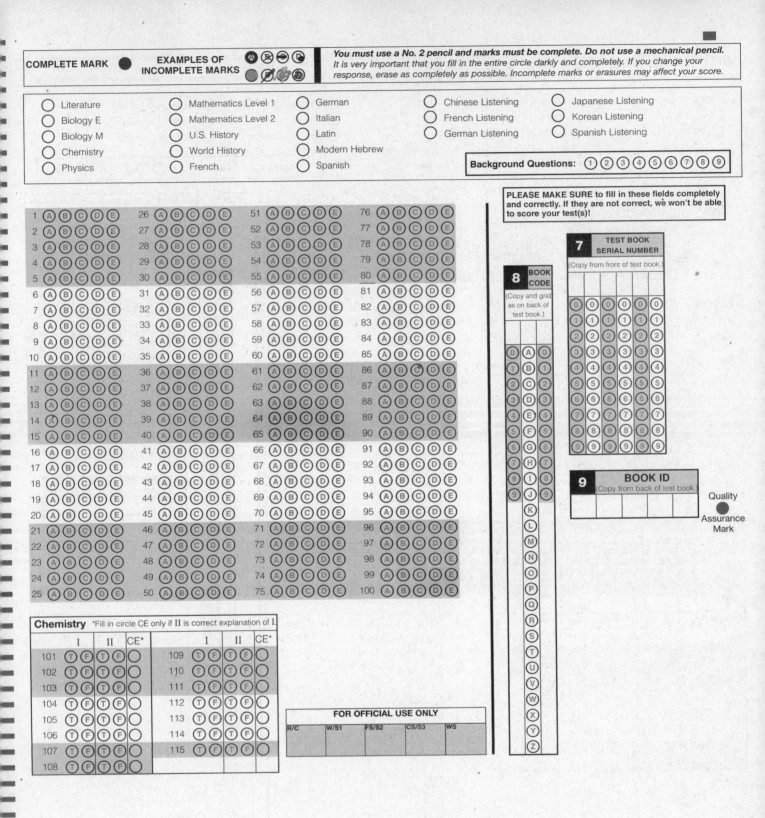

PLEASE DO NOT WRITE IN THIS AREA

SERIAL #

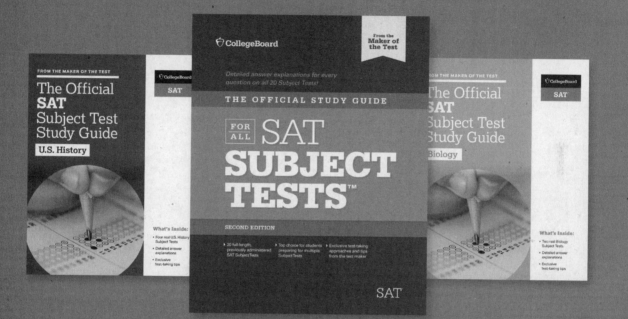

Show up ready on test day.

Watch **free** online lessons
for science from Khan Academy®.

satsubjecttests.org/biology
satsubjecttests.org/chemistry
satsubjecttests.org/physics

There are over 100 videos to watch covering
a variety of science topics. These lessons are
great refreshers to help you get ready for the
science Subject Tests in Biology, Chemistry,
and Physics.

Disclaimer: Playlists were created based on videos available on Khan Academy.
Content is subject to change in the future.

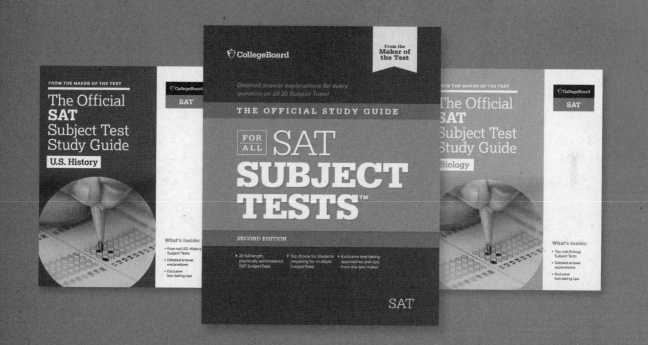

Show up ready on test day.

Watch **free** online lessons
for science from Khan Academy.

satsubjecttests.org/biology
satsubjecttests.org/chemistry
satsubjecttests.org/physics

There are over 100 videos to watch covering
a variety of science topics. These lessons are
great refreshers to help you get ready for the
science Subject Tests in Biology, Chemistry,
and Physics.

Disclaimer: Playlists were created based on videos available on Khan Academy.
Content is subject to change in the future.